IM

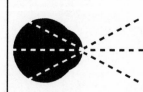

This Large Print Book carries the
Seal of Approval of N.A.V.H.

IM

A MEMOIR

ISAAC MIZRAHI

THORNDIKE PRESS

A part of Gale, a Cengage Company

Farmington Hills, Mich • San Francisco • New York • Waterville, Maine
Meriden, Conn • Mason, Ohio • Chicago

LIBRARY OF CONGRESS CIP DATA ON FILE.
CATALOGUING IN PUBLICATION FOR THIS BOOK
IS AVAILABLE FROM THE LIBRARY OF CONGRESS

ISBN-13: 978-1-4328-6734-8 (hardcover alk. paper)

Published in 2019 by arrangement with Macmillan Publishing Group, LLC/Flatiron Books

Printed in Mexico
1 2 3 4 5 6 7 23 22 21 20 19

For my mother, Sarah

Just wait until now becomes then. You'll see how happy we were.

— SUSAN SONTAG

PREFACE

At the start of the Orson Welles movie *Citizen Kane,* as Kane is dying in his wheelchair, he whispers "Rosebud" and the audience is left to piece together the significance of the word for the rest of the movie. When I saw it for the first time, I was in my early twenties, and I was reading a series of books called *A History of Private Life,* a recounting of civilization in three or four volumes. Each referenced the grand wars, monarchies, art, and politics that other history books focused on, but only as placeholders for what were the real make-or-break major events of history: the stories about the daily lives of slaves and citizens and how they lived, the food they ate, their bathing rituals; the undisciplined sexual habits of the Byzantine court; the heights of beds in Renaissance Italy and what they were made of; etc. So. My ideas about memory, what matters, what to chronicle, were formed largely by that "Rosebud" moment, and further fixed in my psyche by those books, a powerful duo of influences.

Once the hurdles of insecurity were jumped, once I was convinced it was the right time for my story to be told, I started the task of editing the events of my life, making lists and putting stories in order, comparing the big headlines with the tiny little items. Not ever having been one to revel, it's the tiny things that make me happy more than any great accomplishment or glamourous acquisition or celebration. When I was thirteen my mother gave me Colette to read — a book called *Earthly Paradise,* which had lots in it about sensual pleasures. I guess I took it very much to heart. That combined with my natal astrological chart, Libra with a Virgo ascendant, makes me obsessive about creature comforts. What I eat for breakfast often carries more weight than an artistic inspiration or some kind of big achievement. (I now understand why old people are so obsessed with food. I know people in their eighties who talk about their preference for a certain brand of cottage cheese the way JFK talked about Cuba. I, too, am now obsessive with my dietary preferences, and those musings are, more and more, the centerpieces of my conversation.) And so after a great, long meditation, I began this book with the idea to memorialize the tiny day-to-day rituals, even at the cost of leaving out great chunks of my career trajectory. For example, I was much more inclined to remember the long melancholic walks I took in the environs of the Guggenheim Museum during the breaks from rehearsals of *Peter and the Wolf* than the opening night of the show itself.

Through the writing and rewriting of this book I realized I had to sacrifice a few things for "shape." After all, a book that hangs together, that's meaningful in some way, is my ultimate goal, and getting sidetracked helps no one. So I edited. But what I hated losing were the tiny things, the day-to-day history of my own private life. And thus, I worry: Did I miss it? The minutiae? So many microhistories have had such a huge impact on the experience of my life. For instance:

- The pages about swimming, which I have done at the same pool for the past thirty-five years. The minifrittata I ate for breakfast afterwards at a place called Good and Plenty To Go, a small catering facility up the block from the pool. Most mornings of my life I sat at

11

one of the three outdoor tables, dreaming, planning, brooding, freezing my ass off in February, and sweating through my clothes in August. When it closed seven years ago, my heart broke. Had I died around that time, the last words on my lips would surely have been "mini zucchini frittata," thus throwing my personal history, and those who survived me, into a quagmire.

- An in-depth description of the years I spent riding the subway before completely swearing it off. The size of subway tokens and how they changed. What subway tokens actually were; I worry there's a whole upcoming generation who might shrug their shoulders. And especially how I mistrusted Metro-Cards. (I'd have sworn some elfin subway-riding thief was depleting my MetroCard when I was least aware.)
- Our first and only family dog, called Pom Pom, who got the shaft in draft two of this book. He was an apricot standard poodle that my mother acquired sometime in the late sixties. She kept him meticulously groomed, down to his pink-polished claws and topiary cut, and he inspired a collection of

topiary fur coats I did in 2008 — which I hired a poodle groomer to execute.

- Stories about travel that will never see the light of day; trips I took and loved before I started to hate traveling. And not descriptions of the romantic gondola rides in Venice, or fabulous dinners in Marseilles, or gardens in Kyoto where I had more than one revelation. No, these were writings about squalid airplane-seat upholstery; meals eaten on the fly at a Wolfgang Puck concession in a certain Midwest airport I frequented; extraordinary linen sheets in a very ordinary *pensione* in Florence; and the habits and signals of cruising parks in London and Milan.
- And what of smoking? How I loved smoking. How it made me feel like Greta Garbo, and how attached I was to the accoutrement. Details about my favorite ashtray and the jeweled lighter I found with my dear friend Lisa Eisner at the Rose Bowl Flea Market in Pasadena, which led to the design of a costume in an opera I directed in St. Louis. And how I gave up smoking cold turkey fifteen years ago after nearly thirty years of being a slave to

13

the filthy habit.

- Not to mention the house in Bridge-hampton I've occupied for the past twenty-eight years, which has been redone twice but still has the same view from my bathroom of a small oak tree I planted when I got the house. And how I love that tree like a human soul, and how it almost died in one of the renovations. And how it survived. And how each spring to this day I still hold my breath till I perceive the tiny buds of new growth. That house is filled with so much secret history — a volume of its own.

- Shouldn't this book allude at least once to the fact that I've done the *New York Times* crossword puzzle literally every single day of my life since my first year in high school? Isn't that an important feature of my life? Enough so that the name Eugene T. Maleska or Will Shortz might pass my lips as I quietly expire in my wheelchair, dropping a snow globe that crashes to the floor.

I'm afraid some of these microscopic details were cut in favor of a propulsive, gripping story. These little memories that remain, like matches that burn your fingers even after they're blown out; after all my editing, reediting, cutting, and restoring, much as I thought I might be able to control posterity, I fear for those dear little private facts. All these details will, as my husband, Arnold, is fond of saying, "go to dust."

1

I was five years old, lingering at the Avenue U Variety Store, staring. My mother took me there a lot when she went shopping for household things. I made sure she saw me pining there in the toy aisle.

Because I was "artistic," it was expected that more than anything else, I'd want whatever sort of art supplies the store kept in stock in those days: an assortment of chalky tempera paints that came in little jars packaged in shrink-wrap; waxy colored pencils that left nothing but translucent traces of color no matter how hard you pressed; oaktag in random colors; and tubes of glitter, which made my mother wince in anticipation of the mess I would no doubt make. I got paint-by-number sets that were too advanced for my age. I got real toys, too, things like Colorforms and an "age-appropriate" Erector set with scary pointed metal edges that full-grown adults might maim themselves with; today that set would be banned. I got all kinds of toys and games. I wasn't deprived, but the thing I wanted more than anything, the thing that eluded me to that point, was a Barbie doll.

The deluxe Barbie set came with a doll and three changes of clothes. Barbie herself was frozen in clear molded plastic, stuck to a cardboard background, dressed in a zebra-printed bathing suit with snap-on black pumps that seemed to go with everything. On one side of the cardboard was a polka-dot sundress on a tiny hanger, and on the other side a fabulous mink-cuffed, gold-brocade, knee-length coat.

My mother reluctantly took notice of my lingering. She looked over with a dark expression, another hint that there was something wrong with this yearning of mine. We'd had the conversation before, more than once, with the standard conclusion: "Boys don't play with dolls." But I desperately wanted to play with dolls, and she knew that. No matter how long I stared at that Barbie, my mother didn't flinch. But I kept my hopes up. On Hanukkah that year I was given a G.I. Joe, a consolation prize that I never played with the way I was supposed to. The first thing I did was lose the little Uzi; it mysteriously disappeared, and I never made a great effort to find it, since I had no plans to send him into battle. I wanted him out of that dreary camouflage print, but there didn't seem to be any alternatives. His body wasn't the right shape, he had a thick waist, no breasts, and even though I tried for a day or two to change his appearance, it was hopeless. No magic. Joe languished forever after in the toy bin.

Around my sixth birthday I was back at the Avenue U Variety Store with my mother. She was shopping for something mundane like a Pyrex dish or a new nozzle for a hose. I was holding the doll again. It was a starter Barbie, a kind of rudimentary presentation, in a long box, like a coffin, with a cellophane window and only the dress she was wearing: a simple pink, yellow, and olive-green plaid sleeveless job with a slightly high-waisted dirndl skirt and the ever-present black pumps. Perhaps the fact that it wasn't the grand deluxe set, that it seemed humbler, more manageable, appealed to my mother's sense of propriety. I presented it to her, and she took the toy and held it tentatively for a long time, on the verge of a remark. Finally she tossed it in her handcart, which I took as assent. I stayed cool on the outside, but on the inside I was hopping up and down with joy. I measured the minutes it would take to get from that spot — out of the danger zone of her changing her mind — back to the security and privacy of my bedroom, which I shared with my sisters, but I knew I'd have it all to myself till they got home from school.

We went up to the cash register to pay for it. My heart beat faster, my neck tensed for fear that anything should interfere with the transaction. The old man at the register, decrepit-looking, with a cigarette hanging from his lips, leered at my mother and said, "Will that be it, honey?"

The word "honey" hung in the air and irritated me to such an extent that it was physical. My eyes itched, the back of my throat went numb. My mother ignored the sleazy endearment, but I couldn't. I burned. And finally I boiled over. Stamping my foot I screamed, "She's not your honey!" A few seconds of dead air, then shock registered on the guy's face, then a greasy smile. He patted my head, which made me want to bite him. I knew my mother could take care of herself, she was no shrinking violet, but I was outraged that this stranger would take that kind of liberty and think nothing of it, as if he were entitled.

One benefit of my outburst was that it

distracted attention from the Barbie transaction, and before she knew it, my mother was paying for the parcel and out the door. She left the Avenue U Variety Store taller, with pride that I'd defended her honor. And like a dog who disappears with a hard-won bone, the minute we got home, I raced to my bedroom to play with Barbie undisturbed.

I approached Barbie *not* like another pretty face. Of course I made her dresses, but I made up stories for her, too. She was the woman I dreamed of being or befriending. I transformed her with outfits I made from scraps of fabrics and paper I found around the house. One day my mother shortened a dress made of pale-blue crystal-pleated chiffon that she got to wear to an important event associated with my father's business. The scraps were too wonderful to throw away, and she gave them to me. I was thrilled by those scraps and knew immediately what to do. I made Barbie a floor-length boatneck sheath with a fluted hem. I crudely stitched a broad sash that closed with snaps in the back. My focus on constructing that dress was laserlike. I made up a story about how Barbie was wearing the dress to a very important party that would clinch her great success. For fleeting moments I forgot about my mother's angst surrounding my attention to the doll. I was caught up with how best to style Barbie's hair, how lucky she was to have that tiny waist and those long legs, and how well she carried off that blue dress despite the black pumps, which I wished could have been gold or silver or, at the very least, bone.

I proudly presented Barbie in the crystal-pleated chiffon dress to my mother. She acknowledged it with a half-smile, accompanied by a distinctive whiff of misunderstanding. For a long while around my father, I pretended that Barbie belonged to one of my sisters. I don't think he ever realized the doll was actually mine. It was a well-kept secret, our secret, my mother's and mine. We didn't — couldn't — let on to the others. She was protecting me, but more, she was struggling with her own past — a past that didn't embrace effeminate little boys, a past that did nothing to prepare her for dealing with such a son.

To hear her tell it, my mother and I have a lot in common with the biblical Sarah and Isaac. She was named Sarah after her father's mother, and I was named Isaac after my father's father, a coincidence not lost on our family and friends. And the parallels don't end there, according to her dramatic version. In 1961 my mother's doctor considered her to be on the old side for childbirth. She was thirty-six and in good shape, but she was told that having me, her third child, was a risk. It was one she accepted, just as the older Sarah of the Bible took a risk in having her Isaac. My mother was fond of quoting her doctor on the subject. According to him, if we survived I was destined to be either "a genius or a Mongoloid."

We came through childbirth unscathed, but shortly after there was one dramatic and life-threatening event that shaped my perception of the world and especially my relationship with my mother. At the age of four I was stricken with spinal meningitis. The story goes that one morning I couldn't lift my head off the pillow, I ran a very high fever that wouldn't break, and eventually I couldn't be revived from a deep, mysterious sleep. My mother panicked and called the family pediatrician, Dr. Bernard Greenberg, who made a snap diagnosis over the phone and instructed my parents to take me immediately to the emergency room at Maimonides Medical Center in Brooklyn. There's a bit of extra suspense that my mother loves to insert into the tale — about how they couldn't find parking at the hospital, and how my father ran for blocks, carrying my limp body in his arms. He was the hero of the tale, getting me there just in the nick of time for the doctor to inject me full of antibiotics and save my life. I'm not exactly sure why that detail was worth embroidering onto the already dramatic tale. I think it was my mother's attempt to prove how much my father loved me. But over the years it came across more as a hard sell. For one thing, wouldn't anyone run a few blocks if they had a dying child in their arms?

My mother says she never fully recovered from the trauma and describes those days of my illness as the worst of her life. "I wouldn't wish it on anyone." She reacted to the experience in contradictory ways. She overcompensated, examining every cough and sigh. She had Dr. Greenberg on a short leash and was on the phone with him constantly. On the other side of the spectrum, perhaps to purposely distract herself from what she perceived as my physical vulnerability, she and my father went out a lot. I remember missing her, worrying about when she would return, wishing she'd stay home. I'd carry on and she'd say, "Relax, we're not going to Canarsie," which always struck me as funny, since Canarsie, far as it was from where we lived in the Midwood neighborhood of Brooklyn, was not nearly as far as Manhattan, where my parents were actually going. I'd lie awake, sweaty with fear and anxiety, waiting to hear the familiar sound of the car pulling into the driveway.

My mother was deeply anxious about my physical and emotional health. She'd warn against overexertion, and when I was "all sweated up," she'd make me sit still for ten minutes before going out into the cold. Yet when I was actually sick she'd accuse me of pretending. "You're such an actor!" she'd say with a withering look. I was accused of "acting" a lot, whenever I cried or carried on, to the extent that I got confused myself between when I was actually sick and when I was faking it. When she couldn't understand something I was feeling she attributed it to my overly dramatic nature — which, ironically, I got from her. And though she encouraged me to be independent, she also liked knowing what I was up to. She convinced herself that I was fine without her, but then was loath to admit it.

Most of the time she rejected the stereotypical role of the overbearing Jewish mother and seemed to want instead to be a best friend or mentor. This, too, was meted out in contradictory ways. She'd lull me into a sense of friendship, encouraging me in my creative pursuits, and then pull the mother card, stressing the importance of conforming to the family and its preconceived, traditional ideas. She was my cheerleader, filling me with her confidence if I lacked my own. But she felt too bound by the traditions of her upbringing to give me the consistent acknowledgment I needed. However she did it, she helped mold me into a functioning artist. Whether it was direct encouragement, or more commonly, a coded glance or a mysterious comment that helped me to think or act independently. Throughout, though, I could sense how much easier our lives would have been if only I'd been like other boys.

But I wasn't. And for as often as I know this caused her pain, she also related to it, because my mother felt different herself. Simply put, she and I have chemistry — an affinity. She's a woman of words. And wit. And some tricks. And the sands sometimes shift among these attributes. A trick she used many times: If someone called on the phone whom she didn't want to speak to, she would turn on the kitchen tap and bring the receiver close to it and say, "I'm sorry I can't talk to you right now. I'm frying." It was the perfect excuse to hang up, and it

26

fooled everyone across the board. I use it to this day.

We amuse each other to no end, and for all of my childhood and much of my young adulthood, I was her companion. Her confidant. I gave her a sympathetic ear. We spent a lot of time together, and I'm not sure who was more needy of the other. We shared secrets and protected each other from the family, who had some difficulty fathoming us: her, this erudite, sophisticated woman; and me, this creative, effeminate little boy. The confidence we shared cemented a bond, but complicated a traditional mother-son relationship. For all the nights I remember her seated at the edge of my bed, stroking my forehead, comforting me when I awakened from a nightmare, I also remember as many times when she was hard-selling me the virtues of the Syrian-Jewish community we lived in. Next she'd go on about how intellectually let down she was by her peer group, then she would obsess about marrying my sisters off by the ripe age of twenty. We had a great friendship, but I rarely felt like her "son," and she was never purely my "mother."

We do look alike. Anyone would know instantly that we are mother and son. We have the same deep-set eyes. Hers are hazel

27

green, mine go that color when I'm tired or on tranquilizers. I thank her genetic pool for my thick head of hair. All through my childhood she had a dyed black bubble coif. The styling varied a bit from decade to decade — higher in the sixties, slightly curlier in the seventies — but the sheer volume of hair, which she gets from both her parents, bodes well for me into my old age. Even today, at ninety-one, she has a goodly head of it. All her brothers and sisters and I have the same high, thick waist and long, stalky legs. The same small mouth and hook nose. Together we look like a flock of birds. Jewish flamingos.

When I was about seven and a half we moved to a new house and, not long after that, my habit of not sleeping well became a regular part of life. Every Saturday morning I would rise at the crack of dawn and wait for TV to start up (those were the days when most TV stations shut down at midnight). I'd watch one show starting at 4:00 A.M. that taught foreigners how to speak English. Finally, around 6:00 A.M., more kid-appropriate things would appear — shows I loved, like *Dodo, the Kid From Outer Space* and *The Patchwork Family.* By 8:30 I'd have set the table for two and begun cooking an elaborate breakfast for my mother. The rest of the family wouldn't rise till much later, so Saturday mornings meant quality time for us.

Sometimes I'm unduly influenced by the sounds of words. I like to say I became a designer based on how much I loved the sound of the word *taffeta.* I heard the word first spoken at breakfast by my mother, who assumed I knew what it meant. The word filled my head with curiosity, and when I discovered taffeta the fabric, the properties of it, it was the first step in my obsessive study of textiles. Around that time I heard the word "sauté" spoken on TV by Julia Child and looked it up in the *Encyclopedia Britannica,* which stood in the den in a little self-contained wood-veneered bookshelf that came with the set. What I found was more than a definition; there was an illustrated step-by-step guide. At once I taught myself to sauté vegetables and began adding them to our Saturday-morning scrambled eggs, which I knew would please my mother. She and I acknowledged sautéed vegetables in scrambled eggs were *goo-ah-may.* I also precociously learned to brew coffee, and to this day I hoard percolators.

The table setting was important, too. Pouring the milk into a creamer was a fancy touch, and I always remembered her saccharin: tiny white pellets contained in a ceramic pillbox painted with a scene of a girl on a swing suspended from the branch of a tree. In the springtime I would cut some of the orange tiger lilies that grew along the edge of the garage to add to the table setting.

It was over these breakfasts that our great friendship flourished. My mother told me stories of her childhood. She described her obsession with books and talked about her library card the way others talk about their passports. These stories conjured images of a middle-class, Jewish Francie Nolan, the heroine of *A Tree Grows in Brooklyn,* out on a fire escape night after summer night, eating apples and reading books. She would tell me about her early adulthood and her courtships. She spoke about her frustrations with my father and his lack of interest in art and literature. She confided in me when we had cash-flow problems. There were definitely conversations which might have seemed inappropriate for an eight-year-old, but I also remember it was later at one of these breakfasts that she, not my father, told me about the birds and the bees. She insisted that the act only happened as result of a feeling of love, and she said it was

30

something I would eventually want to do. From the description, I found that hard to believe at the time, but to this day I'm impressed by the pure and appealing way she framed the subject. I think one of the reasons I have such a good and guiltless attitude toward sex is because of this first description.

My mother was the most fascinating person on the planet. I hung on her every word. She's a gifted raconteuse and, simply put, she charmed me. She trained me to be her best friend. Ever since, so many of the friendships I've had with women mirror this early dynamic. It runs very deep. I live to be confided in, to bolster a woman's ego, to be asked advice — whether it's about a dress or a deeper, more profound matter. Since this early bond with my mother, I've found myself in many similar friendships in which I'm beholden to a woman who makes herself the emotional center of my life, and me the center of hers. It recurs with varying degrees of success, satisfaction, and neuroses.

During our breakfast tête-a-têtes, my mother often expounded on her theories of style and culture, which I absorbed like a willing disciple, if not a stalkerish fan. While it clearly pained her that my father didn't make enough money to keep up with her wealthier friends, she also warned me against becoming "materialistic." It was a subtle distinction, the wafer-thin line between loving clothes, which my mother surely did, and being "too obsessed." She warned me never to take these style issues too seriously, lest I be labeled *Shallow*. Though a pared-down look was fashionable in those days, I often think my mother's aversion to displays of excess was her way of feeling superior to the women who had way more money, more clothes, better houses, etc. It was how she reassured herself that she had an intangible edge. And my artistic sensibilities — this line I skate between the *dignified* and the *over-the-top* — began with these discussions on Saturday mornings. It was drummed into my head that being smart trumped all else; wit and nerve were the most important elements of style; and money was not everything.

Around the time I was born in 1961 everyone wanted to look like Jackie Kennedy. And although my mother was someone with intense personal style, she was just as enamored of the First Lady and did a lot to emulate her. This was the naissance of the bubble coif. She also kept her makeup neutral — for the only time in her life, she wore nude, peachy-pink lipstick. Eventually she went back to her bright-red lips, though. "You know, brunettes look tired in pink lipstick," she'd say. My mother had narrow "aristocratic" feet like Jackie, who wore a double A, and shoes were always a priority for her. "Your father married me because I had my shoes dyed to match my cashmere sweaters. He thought that was *the end.*" She preferred a pointed toe because it "lengthened" the figure, and she never wore platform shoes, claiming they were "vul-gah" and made everyone look fat.

My mother wore plain clothes mostly, eschewing heavy, ornate embroideries and froufrou. And never jeans — even later, when Jackie O was photographed constantly in jeans, my mother resisted them. Mostly she wore day dresses in stripes and prints, A-line or tent-shaped or shirtwaists, usually without belts because of her straight middle. Around the house she wore swing-shaped, floor-length zip-front robes, in brocade or floral or leopard print, worn with channel-tufted Jacques Levine wedge slippers in gold and silver leather. She held ruffles to a nearly impossible standard of intellect; they had to be "smart ruffles," which were integral to the design of the blouse or dress. I didn't know it at the time, but these were the blocks with which my design philosophy was built. The best collections I ever did were inspired by the memories of how my mother looked in clothes. I also attribute my skepticism — my outright loathing for meaninglessly fancy designer clothes — to my observations of her at her best: pleated skirts and astronaut-collar sleeveless tops; lots of plain, handsome, neutral suits with boxy waists, some with fur trim, and accessorized with simple pillbox hats. Plain black evening dresses "jazzed up" in different ways, with the right accessories. "I'll drape a piece of chiffon," she'd say, onto something plain and make it fascinating. It was ingrained in me that personal passion and real design — the quality of ideas — always outshine the froufrou, especially where expensive designer clothes are concerned.

My mother's take on religion, however, was a much harder sell.

The rules and traditions of the Syrian community weren't clearly spelled out. In those days the subject was left open to individual families for interpretation, and there were subtle differences in religious observances. There was no name for what we were, as in "orthodox" or "conservative." My family kept pace with the majority of the families in the community, which meant keeping kosher at home, strictly adhering to the major Jewish holidays, and observing the Sabbath loosely. We could drive on Saturdays, use electricity, and work, if necessary. I mostly managed to avoid going to temple, except on High Holy days and odd weekends when my parents got around to thinking about it. But some of my greatest memories of family life are of my parents taking my sisters and me on long impromptu drives on cold Saturday mornings to a frozen lake in Upstate New York to go ice skating. We'd stop at a general store on a steep hill to buy sandwiches and Fritos on our way to that lake. I wish those outings represented the better part of my childhood but they don't.

What I remember most is the repression and guilt of the yeshiva. There was definitely less religious structure in our house and in the houses of our Sephardic neighbors than there was in a lot of the Orthodox Ashkenazic Jewish homes of the kids at school. But we weren't nearly as free as the Reform Jews, an example being my mother's two brothers, who fled the community early on. They seemed to have happy families without any emphasis on religion. They lived in Manhattan, ate whatever they wanted, and there was no confusing weaving in and out of religious idealism. From what I observed, it was a smarter way to live, more natural. I admired and envied their freedom.

Yeshivah of Flatbush was considered much better, more prestigious than other yeshivas in the area, it was — we were told by rabbis and community leaders — rated one of the top schools by the "National Board," whoever they were. My parents sought to broaden our horizons a little beyond the Syrian community. A little. But not too much. They wanted to be slightly progressive. We attended Yeshivah of Flatbush with a few other Syrian kids from families who were also aspiring to be less "typically Syrian."

I was stuck at that ugly yeshiva for nine years. Like a lead weight covered in felt, like being smothered by too much heavy wool. Days began at 7:30 A.M. with prayers, then Hebrew study classes, which would last till noon, during which Hebrew was spoken exclusively; after lunch and more prayers came the standard elementary classes like English and math, and the day finally ended at 4:30 P.M. The Torah was full of boring stories about boring patriarchs that seemed improbable to me even at that young age — just propaganda to scare people into submission. I especially hated the story of

Abraham's random sacrifice of Isaac. Since it was a story about someone with my name, I took it to heart. The whole "only kidding" deus ex machina at the end seemed to trivialize my own life, as though killing Isaac was just as easy as not. I considered god to be extremely random and really mean.

At a very young age we were told that assimilating was a bad thing. Not only assimilation into the world at large, but even into other Jewish realms. The Syrians I grew up with looked down on Ashkenazim, and we were discouraged from closely befriending and *forbidden* to — god help us — marry Jews who weren't Sephardic. So confusing. For one thing, it was the "inferior" Ashkenazim who were credited with the more prestigious yeshiva. But it was stressed to me that "Sephardim are the aristocrats of the Jews," which seemed elitist and exclusionary. I hated the idea that I was supposed to keep smart, funny people at arm's length because they weren't Sephardic, and especially so if they weren't Jewish. It was a pattern with my family and a few others in the community. Expose a little, but don't encourage.

While the Ashkenazic rabbis at school were the classic black-hat-and-*payot* variety, the rabbis at Beth Torah, the Sephardic shul my family and I went to, were more modern looking, like the families who attended it. Some were even handsome and well dressed and smelled of Paco Rabanne cologne. But it didn't make me like them any better. As a matter of fact, it felt like a kind of bait-and-switch. I mean: a handsome rabbi who smells of sexy cologne — what the hell does that even mean? The rabbis at school seemed to *try* to look terrible. It was as if the worse they looked and smelled, the closer they were to god. And to some extent that was appropriate. They looked terrible, they smelled terrible, they treated me terribly, and my fear of them matched the physical reality.

The same was true for the women. At yeshiva, the ladies dressed in long skirts and high-necked, long-sleeved blouses, no matter the time of year. They wore wigs as part of the religion where modesty was paramount. The wigs they wore were not glamourous. The opposite, if you can believe such a thing. They wore these wigs to make themselves *less* attractive. Imagine. I couldn't fathom it. And this is coming from someone who really understands wigs. This was so different from what I was used to in my house. My mother and her friends would never dream of *purposely* making themselves ugly.

For those years, I could never tell what I hated more — being at that school, or being away from home. There were times that my whole mind and body rebelled at the thought of being in school. I would make up reasons for staying home, feigning some ailment or other. I did this a lot more than the average first grader, so I was able to wear my mother down and sometimes she would play along with the charade. On days when I went to school, I would panic as soon as I arrived. It felt like I was falling backwards into an abyss. The panic crept up as I left home, increased as I entered the school building, and before I knew what was happening, I was writhing on the floor, screaming. To this day I define madness as the event of not being understood. There is no more alienating feeling, and it feeds on itself. The less the adults around me understood me and what I needed, the more I screamed and writhed. I still occasionally have that "falling backwards" feeling in moments of terrible stress, and even now I'm terrified of losing control like that.

One morning I was so desperate to not go to school that I actually punctured one of the tires of the school bus with a steak knife — not an easy thing for a six-year-old to do. It made no rational sense, but in the moment all I knew was that I was desperate to stay home. If the bus had a flat tire then it couldn't take me to school. So while my two sisters watched in horror, I plunged the knife into the tire with all my might and then ran inside the house and hid in the hall closet, scared of what I'd done, terrified of being spanked or punished. That morning my father had to drive all the children to school in his car — back and forth in shifts — while the bus was fixed. Oddly, he seemed amused by my assault on the bus, and I never heard a word of reproach from him about it. I think he simultaneously respected the sheer planning that went into the tire-stabbing, and was perplexed and possibly even scared by my nerve and determination.

Eventually, on days when I made it to school, days when I would "fall backwards" and have screaming fits, my mother would be called to take me home. This happened repeatedly the fall I turned six, and ultimately I was suspended from school and my parents were told that I wouldn't be allowed back unless they took me to see a psychiatrist.

The school-appointed therapist was full of cautions about what a monster I was at risk of becoming, so my mother decided to shop for another therapist. We auditioned a series of them — some nice but ineffectual, others depressing. There was a chubby man with a red beard who lived in Manhattan Beach, a long drive away, in a brick house set back behind a great sloping lawn covered with snow. There was a Hasidic woman in a particularly awful wig who spoke in a thick German accent and whom I had to address as *Geveret* Galetski (Hebrew for "Mrs. Galetski"). I also remember a man who smelled like cumin and worked out of a windowless apartment in Park Slope. I don't think I lasted a full session with him before my mother hustled me back out into the daylight.

Toward the end of first grade, late one morning right before lunch, my mother showed up at school unexpectedly and took me out of class. This was a major and happy surprise for me. We drove out of the neighborhood and then through the Brooklyn-Battery Tunnel — another really good sign. It meant we were on our way to The City! Brooklyn may have been a part of New York City, but it wasn't "The City." In those early years my family traversed that tunnel only on special occasions — on our way to the theatre for birthday treats, or to visit one of my mother's brothers and their families who lived in The City. Or to go to my father's office on West Thirty-fourth Street, right across from Macy's, where some of the more wonderful scenarios of my early childhood played out, including our yearly visit to watch the Thanksgiving Day parade from his office windows. I always associated great things with driving through that tunnel. I emerged from it feeling like I was on my way to someplace wondrous — a real-life Emerald City.

That day my mother and I landed in the leafy and genteel neighborhood of Gramercy Park. We lunched at the Woolworth's counter on Third Avenue, then walked around the corner to the northeast side of the park, and entered a beautiful old Beaux Arts building. We were taken up a wood-paneled elevator by a doorman wearing white gloves to a high floor, where we let ourselves into someone's living room. It was dark, with shards of light cutting through the shuttered and draped windows. I was immediately intrigued by the décor of the room. Lots of rich damask and red velvet upholstery trimmed with thick fringe, so different from the contemporary, stark, mid-century décor I grew up with.

After a few minutes, a tall, spry old

woman appeared. She introduced herself as Dr. Mossey. In my memory she looks like Eleanor Roosevelt — elegant in a rough-hewn, unselfconscious way. She had thick white hair and wore an unfitted, printed foulard dress with wooly tights. At the time she reminded me of my mother's mother, the quintessential sweet grandmother I called "Meema," whom I'd loved very much and who had died a year or two earlier. I think I loved and trusted Dr. Mossey almost immediately based on this similarity. Her ironic half-smile was like my grandmother's, too. *A curious smile for such a small mouth,* was the thought that ran through my head, *as if a bird is smiling.* There were other similarities — her serenity, and her seemingly limitless acceptance of me.

Dr. Mossey sat us in the living room for about fifteen minutes and talked mostly to my mother. Then she took me into her office, which was decorated in the same plush, old-world, comforting way. For the remainder of the session we were alone. She asked me to draw things and build things with blocks, and I obliged. I was apprehensive at first, afraid to make a mess. My mother was always so crazed about keeping the house tidy, and would complain to me if I left crayons or paints or scraps of material lying around. I'd be in the middle of some art project, surrounded by supplies in various states of disarray, and my mother would snap: "She just left!" — referring to the cleaning lady who had just tidied the house. With Dr. Mossey, though, that seemed the object of the game: to be messy, to let it all hang out. And for the remainder of my sessions with her — which would go on for three years — that's what I remember most. It felt like a social occasion more than a doctor's visit. This friendship was different from the one I had with my mother. Dr. Mossey did nothing but listen. She smiled that bird-like smile. She nodded. Those sessions all those years ago are why I'm so devoted to therapy today. All the associations were great — getting out of school early, emerging from the tunnel and lunching with my mother at the Woolworth's counter (they served one of my favorite food items of all time, which I still long for: a tricolor ice cream waffle sandwich), and then spending the afternoon getting purposely messy with Dr. Mossey's toys and art supplies, which seemed much better than the ones I had at home.

When I came out to my mother at age eighteen, she was shocked and didn't believe me. She referred to a conversation she'd had years earlier with Dr. Mossey, who had assured her I *wasn't* gay. But just the fact that my mother had raised the question at all was an admission that she had more than an inkling. For years I wondered how Dr. Mossey, someone I thought really knew me, could miss such obvious signs. Then it occurred to me that she told my mother I wasn't gay possibly in order not to alarm her or my father, and to prevent some kind of rash action on their part. I thought maybe it was a protective act. Dr. Mossey was deliberately keeping the truth from my mother and giving me the opportunity to figure things out for myself, before anyone could try to convince me otherwise. It was Dr. Mossey giving me a head start.

Therapy got me back in the door at Yeshivah of Flatbush, causing a potent combination of relief and dread. My parents were relieved, and that eased things. My hysterical spells became less frequent. But I went down in that school's history as something of an antichrist. I was a terrible problem to the rabbis and teachers. I imitated them to their faces and I disco-danced to the beat of the daily prayers. I defaced sacred volumes of Torah with sketches of shoes and hairstyles in the margins. I visited the nurse's office on a daily basis, feigning a variety of ailments with the hopes of being sent home. The nurse, a tall, robust woman named Chaya, who looked like a poor man's Ingrid Bergman with short sandy hair, had a pat remedy: She gave me Sucrets — cough and cold lozenges — and sent me back to class.

Toward the end of my days at Yeshivah of Flatbush, there was constant talk of my expulsion. One day, one of the many times my mother was summoned to school to meet with the principal, I was sitting outside his office, and when she arrived I almost didn't recognize her. She had on a drab grey dress, not a stitch of makeup, no jewelry. Even her ever-present red nail polish was missing. Later she let me in on her plan: "If I came in dressed to the nines they'd probably have thrown you out!" A dreary, unkempt appearance would make them sympathetic to her pleas, she thought. And she was right — I was admitted back to school with no punishment. Forget the pen. Dress is so much mightier than the sword!

2

The Syrian-Jewish community had never seen anything like me before. I stuck out like a chubby gay thumb. There wasn't a moment when I didn't feel claustrophobic looking at my prospects there, and yet for those who were suited to it — like my sisters and some of my cousins — it was a mecca, its own little holy paradise closed off to the rest of the world. The only things or people from the outside world that were acknowledged served the community: customers, interior designers, caterers, cheap labor, Shabbat goys (non-Jews who are enlisted to do the things that Jews can't on the Sabbath, such as turning lights on and off). Everything and everyone else was shut out. Even at a young age, I was demoralized by this. And while I had no other experience to compare it to, I knew there had to be a better place for me in the world.

The community was founded in Brooklyn

at the turn of the twentieth century, when a few Syrian-Jewish families fled the anti-Semitism that was prevalent in Syria. Within a short time others emigrated based on stories of easy success in the various New York City industries. By the end of the 1940s they expanded south from Bay Parkway to Ocean Parkway and Avenue S where they erected a temple called Shaare Zion. By the late 1960s the community had grown to such a huge extent that the neighborhood, including the shul, was filled to capacity. Around that time someone got the idea to extend the radius to an area twenty blocks north to Ocean Parkway and Avenue J, a comparatively spacious and beautiful suburban area referred to as Midwood. By the early 1970s, forty or so courageous families who were willing to move to uncharted new Brooklyn territories, my family included, settled there and founded a second shul.

The Beth Torah Congregation was the "new guard" shul, a modernist place that from the outside resembled a brick fortress. Inside the main worship chamber there were no windows; instead there was a massive oval skylight providing natural light that beamed down from the thirty-foot ceiling, giving the room a godly, ethereal quality.

Hung directly below the skylight was a huge, modern light fixture best described as a twenty-foot neoconstructivist bugle hanging downward. It was made up of graduating hoops of brass and supported big brass globes suspended by a huge ball-chain. The fixture was an endless source of distraction for me. As massive and forbidding as the whole scheme sounds, it really was a beautiful room, thanks to the fabulous light and the muted neutrality of the beige- and olive-green color scheme. A tapestry in similar colors by leftist artist Ben Shahn dominated the entrance. Those modern, muted colors felt purposely different from the traditional cobalt blue and burgundy of Shaare Zion.

Sadly, the progressive attitude of the décor didn't make itself felt in the attitudes or traditions of the congregation. It was every bit as repressive as the old shul. Especially for women. For a few years after their migration in the early twentieth century the women wore the traditional hijab — the veils — which guarded their faces from any kind of outside scrutiny. They stopped wearing them by the early 1920s, but the underlying attitude didn't change much. The exclusive purpose of women was to bear children, cook, and keep house. By the time I was born, the women in the community were far from hidden in hijab; they were displayed as commodities to be bought and sold. At the same time, divorce was considered aberrant, and when it did occur it was spoken of in whispers and the offending parties were shunned. Homosexuals were persona non grata — so taboo they weren't even a subject of discussion.

It was a bizarre mix of piety and flash that's difficult to wrap one's head around. The community seemed to place more emphasis on overt displays of wealth — the primary ways in which girls were judged marriageable — than it did on religious devotion. To the Jewish community at large, Congregation Beth Torah would seem progressive. The mere fact that the men could *see* the women during worship in the main temple was considered modern; at times women even waved to the men as they entered. The services took place at a central island surrounded by bleacher-like theatre seats that rose up each side of the room. Women sat closer to the entrance, and men were more centrally located, closer to the action.

At yeshiva, prayers were referred to by the Yiddish word "davening" and were performed in a singsong-y Yiddish dialect and cadence, very different from the Arabic style of prayers at Beth Torah, a style that sounded more like howling than praying. No matter what the style or context, I loathed it. It consisted of men and boys in rows, all swaying back and forth, their mouths full of mumbling, begging god's forgiveness and confessing to sins they didn't commit while ignoring the ones they did. Not to mention the misogynist overtones.

It was easy enough to fake the swaying and mumbling, but what I couldn't fake was the faith. Even though I took part in prayers many thousands of times in those years, and I understood the words when I bothered to actually read them, I never remotely felt any bit of their spiritual meaning. I hated wearing a yarmulke. It never stayed on my head and had to be bobby-pinned to my hair. And after my bar mitzvah, we were expected to daven every morning wearing tefillin, which are sacred scrolls in odd little boxes that are strapped tightly to one's head and to one's left arm with black leather straps. The strap left a long winding welt up my arm that I always associated with the markings from a beating. At school we had to wear something called a tzitzit under our shirts, which was a muslin tabard with long string tassels attached at the corners. It was hot and uncomfortable, and I never got used to it. At services I wore a tallis, a prayer shawl with tassels, layered over my clothes.

When I wasn't daydreaming or considering the engineering feat of the fabulous light fixture, I'd look over at the women and pine to sit among them. They seemed to be having much more fun than the men, who were tasked with reciting the solemn, terrifying prayers. The women weren't pressured to pray, and they never did. Instead they held a kind of fashion show. Each woman's entrance was scrutinized and accompanied by whispered commentary. The latest looks. Major jewelry. Short, short skirts. High, high heels and price tags. Big hair. If not décolletage, then skintight clothing that showed exactly what was going on underneath. Dressing always sends a message, whether we mean it to or not, and these ladies, especially the mothers of all the eligible daughters, meant it to. And the message was: *We're in the market for rich husbands.* Some of the young women may have liked putting themselves on display that way, but even if they didn't, they had no choice in the matter. You weren't going to catch a rich husband in a long skirt and flats. And it wasn't as if any of them had an option of going to college and establishing careers and financial independence. That was out of the question — not even considered.

I observed all of this with a mixture of fascination and disgust. It made me so uncomfortable that girls were viewed as objects up for barter. And pity the girl who was fat or unattractive — she was reviled. Any girl who passed the age of twenty without being married was considered an old maid. If she didn't marry she had no other option than to live at home and become a spinster aunt. Maybe she'd be allowed a menial job in the family business, but nothing more progressive than a sales clerk or a secretary. I'm pretty sure my early exposure to this mix of sexism and fashion-obsession — and my responses of both fascination and revulsion to different aspects of it — influenced, if not founded, my ideas about feminism and style. Certainly growing up in a household with three strong women — my mother and my sisters — who rose to the challenge of the very repression they were victim to, taught me how to be respectful of women and to be considerate of whatever specific social mores they were dealing with.

As upsetting as this objectification of women was, it had its heady sides, which made it more confusing. No doubt it was a tradition based in misogyny, but, boy, were the clothes good! The High Holy Days were like a fashion sporting event. I had my favorites out of a few chic women in shul, but I was always rooting for my mother and sisters, who made their entrances in outfits that were styled down to the last barrette. I have a memory of my mother sometime in the early 1960s, her hair teased into her signature coif, wearing a fawn-colored twill coat-suit with an azurine mink collar and a pale-grey satin pillbox hat. She dressed my sisters in abbreviated grey or pastel tweed suits with Mary-Janes. In the 1970s, as things became more casual, my mother dressed in layered sweaters and boots. And lots of suede; I particularly remember a rust suede A-line skirt with a red fox-trimmed cable-knit wrap cardigan. An espresso-brown knee-length suede coat, lined in mink over a black sweater and skirt. And my favorite shoes of all time, which were YSL — chocolate brown suede and leather wing-tip T-straps with heavy stacked heels. She wore those shoes with everything that year. While my mother was elegant, my sisters went more bohemian in maxi skirts made of patchwork, accessorized with wedge boots. The girls worked hard on those outfits.

It wasn't merely wardrobe and hair that were scrutinized and styled to such a degree. When my eldest sister turned fourteen, she mysteriously disappeared one day and returned a few days later with a bandaged nose. The most exciting part of that event was that Jackie Onassis was espied in the surgeon's waiting room, thereby confirming his A-1 status. (My parents were obsessed with "the best" when it came to things like doctors, and obviously if Dr. Thomas Riis was good enough for Jackie O, he was good enough for us.) When my sister's bruises disappeared after her nose job, my parents took us out for what amounted to a "nose job celebration brunch" at one of the most fabulous places in New York City at the time, a restaurant called Maxwell's Plum. It was Warner LeRoy's first restaurant, a fixture in the city's landscape of see-and-be-seen places with a mod atmosphere, part olde-time saloon, part acid-trip hippie.

In preparation for the High Holy Days fashion parade, my mother and sisters spent days and days shopping for clothes. After all, Rosh Hashanah and Yom Kippur weren't merely opportunities for celebrating the New Year and atoning for one's sins — this was also prime husband-hunting season. Part of me felt jealous of their shopping pilgrimages, while another part of me felt sorry for them. The pressure on them to turn themselves out every week was enormous, and nothing less than their future happiness rested on the outcome. They combed the tristate area. Lord & Taylor. Bonwit Teller. Loehmann's. Another discount place in the neighborhood called Lupu's. (I kid you not. It always struck me as rather funny that someone named Lupu would open a women's clothing store in a Jewish neighborhood.) Up and down Kings Highway they shopped, ending up at Jimmy's, which was a very expensive shop that held special status in the community. Jimmy's specialty was flashy European designer clothes, which weren't necessarily any better or worse than what could be found elsewhere, but their cachet went above and beyond their actual value simply because of their astronomical prices. And since every Syrian family shopped there, it was common knowledge how much you paid for something. My sisters and I were in awe of the clothes, but my mother knew better. She hated the idea that anyone should know what she did or didn't pay for something so we rarely patronized Jimmy's.

That was a big lesson to me: Mystery is the soul of style, not money.

Another aspect of style was simple common sense. No one wanted to be a "fashion victim." My mother used that phrase, which had recently been coined by *Women's Wear Daily,* a lot. One year in the early 1970s Rosh Hashanah fell on a terribly hot day in September. My mother's best friend at the time entered Beth Torah wearing thigh-high suede boots with thick tights and a short dress, a safari-looking Yves Saint Laurent with a lace-up neckline over a ribbed turtleneck. My mother said to her, "Aren't you hot?" Her friend said, "These are statement boots. I'm making a statement." Later, my mother said to me, "Yeah, she was making a statement, all right. A statement about what a moron she is."

My sisters were gorgeous. Norma, who was nicknamed Bridget after Brigitte Bardot, was my father's favorite. She was born with blond hair and blue eyes, an anomaly in a family of hazel-eyed brunettes. Norma easily grasped and held on to all the responsibilities of the eldest child. There was never an issue of who had priority in the house among the three of us; Norma had first dibs.

Marilyn was even more beautiful and a

little more complicated. My mother insisted on her having a Louise Brooks bob, which traumatized Marilyn. When she finally got to pick her own hairstyle as a young teenager, she grew her hair down to her waist. She was the middle child, and my parents' love for her was a bit more conditional. By the time I came along there were even more conditions on love, but as a trade-off, there was less scrutiny. Marilyn was considered "high-strung," something I was accused of as well. She was nervous and easily set off, and she was difficult about eating. My mother sometimes had to force-feed her. Once when she was about seven, Marilyn locked herself in the bathroom in order not to eat dinner. My mother borrowed a ladder from the next-door neighbor and climbed up and through the bathroom window. Marilyn describes that scene: my mother's face appearing in the window out of nowhere, like something out of a horror movie. Marilyn didn't eat for the same reasons that I overate. It goes back to the nervous energy around the subject of food in our house, as well as comfort; and having too much, or too little, or just enough love. It came from parents raised in the Depression, who were always scared of being plunged again into poverty, and who care-

58

fully, scrupulously balanced love and food, wealth and food, food and truth.

My chubbiness, my homeliness, was contrasted with my sisters' beauty. For every sympathetic sideways glance I got, they got smiles, oohs and aahs, heaps of clothes, all the wonderful things reserved for beautiful girls. They were thin and lithe, and my mother, like so many mothers of the time, got into the habit of treating them like cutout paper dolls. She took them shopping constantly. It was a bonding ritual. My mother's favorite store was definitely Loehmann's, which was a Brooklyn institution and a mecca of discounted designer clothing that in its heyday had locations all over New York and its outlying suburbs. When they came of age, my mother initiated my sisters into shopping there like other families might initiate their offspring into Freemasonry. It was a major event to show up at exactly the right time on the right day when one heard rumors about new merchandise coming in from one or another designer brand. At our Saturday breakfasts my mother was full of stories about the original location in the basement of Mrs. Loehmann's house on Nostrand Avenue in Brooklyn. Mrs. Loehmann would sit on a big chair "like a queen on her throne," shouting orders at everyone, from the staff to the customers. There was a story about the day the actress Abbe Lane was there shopping with her husband Xavier Cugat, who was dressed elegantly in a handmade tweed suit. In his breast pocket, instead of a pocket square, he had a teacup-size Chihuahua. The number of times my mother spied Lauren Bacall there made it sound like she was a regular, too. "She would fly in from Hollywood just to shop at Loehmann's. No matter what, there's nothing like it anywhere else in the world." About that my mother was right. Originally Loehmann's was a store that sold actual designer first samples, which were made "like diamonds" under the loving supervision of the designers whose labels were cut out just before the samples were shipped there. My mother and her friends could detect a real designer piece from whatever part of the label that remained. They recognized the exact shade of oyster or ivory of that house's label and even the tiniest shard of a "P" or a "T" meant it was a real Pauline Trigere or Traina Norell. It was like striking gold. It was before designers archived their clothes. It was before discount retail was something that everyone just expected. It was a very special place, and it breaks my heart that it's gone for good.

Starting at the age of six or seven, I was brought to the Loehmann's flagship store in Brooklyn when I stayed home from school on some health pretense. My mother would place me in the corner of the big communal women's fitting room with a coloring book. I'd sit in that room, ignoring the coloring book and instead observing the broad range of women of all shapes and in all states of undress.

"There is no fashion without foundation." That's one of my favorite quotes from Christian Dior. Well, I learned all about foundation — that is, underwear — in that dressing room. Underclothes in those days were huge. Panties were the size of pillowcases and came right up to the waist. Bras were longline and came right down to the waist. Slips. Half and full, trimmed in lace, made in the most disturbing colors, meant to be flesh tones but more the colors of prosthetic limbs. The smells trapped inside the synthetic girdles and shapers: sweat, oregano, camphor, all masked with lavender and orange blossom. Women had bigger breasts — real breasts. And such hair. Hair was bigger and sillier when I was a kid. If a dress didn't have a very long zipper in back, if you couldn't step into it with no part of that dress coming near the hair, it couldn't be considered for purchase.

The women who undressed in front of me probably assumed the seven-year-old boy in their midst was paying no attention to them. But in truth I was studying them — their anatomy, their choice of underwear. Without realizing it at the time, I was beginning a lifelong study of the psychology of women and how they dress.

While I would never judge a woman by such a silly thing as lingerie, I have noticed that the degree to which she cares about her general appearance doesn't only exist on the outside. Fashion is not for everyone, but if a woman is into clothes, the subject usually begins with her choice of lingerie — and that affects the way she sees herself. I used to meet thousands of young models. I remember one who went on to become a big star. When we first met she was a teenager and a mess — including her lack-luster bra and panties. Within a few months of hitting it big she arrived at fittings with the most gorgeous underwear (not to mention a perfect landing strip), her lingerie telling its own coming-of-age tale. That young lady's upgrade was due in part to the scrutiny of every great stylist, hairdresser, and makeup artist in the fashion world who had their hands on her in those months. But it was mostly because she *loved the subject.*

The women in the Loehmann's dressing room chose their lingerie with care. And in my assessment it wasn't qualified by the distinction between plain or lacy. Even the simplest bra was well-kept and beautifully selected and fitted. I sensed the effort that went into this lovely underdressing was done by each woman to please herself. The feeling of the fabric against her skin, the image she reflected back at herself in the mirror. The lingerie was a manifestation. This, I think, is what occurs when a woman sees a shoe or bag or hat that she feels she must have. She doesn't think, *Oh my god, I wish that were me.* She thinks, *Oh my god, that is so me.* She doesn't want it because she's aspiring to be someone she's not; she wants it because she already feels like that woman on the inside.

My mother made some of her most important fashion discoveries at Loehmann's. And that was the word she used, too — *important.* Only she pronounced the word, in perfect Brooklynese, *im-PAW-tent.* If a blouse or a shoe was *important,* then it could make your whole outfit. The most important piece my mother ever acquired at Loehmann's was a

Chanel suit — a ready-to-wear sample with the labels cut out of course. I think it was the only Chanel to ever find its way to that store. The suit was made in an oversized black-and-white houndstooth bouclé with black braid, gold buttons, and orange silk lining.

Back then the most worshipped designer in the Loehmann's dressing room was Norman Norell. Some say he was the first American to rival the European houses in originality and beautiful quality. He was known for his sophistication, and for his clientele: Lauren Bacall, Marilyn Monroe, many of the first ladies of the time. Even with the label cut out, Norell was the most *important* of all. The biggest fights in that dressing room were over Norell. In those days there were dressy pants ensembles referred to as "pajamas" that were worn in the same context as evening dresses. One day my mother found a Norell pajama ensemble, and it was like she won the lottery. A hush fell over the room. My mother was a perfect designer sample size, which was a great source of pride for her (and the entire family), and when she put on the Norell pajamas they fit perfectly — inspiring even more jealousy. Norell's collection that season had a nautical theme, so the ensemble was sailor-inspired — off-white chiffon with a midi collar, navy-blue satin trim, and a pussycat bow. The matching crystal-pleated chiffon pants were made to look like a skirt, and only if you entered a room doing the splits could anyone have realized you were actually wearing pants. That little secret made those pants all the more glamourous to me.

My mother had a special talent for putting things together. "Cheater pieces," things with lesser provenance, were regularly mixed with designer clothes. Even reconstructions. Once, while window-shopping on the Upper East Side, she spotted a fabulous sweater. It was pink angora trimmed with pink marabou feathers at the shoulders, the most glamourous and inventive sweater I'd ever seen at that stage of my young life. We knew it was too expensive for my oldest sister, Norma, judging by the exclusive-looking storefront of the boutique. But my mother made note of it, and a few weeks later she found a sleeveless pink angora shell and trimmed it with matching marabou feathers she bought at M&J Trimming. My sister wore that sweater to her sweet sixteen, and it made a real sensation.

From the time I was born till I moved out of the house at twenty, the quest for clothes was endless. Dresses, boots, coats, sweaters. It was a full-time job for my mother, one that she took to with a palpable joy. She and my sisters would arrive home with overflowing shopping bags, the contents of which would then be hashed out. They'd try on clothes and ask my opinion, which is odd considering how young I was. They valued what I said and gave me power to approve or veto things. I don't know how I got the position of family fashion and style arbiter, but it's one I stepped right into with great relish and aplomb. And when my mother didn't agree with my pronouncements she'd say, "Excuse me, *Mr. Designer.* What did I do all those years before you were born?"

I would go so far as to say that between my mother's wardrobe and dressing my sisters, clothes were the number-one obsession in our household for those years when my sisters were "on the market." I might have envied them this level of care and attention, but even then I knew that the fun of dressing up had to be outweighed by the stress they felt in relinquishing all power to influence their own futures. Girls were married as young as sixteen, and if they weren't married by eighteen or nineteen, people started to worry. By the time they were twenty they were old maids. There was nothing that my sisters or any Syrian girl could do to move the process along. They were expected to wait for the right eligible Syrian boy to notice them and pluck them out of the chorus of hundreds of other girls vying for rich husbands.

While my sisters were being groomed for marriage, I wondered what was to become of me. At that point gender identity didn't present itself as a problem because the very idea that I might have a choice in the matter was preposterous. I've always identified more as a woman than anything and if times were different I might have chosen to become a female in appearance; in a lot of ways I operated in the family like a third daughter more than as an only son. Concepts such as "gender orientation" and "sexual preference" weren't spoken of in any terms, especially not to children. Back then, heterosexual was the only option, so I hid my real self. But the older I got the harder it became to conceal what I was really feeling. And though I might have been good at shifting shape, accommodating myself to my external reality, I was never any good at lying.

The visions I had of my future had mostly to do with fulfilling my dreams about art, show business, design, but also dreams of being fully understood. There were absolutely no available examples of what I wanted to be. Literally none. My parents, my teachers would never have accepted, even with my overt effeminacy, that I wasn't straight. What I wanted was a life where I wouldn't feel so ashamed of every aspect of myself, from being overweight to being girlish. Even before I knew exactly what it was I was ashamed of, I felt shame. I had no real understanding of myself, just a constant vibration, a faint register of dread that followed me around and sometimes erupted into mysterious depression or uncontrollable fits. I didn't know what or why or how, but great, destructive shame was hidden on a rooftop somewhere, stalking me, like a sniper.

3

I was born homosexual. Very early in my childhood, I remember lying in bed, awake, anxious, calming myself by imagining that I was in the arms of a man — an adult man. This wasn't a sexual fantasy. It was my "husband" and we floated on a raft, my bed, in a large ocean where no one could reach us. For years I slept with two rag dolls I'd made, and I'd fantasize that they were our children. This man who was my husband didn't really have a persona. If you asked me to describe him, other than the fact that he had dark hair, I couldn't. All I know is that night after night my husband and I floated with our children on our raft, and that was the image that made me feel safe enough to fall asleep. As a child, I had no idea about sex or sexual attraction; I felt love. And these romantic, loving feelings were for men. Sex wasn't a factor until later.

As a young boy, as young as I can remember, I flirted with men in the way some little girls might — innocently, but craving their attention and wanting to charm them. When I was nine I was sent to Manhattan Beach Day Camp, and there was a counselor who I was just mad about. His name was Mike, and he was in his late teens. He had dirty-blond hair, a long beautiful body, and traces of a goatee. He noticed my attention and without ever breaking heterosexual character, he made me feel accepted and appreciated. It seemed that the only way to communicate with the other counselors was via sports, but Mike was different. He was interested in my arts-and-crafts projects, which were the saving grace of my otherwise miserable days.

One of the great moments I recall of being seized by major artistic motivation occurred while I was at that camp. There were two evergreen trees that grew side by side, one slightly taller than the other. I looked at those trees and instantly knew exactly how to reproduce them on the page. I knew, perhaps from having unconsciously soaked up other paintings I'd seen, how to make my brushstrokes evocative of the texture of needles and branches. And I added a lot of blue to the dark green watercolors to capture the late afternoon August light. I painted in the camp's art room, well away from where I'd seen those trees, and Mike exalted my painting and my talent. It was by far the happiest moment of that summer.

I also felt a special affinity with my mother's brothers, both of whom left the Syrian community behind. My mother's brother Harry worked as a nuclear physicist alongside luminaries such as Wernher von Braun and Enrico Fermi until he chose the more lucrative business of retail. He and his brother, Sam, opened a chain of discount variety stores called Everyone's that disappeared about thirty years ago, but which had a kind of ubiquitous place in the New York City landscape almost in the way "Azuma" or "Buster Brown Shoes" did. Harry married a non-Syrian-Jewish woman named Deanne, which didn't go over too well with the family.

Deanne was a strange bird. She dressed in big, colorful printed caftans trimmed with feathers and sequins and wore oversized sunglasses indoors and out. Stylish yes, with big mood swings, which I think had a negative effect on my uncle and her two daughters. But I liked her. She had a cosmopolitan group of friends. Her best friend, Michael Sherman, was the first out homosexual I'd ever encountered, and I was both madly intrigued and terrified of him. I remember my aunt invited him to join us at the Silver Gull Beach Club in Breezy Point, sometime around 1968, where my parents rented a cabana for the few summers we weren't on the Jersey Shore. He arrived wearing a Pucci-print bikini that was clearly not a men's swimsuit; the matching minidress as a cover-up; a bowl haircut with bangs; and huge bug-eye sunglasses. He also had an extremely effeminate manner that he was not at all ashamed of. Staring right at him, as a child does, I asked my mother if he was a man or a woman, which made him giggle. He and my aunt Deanne were from the outside world. They spoke of fancy things. Fashion. The Arts. " 'F' Island," which was the affectionate name for Fire Island in those days. Deanne's mother was a painter named Julia Sherman (oddly, no relation to Michael), whose paintings hung in their home in Sands Point, Long Island, and in their glamourous apartment on Park Avenue. The paintings were huge, colorful, geometric compositions in the mod, psychedelic color palette of the late fifties and early sixties. I pored over those pictures as a little boy, and they influenced my sense of color in a profound way. Now they hang in my cousin Arlene's apartment, and they still fill me with an inexplicable lightness that I can only attribute to the happiness I felt as a kid in that cosmopolitan world that was so far away from the community.

My mother's brother Sam was my very favorite, even though we didn't really spend enormous amounts of time together. I always thought he would have been the perfect father for me. My mother had an especially close relationship with him — he was the first boy born to the family and closest to her in age. There is the sweetest picture of them circa 1935 sitting on a baby elephant at the circus, which describes their relationship to a T. They're holding hands, soul mates, my mother's gaze strong, my uncle Sam's vulnerable. He's sweet; she's protective. In that photo they live in a bubble of sibling intimacy that dreams are made of.

As long as I can remember, Uncle Sam's presence in my life brought enlightenment and joy. One Hanukkah night when I was five or six, in the early dark of daylight savings, Uncle Sam opened the Bronx branch of Everyone's, which had an extensive section of discount toys, to all his nieces and nephews. There was a considerable number of us, at least eight, and we were allowed to get as many toys as we wanted. I will always remember that night, driving through the Bronx, the filth of the city winter, traffic lights reflecting colored blurs on the icy streets. Scrambling through the aisles in that store, grabbing toys with total abandon. Ecstasy!

Uncle Sam was tall and good-looking; he had a solid, neat appearance, and thick hair that turned very white when he was in his midtwenties. (My mother also had white hair by her middle twenties, which is when she began the lifelong chore of coloring her hair; I was looking forward to being prematurely white and was really disappointed when my hair didn't turn by my middle twenties.) He had an easy personality, an uncomplicated way of thinking, so deeply logical and plain. He expressed himself in that direct way, too, and had a wonderful, deep, round laugh like Santa Claus, which I notice is the sound I produce now when I laugh. He and his good-looking, zaftig wife, Sandy, made an unusually handsome couple. They weren't constant visitors the way my mother's youngest sister, Aunt Adele, was, and I always assumed it was because they lived in Manhattan, as if it were the farthest place from Brooklyn on Earth. In truth, I don't think Sandy and my mother got along. Sandy, like my aunt Deanne, wasn't a Syrian girl, which was a huge strike against her. I'm sure Sam and Sandy felt alienated in many of the ways I do now, but if Sandy did hold a grudge against my mother in particular, I feel she was justified. The story goes that when Sam and Sandy first got married my uncle suggested to his new bride that she go shopping with my mother in order to bring Sandy's personal style up a notch or two. As you can imagine, Sandy wasn't thrilled with that idea.

One Saturday afternoon when I was about ten, Uncle Sam — who collected art and dabbled in painting — took me to an art-supply store in Greenwich Village, where he bought me an entire set of oil paints, brushes, turpentine, linseed oil, and an easel, all contained in one of those wonderful wooden art boxes with the compartments and the slide-out palette. I was so proud of that box. He brought me back to his home studio and began teaching me how to use oil paints. We met every Sunday morning for a few months and I learned a great deal quickly and began painting a lot. A few summers later, when I was fourteen, I spent most of my days and nights on the porch of the huge old farmhouse my family rented in Deal, New Jersey, using it like an outdoor studio, painting for hours and days on end. I have memories of being in such a state of deep concentration that summer, I wouldn't even notice a rainstorm until the water slanted into the porch. By the end of that summer I had produced about twenty pictures that I entered into a local art show in nearby Long Branch. I sold two pictures. One of them, of a ballerina, was purchased by Uncle Sam.

I always had the powerful sense that my uncle loved me and accepted me not despite who I was, but because of who I was. When I was five or six the family went to a local street fair in Brooklyn, and my parents put me on a ride made up of mini fire trucks that went around in a circle, like a merry-go-round. There's a picture of me on the ride wearing striped coverall shorts. I thought it would be funny if I pretended I was in a parade, and I started posing and waving in an effeminate way, like a homecoming queen I'd seen on TV. As I was doing it I perceived that familiar hint of dread, I could sense shame lurking. My dad turned away. But Uncle Sam seemed amused. He waved back and smiled at me.

My parents did their best considering the time and circumstances. They just wanted me to fit in, and they tried not to appear too disappointed that I didn't. They wanted me to be thin and athletic and manly. They hated that I was mostly at home in the garage playing with puppets, or sewing, or painting. Even practicing the piano too much got on their nerves. They constantly encouraged me to play outside in the sunshine. (I think it's the reason that to this day I hate summer weather and sunny days.) The way they coped with my specialness was to look away — something I was completely aware of.

None of this was surprising given that homosexuality was completely out of the question at that time, especially in the Syrian community. Yes, there were people who wandered in such as my aunt Deanne's friend Michael Sherman, but he was way outside the mainstream and someone who came across even stranger and scarier based on my parents' dicey reactions to him. The entire subject was denied any space or expression whatsoever. My mother claims she didn't even know what homosexuality was until she was thirty. And no matter how much bullying I experienced for being a "faggot," no one could really fathom what it would mean to really *be* one. I don't think my detractors had enough understanding of homosexuality to make the physical correlation. The same was true of me. While I fantasized about lying in the arms of a man, I didn't realize the sexual or political implications of that fantasy. It was before I had any real sexual desire that I understood, so it didn't quite feel like I was keeping it a secret. These were, for lack of a better descriptive word, *romantic* feelings I had — I couldn't imagine acting on them, nor did I have a particular idea of *how* I would act on them if given the opportunity. And it wasn't like I had anyone soliciting me about these feelings. Certainly not my parents. None of my relatives. Not Dr. Mossey.

God was certainly no help. According to what I was taught at yeshiva, god hated everything about me. He hated "graven images," any kind of art, which is what I spent most of my time creating. And he hated homosexuals — they were supposed to be stoned to death, an idea that got more and more terrifying as I got older and understood the specific reference to me. Art and my natural attraction to men are as much a part of me as my own nose. If god hated those things, I concluded, he surely hated me. On numerous occasions my father backed this up with proclamations like "I think all fairies should be lined up and shot." And while that threw me into a state of panic, I didn't think I'd ever have to reveal my feelings to him — or to anyone else for that matter. My modus operandi was a neat combination of hiding and denying.

But while I could hide my romantic crushes on men, I couldn't change my effeminate demeanor. The fact that I was utterly different from the other boys at school and shul was obvious to everyone. Bullying was a regular occurrence throughout my childhood. Mockery. Insults. Pranks. And not just from kids my age. From older kids. *From rabbis.* I was lucky because I was resilient. And most of the time I did a good job of staying away from possible sources. I preferred to be alone with my puppets and my TV set, and when I did interact with other kids, I chose carefully — I knew I was safe enough with my cousins, who had to be civil with me, and with my one close friend Jackie Gindy, whom I idolized.

Jackie and I are exactly the same age and had been in Yeshivah of Flatbush together for a number of years before we noticed each other and formed an unlikely friendship. Jackie couldn't have been more different from me. He was thin, good-looking, and beloved in the community, even in the fifth grade. He came from money, and in that community as elsewhere, people acknowledge that as a lovely personality trait. But it would be unfair to suggest that Jackie's popularity came solely from his looks and money. He was sweet and easy to get along with, and radiated warmth and a kind of happy vitality. Everyone loved him — he was impossible not to love — and the more beloved Jackie was, the more that engendered a lovely life, and on and on went the cycle of positive reinforcement.

The classes I shared with Jackie were always brighter and happier places because he was there. He held an enormous amount of power in the social realms at school, and he wielded it benevolently, often putting off my detractors without trying or even saying anything; he only had to enter the scene. People knew we were friends, and they treated me better in his presence. I couldn't really understand what our bonds were based on, but I knew they were deep and real and that I had his loyalty.

I didn't always possess good character judgment. One day when I was ten or eleven, outside the synagogue, one of the boys I thought was my friend lured me into performing one of the female impersonations I had begun doing around that age. I must have been delusional not to see this coming, but what ham can resist being asked to perform? At first the small crowd seemed rapt. I was doing Streisand — "Don't Rain on My Parade," probably the best number in my repertoire. Then the crowd grew, and by the middle of the number, the taunting started. I tried to ignore it, but after a while I realized the whole thing had been a setup. Finally I stopped. I had the presence of mind to shout, "You don't appreciate greatness when you see it." To which the kids responded by making a ring around me; there in the entrance to shul, they danced as if doing the hora, chanting over and over, "We appreciate Ike! We appreciate Ike!" (Ike was a nickname for Isaac that I detested.) As impervious as I tried to be, that was a bad day.

I was most scared of exposing my family to the ridicule. I would avoid my sisters at school for fear they would get a glimpse of the taunting. Walking to shul on a holiday was an ordeal. Approaching the entrance to Beth Torah meant navigating a gauntlet of insults from the other boys. I'd make any excuse to walk alone so as to more easily dodge the group of mean kids that seemed always to await me there. My mouth would run dry in expectation of some horrible

scene and the shameful prospect that someone would tell my parents, or my sisters
would see and feel implicated by association. My parents must have been aware of
the situation — certainly my sisters were.
But they never spoke of it because I think
they understood that I preferred it not to be
an issue. It helped me persevere to think of
it as my own problem that I could keep
under control. And on good days I relished
defending myself against bullies. It rarely
got physical, it was mostly words, and I
think learning how to defend myself against
those bullies is one reason I have no problems calling on words when I need them.

I was born with a lot of fight, and with an
optimistic streak that I think I got from my
mother — no matter how sad or depressed
I get, I go on. I was also born with the great
knowledge that feelings don't lie. I don't
know what taught me that lesson; perhaps a
lot of artists are born with an innate sense
of trust in their feelings, and perhaps the
undercurrent of my mother's support imprinted that message on me, too. I gathered
that being different was a good thing. I had
no desire to be the same as the boys who
played basketball and conformed to what
everyone expected of them. I didn't challenge them — there was no point in that.

But I also didn't try to be anyone other than who I was.

Sometimes public shaming took me by surprise and there was no escape. The summer I was eleven my parents sent me to Camp Winadu, an all-boys sleepaway camp, which was largely attended by Syrian-Jewish boys. I've blotted most of that horrible summer from memory, but I can tell you that I wasn't the boy with the sun-kissed skin out on the lake water-skiing. I was the fat boy in the arts-and-crafts shed making découpage. On the odd days when I wasn't hiding in the woods by myself, I was hiding in the woods and doing female impersonations for small groups of kids who would find me there. At the end of that summer, the counselors did a send-up show featuring parodies of some of the campers. One of the counselors dressed up as a girl, with a wig, a dress, and a tulle stole. As I watched the crude performance and listened to the other campers howl and hoot and jeer, it slowly dawned on me that the "girl" in the show was meant to be *me.* That it has the power to embarrass me even now is a testament to how deeply mortified I was. It was one thing for me to emerge occasionally among all the small-mindedness, racism, sexism, and homophobia, and embrace my oddness publicly doing female imperson-ations and puppet shows. It was another to be broadly ridiculed so publicly, and by adults who were meant to be looking out for me. It made for a deeply felt, at times very sad, reality.

For the most part I lived by operating in a state of denial. Not a denial of who I was — rather, a denial of my environment, and that it had any particular power over me. It was a form of self-preservation, but it was also a great test of self-awareness. To put it crudely: *How else would I know I was a sissy if it weren't for bullies?*

4

If my mother colored my existence, my father outlined it. He stood in contrast to her in almost every way. She had a command of the language; my father expressed himself awkwardly. My mother grasped the modern world while my father's view of it was narrowed by his past. And yet no one can say they didn't inspire my sisters and I to live a better life than the ones they had as kids, and to move further forward than they were able to as adults.

Parents in those days were not the friendly caregivers of today who agree with their child's every utterance and peccadillo. In the middle sixties and seventies there were still winners and losers at ball games; big, scary accidents on unsafe, concrete jungle-gyms; playing in the street till all hours; and riding bikes to the ends of the Earth. When I was growing up, parents demanded re-spect, awe; they were people who put conditions in place, who did not stand for deviance from any of the plans they laid out. My mother was the day-to-day disciplinarian, every once in a while threatening to slap us, her hand hovering in the air or reaching for her slipper, which meant something worse. Her threats were more amusing than terrifying. If we expressed our dismay or disagreed with her in any way, she'd shoot us a deadly glance and we'd get the standard "Well, you're stuck with me!" — which covered a lot of ground those years. My father was the overlord. The unpresent presence. The threat of a formal spanking if we really got out of line — more emotionally terrifying than physically painful. He wasn't involved in the small business of the household. He'd arrive home from work late in the evenings, pour himself a Dewar's on the rocks or a Mateus Rosé, although he was not a drinking man. After his first heart attack the doctor told him an occasional cocktail would do him good. So he used the cocktail more as a way to tune out than as something to overindulge in.

My father, Zeke Isadore Mizrahi, was born into the garment trade. His father was a tailor in Syria who worked as a ladies' clothing cutter in a sweatshop in SoHo after he emigrated to the United States shortly before 1920. I don't know if it was due to some failing on his part, or if it was a result of the hardships of the Depression, but my grandfather had a tough time holding down a job, and my father described his upbringing as "dirt poor." Both my parents were born the same year, 1927, two years before the great crash of the stock market. There were nine children in my father's family — two girls and the rest boys, and all seven of the boys shared a single bedroom. He and his brothers would go with their father to wholesale food markets where they would buy huge sacks of rice and lentils and other cheap provisions that they'd survive on for weeks. My father was forced to drop out of school before the seventh grade and find odd jobs in sweatshops to help support the family. Eventually he learned his father's trade as a cutter, his gateway into the garment industry.

In 1957 my eldest sister, Norma, was born, and my father had made a name for himself in the community as the owner of one of its most successful childrenswear businesses, making mass-market coats and suits for little boys. Two years later, when my sister Marilyn was born, the company was so successful there were plans to take it public. Two years after that, when my mother was pregnant with me, the public offering failed, and my father lost everything. But he was resilient. He reestablished himself by frequenting a coffee shop in the garment center that in those days was a kind of industry meeting place. He sat there morning after morning and finally met his next partners, with whom he would from a manufacturing concern. Together they founded a company called Rydal Mfg., makers of little boys' coats and suits, with headquarters at 112 West Thirty-fourth Street, in what was regarded as the premier childrenswear showroom facility. My father not only overcame the blow of losing his business while having to support a young family, he started a new business in the ashes of the old one. That was a great lesson to me and my sisters. When I went out of business in 1998, I thought back to this history and puzzled a lot about the idea of reliving one's parent's mistakes before embarking on one's true purpose.

While my father was bred for the garment business, I always thought of his trade as a sort of fallback for him. As a young man he'd been a drummer for a big band — his professional name was Zeke Manners (not to be confused with the country-western star) — and became well-known on the local circuit. He had a fantastic sense of rhythm, and years after he gave it up he used to play the drums with his hands on any surface available; accompanying the radio or just eating up nervous energy in the car while waiting for a light to change, he played the dashboard as though it were a conga drum.

The stories he told of his days as a drummer, which he meant as a cautionary tale about the debauchery of misspent youth, brought out the opposite reaction from me. I was fascinated and couldn't understand why he'd left it all behind. He drank a little. He even smoked reefer. He fell madly in love with a non-Jewish woman, and they moved in together. Their romance ended when two of his older brothers hunted him down in his "love nest" and "beat sense into him." *Sense* meant finding the right Syrian-Jewish girl and settling down in a reliable business and having kids. Although I was one of the kids that resulted, I was never convinced it was a good thing he turned his back on his musical career, not to mention this woman he seemed to love. I often thought that the years he spent as a drummer were his happiest.

He and my mother started dating in 1956, after they met at a community dance. They were the same age — thirty — and for her it was a crisis, since she was considered way past the marriageable age in the community. They had actually met once before ten years earlier at another community party when he'd asked her to dance and my mother said she "turned him down flat." When they met the second time, however, my mother was more amenable. She didn't want to be an old maid and still held on to her hopes of starting a family. Forever after, my mother maintained the upper hand in the relationship and never tired of telling the story of their first meeting.

My mother, Sarah Esses, did not lack for a healthy self-image. She was born in Brooklyn, the oldest of eight. She ruled the house even then. Her immigrant Syrian parents didn't speak great English, so from the time my mother learned to read, they relied on her to translate from English into the broken Arabic she spoke.

Here's a bit of questionable family lore — a story my mother loves to tell: Sometime in the early 1930s, when she was six or seven years old, a couple of Hollywood scouts came to her neighborhood in Brooklyn looking for talent. They noticed the beautiful Sarah Esses and knew immediately that they had a star on their hands. They took her to a local portrait photographer to take her picture. The picture is evidence that the story has some basis in truth. She is hauntingly beautiful. Draped like a cherub, perfect ringlets, searing, deep-set eyes staring directly at the lens. Apparently the minute the powers-that-be saw that photograph, they pressed the talent scouts to sign my mother to a contract. But it was not to be. Her parents were quick to refuse. No daughter of theirs was going to ruin her life and become a child star, and no one was moving to Hollywood. I often wondered why my grandparents took Baby Sarah for the portrait sitting in the first place. Was it to taunt the scouts? Was it to prove to themselves that they indeed had a beautiful daughter with star quality? My mother insists that those very same talent scouts discovered Shirley Temple a few months later. I have a framed print of that photograph — it lives on a shelf in my den as a symbol of my mother's great missed opportunity.

My mother's father in particular adored her, and in his eyes she could do no wrong. My favorite illustration of his blind worship occurred when she was first learning to drive. She was always a rather bad driver, bumping awkwardly back and forth into parking spaces, quipping, "Well, that's what bumpers are for!" But when she first got her license as a teenager, she was particularly bad. One day she was driving her father to Bradley Beach, a resort town on the Jersey Shore where a lot of Syrian Jews spent summers. On the road that day she was honked at, shouted at, cursed, and aggressively passed by the other drivers she managed to piss off. Finally her father turned to her and said, "What's the matter? They never saw a pretty girl drive a car before?"

My mother was something of a celebrity in the Syrian community, and especially among her extended family. She created her own mythology, taking the simplest events of life and elaborating and editing them to the point where they became pure melodrama. From the time I was a young child, my mother captured my imagination with stories about the many men whose marriage proposals she'd rejected, usually at the insistence of her parents, who didn't think there was anyone good enough for their daughter. One suitor proposed to her at a rooftop party he threw in her honor, while offering her a perfectly matched strand of pearls. When she rejected him, he violently ripped the pearls apart and they went streaming and bouncing across the rooftop into the dark night.

She was close to her siblings and looked upon her younger sisters more as daughters, doing their hair and fixing their dresses, and her younger brothers more as peers, playing baseball and other sports with them. My mother's family had their share of money woes, but never terrible enough for them to go without food, clothes, or schooling the way my father's family did. The fact that my mother finished Brooklyn College and actually worked briefly as a secretary on Madison Avenue (albeit for someone named I. Shalom, one of the founding fathers of the Syrian community) was amazing for the time. Among other things, it positioned her for a world of interests outside the realm of the Syrian Jews.

Window-shopping became an obsession for her. She would study the windows of Saks Fifth Avenue and Bonwit Teller (which at the time was on the corner of Thirty-eighth Street and Fifth Avenue). There's a story about a bias-cut striped sundress she saw in the window at Bonwit and just had to have. She passed that window and longed for that dress for weeks. Finally she saved the money to buy it. She wore it to a very important party in the community that summer and "made a hit." Her sophistication stood out among the other girls her age who wore homemade dresses or ones that were bought in the local Brooklyn shops that my mother had already outgrown. That prized dress stayed in her closet for years, a symbol of her fashion independence.

There were also negative ways in which my mother stood out in the community. She was a very smart, pretty girl with a drop of worldly exposure and a library card that was in constant use. But by the community's estimation, she deluded herself into thinking she had all the time in the world to meet the perfect person on her own terms, fall in love, and fulfill the obligations to wed and set to the task of reproducing. The older she got without being married, the more she became a symbol to other girls in the community of what exposure does to a girl. If let out of her restraints, if educated, a girl might get ideas other than the simple ones about getting married and creating a family. When she reached her late twenties my mother woke up, looked around, and realized the community in which she had always felt like a princess now considered her an old maid.

My mother made up her mind to marry

my father when they were out on his sailboat (bought at a time when he was making a lot of money in his first successful business). There was some unexpected bad weather, and his ability to get them to safety struck her as an augury for a nice, well-provided-for future. She speaks of the romantic scene on the beach, him wrapping her in his sweater against the harsh wind. She "fell in love with him that day." He was "street smart," according to her, something she needed in her life. They always appeared as a somewhat odd couple to me, but my father appealed to my mother as a provider and a solution to her waning marketability. She knew she could have — if not the great intellectual meeting of the minds she always dreamed of — a good life with him. It always seemed to me that my dad saw himself as having moved up in the world by marrying my mother. My mother, on the other hand, had an inkling of doing the opposite.

Still, when my mother married my father at the impossibly old age of thirty, she knew it was something of a miracle that she'd received one more chance to fulfill what she was bred for. It seemed all her prayers were answered, and the way she describes it, the first eight years of their marriage were ecstasy. She immediately got pregnant with my eldest sister, then another daughter two years later. Pressure was mounting for her to bear a son, which was what every family wanted in those days. (Shockingly, in that community it's still a major priority.) And then I came along.

The two or three years after my birth my mother always refers to as her happiest time. She was ecstatic being home with her babies, away from all other worldly cares. She didn't speak to anyone outside of her closest relatives and friends. She didn't read newspapers, only books. She didn't let anything pierce the bubble of happiness she had created for herself. Even when my father had his financial troubles, my mother claimed the rewards of motherhood over-came any of those pressures.

Memories of my father are mixed and complicated. There were tender moments here and there, but for the most part it was more like a standoff between us. I think he was as baffled by this preexisting disdain as I was. He was disappointed in me — his artistic, effeminate son — and I feared him. But these feelings were inborn, as inborn as the warmth and closeness I naturally felt for my mother. Even as an infant I'd scream and carry on if he so much as picked me up, and I wouldn't stop until he handed me back to her. As an older child, I don't recall thinking there was anything particularly amiss; it was simply a fact that though we "loved" each other, we didn't really like each other. It wasn't until later in my life when I made it out of the community and saw other, closer father/son relationships in action that I felt like perhaps I'd missed something.

He could be genuinely charming, thoughtful, and loving. When he was feeling happy and lighthearted, he was fun to be around. He had an idiosyncratic, Runyonesque sense of humor and would repeat bad jokes until they became funny. He entertained all of us with Danny Kaye-ish gibberish-French. He had some good sayings: "That was a treat instead of a treatment" when he liked something. And a dubious one: "Are you really going to hock me a Chinig?" when he felt bothered. When I was a toddler, he would stay home in the mornings and watch a show called *Romper Room* with me and my sisters. The show was like a virtual TV nursery school, with a teacher named Miss Louise who called good children "do-bees." That was a sweet nickname he called my sisters and me. Most times, when he'd leave the house he'd say to us, "Be good do-bees!" But his idea of affectionate patter sometimes backfired. The other nickname he had for us was "Dummy." As in, "Dummy, pass the salt." My mother hated it. My sisters and I were smart, so it's not as if this crushed us intellectually, but being called dummy every day for years in whatever context does a kind of damage eventually.

He could be callous and bigoted. He regularly used slurs such as the "N" word and "fairy." "Those faggots," he'd say in the front seat of the car, pointing to men we saw walking together in New York City. The epithets, and the hatred I sensed behind them, terrified me. Racism and sexism were imprinted on my father from early on. It was his upbringing, but it was also the country's upbringing. He was no more racist than the average American at the time. I sometimes think he took the disparagement he endured for being a Jew as an affirmation that it was okay to disparage others lower down in the pecking order. Not to apologize for my father, but he died in 1982, before the awakenings of the last thirty-five years, before the modern day that landed us (I like to believe) on another level of cultural and sexual integration. If he had lived longer, he might have learned better, along with the rest of the world, and understood the evils of discrimination. My mother often forgave him by blaming his poor background and the terrible domestic violence that compounded the problems in his household growing up. I always wondered how he made it through as such a nonviolent and otherwise gentle guy. He was terribly abused by his father, who used belts and even baseball bats to beat his children. Yet as horrible as the beatings were — and his stories gave me the sense they would have been considered extreme even then — he never said one ill word about his father. He spoke almost sentimentally about the beatings, as if such things were a common practice in every family. He seemed to equate those beatings with a bygone kind of love. The thing that was most troubling was the mixed message he sent me about the subject. Again and again he'd note how lucky I was that I wasn't beaten similarly, while intimating that I might have been better off if I had been — as if he were a better man for having endured those abuses. He occasionally "spanked" my sisters and me, which felt humiliating, but never came near the violence he lived through.

To this day it's difficult for me to stay

angry with my father, because my memories of him are so divided. I remember how secure I felt dozing off next to him on the sofa at night while we watched TV. At other times, though, when I checked his spot on that very sofa, he was so utterly zoned-out that it was as if he had a "Closed for Business" sign across his forehead. I took it personally at the time, as if he didn't care about me. But I think the truth was that his life exhausted him, and it was all he could do to stay awake after a long, hard day at work. And it would get worse after his first heart attack, which he had at the age of forty-two.

Even with their differences, there was a lot of real affection between my mother and father. My mother was often frustrated by his shut-down affect at home, but once in a while I noticed them sharing a private joke, and more than once I noticed them spooning in bed together in the morning. They shared a similar sense of humor. All through the 1970s, as my mother got deeper and deeper into her forties, he would tease her, "If you don't watch out I'm going to trade you in for two twenty-twos." The joke could easily have landed wrong, but it always made my mother laugh, and would snap her out of a bad mood. They maintained a number of inside jokes that dated all the way back to their honeymoon in Niagara Falls. A guy named Lou ran the bed-and-breakfast where they stayed, so forever after my mother and father called each other "Lou" or "Louie." Significantly less educated than my mother, my father didn't know you had to qualify the word *personify* with a noun (such as, "you personify grace," or "you personify humor") — he thought the word *personify* was a superlative all on its own, and even after she pointed out the correct usage, they would lovingly say to each other, "Honey, you are personified!"

By the time I was in grade school, my mother's contentment with her domestic bubble had worn off, and she grew depressed with her life as a housewife — although she couldn't imagine doing anything to change her circumstances. Her disenchantment often led to an afternoon Valium and a lie-down on the sofa, when we knew not to talk to her.

Her ticket to freedom was her library card, and she read everything from Henry James to Philip Roth, and could speak intelligently about both and all points between.

And she had me.

I listened to her problems and was sympathetic. I understood how frustrating life in the community could be for her, living among people who didn't read and only talked about superficial things like clothes and cooking. I'm sure she felt limited by the confines of wifehood and motherhood as defined by the narrow-mindedness of the community she so loved and revered. Still, I couldn't argue with my mother's own decision to stay put in the community. Although she must have felt squelched, she was loved by her husband and kids. And she was no shut-in — she went to theatre and museums, she engaged with the outside world. The same couldn't be said for other women in the community, who were so removed from the world and so uneducated they were barely literate. They didn't read, and they considered my mother odd for being versed in things like literature and the arts. I could never fathom what it was that made these other women adhere to old ideas about womanhood that hadn't changed for centuries. I think part of it was the promise of wealth. Great homes, clothes, and cars were the incentives with which men kept those women on such a straight-and-narrow line. My mother was coldly practical in her assessment of why women should stay with men who treated them badly — they should "stick it out" for the sake of their kids. There were terrible stories about women who were abused by their husbands. One of my mother's close friends was married to a man with a terrible temper who regularly raised his hand to her. We argued all the time about what she should do. I thought that anything was better than living with him, but my mother would say, "What else can she do? She has no training, no skill. She can't get a job. How are her kids supposed to eat?" And she had a point. In the context of that archaic world, I suppose women had no choice. Still it bothers me that for all my mother's smarts, she defends the community and the system that looked away from that kind of abuse. And to this day she laments the misfortune of any woman who finds herself unmarried at the age of thirty.

Most of the great girls I knew in the community who couldn't rationalize a way out ended up with men way beneath them. Girls who might have had careers had they not been shackled to these old beliefs. My sisters were talented, brilliant girls who were held back by that brainwashing. And still my mother encourages her grandchildren and great-grandchildren to think along these lines. She simply can't fathom how a woman might make a life for herself without a husband. Based on what I witnessed, I couldn't fathom how a woman could make a life for herself *with* one.

5

I have almost no memories of my life prior to having meningitis, but I have these family pictures to remind me of the ways in which my body always seemed to present problems. In early pictures, I'm wearing leg braces to correct bowleggedness. When I look at these pictures now, I see a standard-sized, healthy three- or four-year-old boy, but there's a deeper sense memory underneath of always feeling ashamed of my body. There's a slightly later picture of my sisters and me standing on the beach. They're beautiful little girls wearing matching black maillots, looking tall for their ages, and slim. Then there's me. I'm sitting in the sand, wearing a striped singlet with a little navy elastic belt. Even at that young age I felt more comfortable in a bathing suit with a top that covered my belly and chest.

I swam wearing a T-shirt for years. I was always horrified at the thought of being without a shirt, and I often wonder if this innate shame might have been some deeply felt wish to have another anatomy, the anatomy of a woman. Ultimately whatever that was transmuted itself into weight dysmorphia. I've always attributed the shame I felt about my body to being fat. By the age of twelve I was five feet eight inches tall and weighed 250 pounds. Then began the nightmare of weight control that has been the bane of my existence for as long as I can remember. My mother's concern about my weight was complicated by the fact that my father was also overweight — something that bothered her tremendously. As an adult my father overcompensated for the food deprivation of his childhood, and by the time he was thirty-five he had a huge gut. He wasn't the tallest man. Five foot seven at most. His suits all had outsized waists, and his belts were as long as dog leashes. Not only did I not want to be like my father, I was aware that my mother didn't want me to be like him either.

There were so many complicated scenes between me and my mother involving food. The lunches I took to school were different than my sisters'. In my brown-paper lunch bag I got all kinds of diet foods: individual packages of melba toast; fat-free, kosher cheese; tuna salad without mayonnaise; and fruit. Meanwhile my sisters got sandwiches, potato chips, and cookies. At night before bed, my sisters and I got glasses of chocolate milk, which stood on the dresser in the bedroom we shared. My chocolate milk was much darker than my sisters' because mine was made with skim milk. And they thought I didn't notice.

I recall my mother's watchful eye on me at mealtimes, scrutinizing the portions I ate. During the week my sisters and I typically ate dinner with our housekeeper, Maureen, before my father arrived home from work. Maureen was like a fun aunt. She was easy and uncritical, a constant source of companionship and love. I was no easy weight to lift, but she managed to hoist me onto her hip effortlessly, no grunting, no loss of breath. It was a major feat wedging my heft into the playground swing seats, which were like little sedan chairs with slide-down metal safety bars. But somehow skinny Maureen hoisted me up and jammed me in without making me feel self-conscious. When the Good Humor man would show up on the block, my mother would place a quarter in my hand and say, "Don't buy the ice cream. Save the money till you have enough for a toy." I would get Maureen to walk me around the block, where we'd meet the Good Humor man on his next stop. I'd buy the ice cream and eat it, out of my mother's sight.

It was always confusing how my father could be so closed-minded about black people, using terrible racial slurs, and then be so friendly, even familial, with Maureen. I felt that duplicity deeply. I felt an awkwardness, a resentment, when he came home evenings, into the house, which was otherwise dominated by a comfortable culture of women and girls. I was happy at home with my mother, my sisters, and Maureen. It felt like an invasion when he came home from work. It was life as usual, acceptance, love; then he'd enter the picture, I'd feel his reserve, his disappointment in me. I knew he sensed my longing to be seen as the person I was, instead of the person he wished I was. I knew there were things I wasn't doing with him: manly things like sports and carpentry, which was one of his hobbies. There were endless references to mysterious responsibilities and heavy burdens I was to carry as the only son. I felt the ominous approach of these obligations as I got older, along with a deficiency in me that would need to be made up — a kind of paying of the piper, some sort of terrifying reckoning always seemed imminent in his presence.

On the complete other side of the spectrum there was Maureen. She was an attractive Southern woman with long, slender legs, medium-brown skin, and dark-brown coiffed hair, also like Jackie Kennedy's. Maureen lived with us six days a week and was quite mysterious about her personal life. I couldn't accept that she had any other reality besides the life she led with me. If our family went out to dinner, to a place called Lundy's in Sheepshead Bay, or to the Palm Court in Manhattan, I was incensed that Maureen wasn't invited to come with us. I didn't understand why such a dear presence in our lives wasn't considered essential to a family outing. As my way of making her feel included I would bring her sugar packets as a souvenir of the dinner she missed. When I presented them to her she'd put them in the pocket of her uniform and remark that coming from me they were "too special to ever use."

Maureen's easygoing, judgment-free lifestyle made far more sense to me than the rigidity of the rules and regulations of our family. Hearing the fun stories about her Christmas celebrations made our holidays, and the Jewish religion in general, seem dark and miserable. I aspired to a life full of ease and Christmas presents, as opposed to the dour holidays and guilty fast days. Yom Kippur in particular is the most solemn day of the Jewish calendar — fasting and atoning are the only things allowed during those twenty-four hours. The first year my sisters were old enough to go to temple, I stayed behind with Maureen. When the family returned they were scandalized to find Maureen and me blasting the family Victrola and singing at the top of our lungs along with "Message to Michael," a Dionne Warwick record we loved.

When I was eight years old I was devastated because Maureen announced that she was leaving our family to work for the Mattel toy corporation. She was my lifeline to the outside world. When she left, I was entirely on my own. With no one to tell me about Christmas or play records with on Yom Kippur, my existence at yeshiva and within the community seemed even more like a jail sentence. I consoled myself with the knowledge that if I had to lose Maureen, at least she was going to a better place, to work for the company that made Barbie dolls.

No doubt this dreadful body shame I was

born with made me acutely sensitive to our culture's obsession with beauty and physical worth. I was surrounded by judgment: fat versus skinny, tall versus short, blond, brunette, almond eyes, hook nosed, busty, hippy, etc. I've always found that no matter what, curvy women dream of having stick figures and thin women go to great lengths for breast or butt implants. Any kind of fashion sets down its demand for a singular kind of perfection; one way or the highway. It translates essentially as one large punishment on women. Only recently are we beginning to acknowledge that beauty is a broad subject, one in which all people can participate. But when I was a kid women were only considered beautiful if they were between a size four and a size ten, with small noses and straight hair. Skinny women judged zaftig women, often implying a speculation about their virtue, while full-figured women felt sorry for those without obvious anatomical gifts. Women themselves were guilty of proliferating these convoluted ideas, and I was an observer of the sort of chatter that went on among my mother, my aunts, their girlfriends, and eventually my sisters.

"She's fat. If she was my daughter I'd lock her in a room till she lost all the weight."

"She's too skinny. A man likes a little meat on the bone. It's no wonder she's not married yet."

"Her hair is all wrong. If they were smart they'd take her to have it ironed."

And the greatest sound-bite of all time, my mother's favorite way of describing someone she considered ugly: "She's a thing."

As a not-very-good-looking kid, I organically acquired my own ideas about beauty. I thought of tiny noses and perfect features as trite and fell in love with atypical, offbeat faces. One primary example was Barbra Streisand. I know I sound like the gayest thing in the world, telling the story of how I fell in love with her at age seven, but I'll go one step gayer and say that she saved my life.

In the 1960s, if you wanted to see a movie, you had to make a special trip of it. And when you went to a theatre like the Criterion on Broadway and Forty-fourth Street, the experience was as grand and exciting as any live theatrical event. The theatre's red-and-gold interior had an old-world feeling, like a palace — a real sense of contained excitement. It was all so dramatic — the crowd, in those days people actually dressed up to go to movies; the ushers, the sconces, and my favorite thing as a kid: a curtain that parted slowly while the lights dimmed and the picture began, as dramatic as any live performance.

Funny Girl grabbed me from the opening credit sequence: photos of old New York retouched in eye-poppingly bright colors and juxtaposed next to equally colorful titles. And then Barbra came on. I think what really got me about her was that she didn't look so unlike my own sisters. She didn't talk so unlike them, either. And yet . . . *Who is this extraordinary woman?* All that boring religious stuff about being Jewish I learned in school — that meant nothing to me. Far more powerful was this vision of a beautiful Jewess, full of talent and personality! That was the moment I became aware of an outside world, a tangible reality — something I could pursue. There had been a few glamourous moments I bore witness to earlier on TV, but finally, sitting in that theatre, I understood that there was something wonderful out there on a grand scale — something to aspire to. All that color, all those magnificent Irene Sharaff costumes on those gorgeous, statuesque women, so artificial, made-up and coiffed for the gods. I think it was that movie that sparked my obsession with color (and my

113

obsession with wigs and eyeliner). The women in that movie substantiate my claim that bodies were bigger back then — and shown to their best advantage in the draped and jeweled costumes. (Our idea of what is acceptably thin has really changed. The beautiful showgirls in *Funny Girl* would be called fat now.)

It's such a cliché: a kid sitting in a dark theatre, the world opening up — a kind of shifting. And yet that's truly the way it happened. Inspiration presented itself to me, perhaps not for the first time, but fully fleshed out and definitely in its most potent form to that point. That moment marked another first for me. This flood of inspiration was accompanied by a feeling of dread and a hint of resigned exhaustion. That particular mix of emotions has become a regular event in my life. Whenever I feel most inspired, I'm simultaneously struck by a feeling of sadness and exhaustion at seeing the distance left to go, the labor ahead to achieve anything near to capturing perfection on that level.

But it was a small price to pay for having so much possibility open up before my eyes. From that day in the movies I knew that the world that I'd been born into wasn't the one I had to stay in. Escape was inevitable.

■ ■ ■

My early life might be described as hope-less. Stuck in a school, in a neighborhood — to some extent a family — I didn't belong in. But by the time I turned nine my world changed. I lost Maureen. I found Streisand. We moved into a bigger house in a new neighborhood. In the spring of 1971 my mother took me to see a matinee of Stephen Sondheim's *Follies,* and after that, literally *everything* was different. I was definitely too young to get the true meaning of the show — an ironic telling of show-business tales — but I took away my own truth about it. I loved the music and the production. I also took away the ennui, the neurosis, and the sadness of the characters — all qualities I recognized in myself.

The house we moved into was a huge old thing with six bedrooms and a detached garage whose access was blocked by the extension my parents had built. Nothing could have looked more ordinary from the outside than that garage, but when the door opened, it revealed my fabulous, glittery puppet theatre that I created that very year, inspired by having seen *Follies.* My theatre was a glowing, spangly, pink-and-gold thing, a light in the darkness, a happy place I could see in my mind's eye even before it was real. I named my first full-scale puppet revue *Follies,* but my puppet version wasn't a reproduction of the Broadway show. Mine was more a sequence of fluff — unrelated numbers about glitter and lights. The musical numbers changed from month to month; I put in new ones as I created them. I set many of them to movie-soundtrack overtures, and my puppets danced in over-the-top costumes I made, inspired by the fabulous showgirl rigs in *Funny Girl* and *Follies.*

When we first moved into the new house, the only things in the garage were some wood scraps, old doors, and a rusted cast-iron swing-frame that was stored in the center. But I saw a theatre. I saw the opposite of my life. A complete escape. Through these puppets I could express every aspect of my creativity: writing the shows, making the scenery, selecting — sometimes composing — the music, creating the characters, guiding their every step, their every wardrobe choice. The puppets themselves were naïve labors of love. Crude marionettes, each about a foot in length, made of dowels, with no sense of proportion or perspective. Huge heads carved out of balsa wood that I got at the local lumberyard. (I nearly killed myself so many times carving those heads with an X-Acto knife I procured from the craft store near school. My hands were always covered with cuts and Band-Aids.) Comparatively tiny bodies, hinged at the waists with eye-screws. Garishly painted faces and coarsely stitched costumes fixed with fish wire to the control sticks I made from wood scraps and which rested in the riggings at the top of my theatre.

It wasn't one show, it was many shows, a grand variety show with a huge cast of characters. A colorful, glamourous world of shows, an amorphous *Follies*. And it was there in that garage — in that theatre — where I began to feel okay about my life. It felt like my home, like a hideaway. I kept a stray kitten there for a while and smoked my first cigarette there.

My parents weren't exactly proud of this puppet dalliance. They didn't encourage the theatre so much as tolerate it. Yes, I sought their approval. And when they gave it, I felt good. Yes, I loved the audiences that amassed in the driveway, but I didn't do the shows for that. I didn't do them for approval or acclaim. I did them for the same reason I do what I do now: for the boundless pleasure I take in the simple act of making things. A distraction away from common, boring reality.

It was around this time Dr. Mossey gave my mother books about "the gifted child" to read. I assumed this was about me, and I got the implication of the word "gifted" immediately. It meant having the ability to live a heightened, less-boring life. I was gifted with the ability to pursue beauty, to make and surround myself with things I loved.

Freezing cold, boiling hot, it didn't matter what the weather, I was out there working. The garage wasn't electrified. All of my electricity — work light, stage light, and an old space heater I got from our neighbor Mrs. Jenner's garbage — came from a single extension cord that I snaked out of the house from a dinette window and into the garage. This cord was the sign to my mother that I was out there busy at work on my latest production. My commitment to that puppet theatre was obsessional. At that point I was choosing between creativity and the dark side of the gift, serious depression. The boredom of the real world. Sitting in front of the TV for hours watching reruns of *I Love Lucy,* eating compulsively, enduring overwhelming levels of fear and dread about not fitting in. My choice was to wallow there or become the star of another world of my own making. It's a pattern that has repeated itself again and again in my life. Unless I'm making something — unless I'm working — I'm fighting off fear and some form of sadness.

Another strong influence on my puppet theatre was seeing the Rockettes. In those days when you went to Radio City Music Hall to see a movie you got a stage show first. One of the great technical break-throughs I made was constructing a line of eight identical dancing-girl puppets that moved and kicked their legs like the Rockettes. In my biggest numbers — the opening set to the overture of *Gypsy,* and the finale set to the overture of *Funny Girl* — the climax was the appearance of these — my own personal Rockettes. They sparkled in their costumes, and kicked up their right legs (it was way too complicated to get both legs to kick), which were made of wooden dowels, jointed at the knees with eye-screws and covered with lamé knit tights that ended up looking more like pants. They were controlled by strings that connected to two old sticks, one attached to their knees and one to their ankles. This might seem like a major accomplishment for a ten-year-old, but in my mind it was a great disappointment. I envisioned thirty-six lithe, gorgeous

119

puppets, with legs like the Rockettes themselves, all dancing in lines, breaking into geometric shapes, some facing back, others forward. And all I could physically manifest was eight clumsy static puppets in pants.

The entire stage rigging was a hand-painted, glittered mess of remnants and leftovers. Set into the swing-frame at about waist level was a wooden stage made from an old door, open to the top, over which I perched behind on a tall stool, pulling the puppets' strings. The puppet controls rested on a rack that was part of the original swing-frame, located high up on the armature, masked by the top of the proscenium. I assembled and revised and drilled holes in my theatre. If something sagged on one side, I figured out how to bolster it with a board or an odd piece of plumbing from a discarded sink. The audience sat on anything that resembled a chair, or on a "bench" that was really an old metal radiator cover. I spelled out "Follies" on my Lite Brite, which I hung above the stage and at the climactic moment, timed to the music for the greatest dramatic effect, I'd plug the Lite Brite into the already-overloaded extension cord. Usually that moment got applause.

My theatre might have been a mess of

junk on the inside, but my audience, which consisted of neighborhood kids, never knew. And what I saw in my head while I pulled those strings and manipulated those shows was perfection. That's a skill I developed way back then: the ability to press forward with the perfect picture in your head regardless of what the actual picture is. Even if it's junk onstage, in my head it's beautiful. To this day that's the main reason I hate looking at any kind of footage of myself, I hate hearing my voice on any kind of recording: Because of the discrepancy of what I see or hear in my head versus the reality of what exists.

The backstage area and all of the inner workings, including where I stood and where I kept the tape recorder, was concealed by old boards and fabrics stretched over frames. I decorated these with my own Magic Marker versions of Joe Eula–style fashion illustrations. The centerpiece was my blown-up copy of his impressionistic drawing of Liza Minnelli for her *Liza with a "Z"* album cover. Eventually there was a puppet version of Liza who was the star of my *Follies.* I mixed in cutout magazine images of Liza and Judy Garland on the proscenium, and in tempera I painted WELCOME and HELLO and other inviting words.

I was mad about *Liza with a "Z,"* which I'd seen by chance on TV. I eventually got the recording, and I listened to it constantly at top volume, which drove my mother crazy. I also set a bunch of numbers to it. I adored Judy Garland especially. I was aware of her from watching old movies on *Million Dollar Movie,* which was on TV every day when I came home from school, or *The Late Show* on nights when I was awake late. I loved the idea that this woman could embody so many incredible characters. I had a compilation album of her hits and modeled a few of my puppets on her. Between Streisand, Judy, and Liza, I never wanted for inspiration. They suggested my whole theatrical oeuvre, manifest in that junk kaleidoscope of puppetry.

I constructed a pulley system for my curtain, which was a yard remnant of gold lamé that I got from the local fabric store, Midwood Trimmings, where I bought all of my cloth and notions. It was my routine to stop at Midwood Trimmings on my walk home from school, and I'd spend forever browsing. I used the money that I swiped from my father's dresser, usually small change, occasionally a dollar or two when I was feeling really bold. He must have known

I was taking it but he didn't acknowledge it, and I was careful not to go overboard.

Midwood Trimmings was a dark mess of a store on Coney Island Avenue in Brooklyn, with a window display that had not changed since the store opened in what I'm guessing was the 1950s. It was always empty except for the woman who ran it — in my memory she's a Hasidic woman who wore a scarf on her head and spoke to me only to say hello and goodbye. She stood there behind the counter engrossed in something and didn't bat an eye. Occasionally I bought half a yard from a musty bolt of felt, which was easy to work with, since the edges didn't need finishing. But mostly what I bought came from the bin of remnants. That bin had mystical properties; it often wasn't replenished for months at a time, but no matter how many times I went through it, I always found something to work with. On the surface, the fabrics at Midwood Trimmings were ordinary, but I quickly learned the compensating benefits of sequinning, Be-Dazzling, and hand-painting.

If the resources at Midwood Trimmings weren't sufficient, I would look elsewhere for supplies. Our linen closet was a favorite resource. My mother often complained that household items such as daisy-printed dish towels or plastic flowers that were lying around the house might go missing when I was in production. Table accessories like figurines or even plates and bowls took on new life when glittered or painted or découpaged. One stage setting centered on a fountain, which I constructed from a series of shallow bowls that I somehow managed to stack between dowels. I painted them and strung shredded Lurex strips between them, simulating running water. I had a roving eye and no piece of detritus escaped my scrutiny. I built staircases and doorways out of cardboard for my marionette stars. Oak tag sold for seventy-five cents a sheet at the local five-and-dime, and I went through sheets and sheets of it, painting and decorating them as backdrops.

When my current revue was fully planned and costumed, I opened the garage door, and that was the signal to the neighborhood that the theatre was open and my show was about to start. I knew some of my audience, but not all. It was mostly children my age or younger than me, although older kids would often wander in. The show was free, and I had many repeat audience members. Three of my cousins who lived a few blocks away came often, and two kids that lived across the street were regulars, a brother and sister for whom I later babysat. Every once in a while some of the neighborhood bullies would drift in to taunt me, older boys I didn't know, but for the most part my audiences were friendly.

Every once in a while I'd do a show for my cousins after a holiday dinner, and an uncle or aunt would wander in holding a drink, amused or baffled. For the most part the kids who watched my shows were entranced. I could feel their attention and energy. Like any child performer, I had a natural, untaught sense for when I had my audience's attention. Even while I was fully immersed in making the puppets dance, I heard their laughter — and even more so the good silence when I knew they were listening. I learned a lot about gauging my audience from that time, something that is second nature to me now.

Going once a month with my parents to a show or a ballet wasn't enough. I started going on my own, pursuing theatre and the performing arts with a kind of compulsion. The first play I took myself to see was a revival of the musical *Irene,* starring Debbie Reynolds. This was in 1972, when I was eleven. I saw an ad for it in the newspaper, and on a random winter Saturday I took the train into the city by myself for the first time. I told no one. I don't remember where I got the money. I bought a balcony seat, which cost very little. Everything happened effortlessly that day — as if it were meant to be. I concentrated so completely on that show that I lost track of everything. Even during the intermission, I was transfixed. Riding the subway home felt like floating in a bubble. It was a small, encouraging sample of the freedom that existed when I was left to my own wits in New York City. I knew from that experience that if I could get away, I could give myself what really mattered, and I wouldn't need anyone's help. From that day forward I knew I could take care of myself.

6

In front of my puppet-theatre garage was the house we lived in. It was in the Midwood neighborhood of Brooklyn, close enough to Yeshivah of Flatbush that my sisters and I could walk to school. It was a huge Dutch Colonial house built around the turn of the century, with a front lawn, three stories, an attic and unfinished basement, plus a yard, driveway, and my garage. It was a big step up from the two-family rental we'd been living in. My father's business was doing well, and the move was a reflection of that. My parents remodeled the house before we moved in, but it never felt quite finished. There was always something either in progress or broken, and my mother was overwhelmed by the upkeep of it. All she wanted was a settled, elegant life in the new house. While for my father, someone who was good with tools and had a real appetite for an ongoing construction project, it seemed like a dream.

Typical of my mother, she found a way to make our new home stylish, but without paying loads of money for it. At first she considered hiring a woman from Bloomingdale's to decorate, but she discovered that "unless we want our house resembling a Bloomingdale's chair showroom, we better look elsewhere." So while her friends' homes were being decorated extravagantly by famous, highly sought-after interior designers like Angelo Donghia and Joe D'Urso, my mother hired someone with considerably less celebrity but who had a reputation for taste and sophistication. Just the name sounded distinguished to me: John Banter.

Observing John Banter at close range, I discovered he was different from most other men. Though not dressed in a Pucci bikini like Michael Sherman, he was not at all like my father or my uncles or any other men I knew. He was slim and good-looking and intimidating. I still had no real idea what homosexuality was — I didn't even know the word. I didn't associate the words "fairy" or "faggot" with any particular sexuality; I did know they were pejoratives I was hearing more and more. I certainly made no conscious connection between these concepts and John Banter, but he fascinated me, and I sensed he and I shared an affinity — though I was far too shy to speak to him.

When John Banter finished the house he came to lunch and my mother served him a Middle Eastern hors d'oeuvre — a small, spicy, cheese empanada called *sambusac*. I was hidden in the kitchen, peering in; when he bit into it, he said, "Sarah, this is a little bit of heaven. I must have the recipe." I watched him carefully from afar whenever I could, and his presence in our lives for that brief moment made me feel better and hopeful for some strange, unknown reason. On top of everything else, I was proud that my family went to the lengths of hiring someone as obviously tasteful as John Banter to decorate.

My parents' renovation of the house was an attempt at a loving restoration with modern additions. They added a den and a dinette in the back of the house (from which snaked the extension cord that powered my puppet theatre). At the front of the house, in place of what once was a screened-in porch, they built a rectangular windowed "conservatory," where the light-walnut baby grand piano lived. The floors in the main part of the living room and dining room were beautifully restored, dark-stained cherry parquet, the upkeep of which was a constant concern to my father. There was always some sort of roll-down preventive rug-scrap or mat. The color scheme of the living room was based on a mustard-colored Schumacher chintz print that covered two dark-wood Louis XVI armchairs and the valances above all the windows in the room. The engineered area rug was matched to this mustard color and inlaid with flowers and stems that set off the browns and blues in that chintz print. A small bull-nosed brown velvet sofa and a chrome-and-glass "Barcelona" coffee table added a note of midcentury classicism.

There was a step-down into the addition, the "conservatory," where the flooring changed to turquoise shag carpet. It was a cold, exposed space, revealed to the street by three walls of paned windows. Through the satin-striped sheer curtains you could feel the presence and shadows of the neighborhood outside. I often imagined that people could hear my playing on the street, and I fantasized that someone out there would be captivated by my piano-playing shadow, and we'd meet and fall in love like something out of a Brontë novel.

■ ■ ■ ■

By the time I was twelve, insomnia was a foregone condition. The most prominent and controversial factor in my bad sleeping habits was a small, portable TV with an oyster-colored pebble-textured plastic case. My parents bought it for themselves, but I commandeered it, and it became a permanent fixture in my bedroom. There were mixed opinions about its influence over me: Was the TV there to make me feel less alone when I couldn't sleep? Or was it the very thing keeping me up at night? Around my twelfth birthday the TV was confiscated, my parents settling on the latter hypothesis, that it was the TV itself that was keeping me awake. But I carried on so vehemently and for so long that they finally gave it back to me. I remember the feeling of relief and triumph the night I got it back, as I tuned in to the Johnny Carson show and watched with special relish.

The following summer the little oyster-colored TV met a horrible end. One night my sister Marilyn claimed to hear it through the paper-thin walls of the summer rental we were living in. She caused such a huge ruckus at 3:00 A.M. that my mother was awakened from a deep sleep and barged into my room — a zombie arisen from the dead, ecru-colored tricot-and-lace nightgown flying behind her like the exhaust from a broomstick. She leered at me through half-open eyes, picked up the TV and threw it to the ground, where it shattered into a thousand little pieces, then exited in another wave of nightgown lace. Part comedy, part trauma, my sister and I burst into laughter — what seemed at the time like our only logical reaction. That event did not set me back in my TV watching for long, though. The next day my mother felt so guilty she bought me a new, slightly larger, lighter-weight, portable TV in a shiny black plastic case.

There was an appearance of affluence to our new home and neighborhood, even though it was a financial stretch for my parents at the time. After hiring John Banter and renovating the rest of the house, they could never afford to finish the basement. The paneled basement rec room they'd imagined — and that all the neighbors had — was not to be. It remained a raw underground reminder of their aspirations versus their financial shortcomings.

The basement, like the garage, was another area that I commandeered as a creative center. It had low ceilings that felt like they were on the verge of collapse, poured-cement floors, and crude makeshift lighting with exposed wiring that always seemed seconds away from an electrical fire. My mother kept an extra freezer and refrigerator there, also a store of canned and dry goods. And soda, specifically Tab, cases and cases of which were delivered by the local drugstore and kept on top of an old, rusted, metal cabinet right by the stairs. I was the only kid in my neighborhood who was allowed to drink as much Tab as I wanted. I imagine it had to do with my mother's desire for me to consume fewer calories. It was my much-loathed job every night after setting the dinner table to act as soda sommelier. I descended to the cellar to bring up the six-pack of Tab and fill the ice bucket. Inevitably the ice would crash to the floor, which would elicit another "She just left!" reproach from my mother. Tab-fetching and ice-bucket-filling were considered the kind of manual labor that boys should do, making it the more detestable to me. All physical labor — any kind of heavy lifting — in our household was male-designated, and if I ever complained or asked why one of my sisters couldn't do it, my mother would say,

"You want your sister to drop her womb?"

When I wasn't being sent there to retrieve Tab, I loved the basement. There were horror-movie elements to it, like creaky stairs and dark, spiderwebbed corners. But I consciously overlooked all of them because it had so much to recommend it as a workspace. My father set up a woodworking shop in the corner farthest from the stairs. He never used it, though, so I took it over when creating sets for my puppet theatre, and later for building a portable hand-puppet theatre, which I used for years when I worked birthday parties. I never put a tool back in its proper place, and I abused tools that were never meant to be used the way I used them. Saws that weren't meant to saw through metal, or drill bits that were the wrong size drilling into something that was never meant to be drilled into. Every once in a while, when the house needed a small fix, my father made an effort to give me lessons on how to properly use a screwdriver or a hand wrench or a power saw, but I was way too impatient to learn about tools. I came really close several times to drilling right through my thigh, or setting the house on fire when heating colored candle wax for puppets in my Thingmaker (a hot plate that made figures out of something called Plastigoop, the kind of insanely dangerous toy we all had in the 1970s).

Around my tenth birthday I started noticing the fashion magazines my mother brought into the house every month. My sisters seemed to be properly engrossed in things like homework and movie dates with friends on weekends, while I studied the magazines and their pictures of women in fancy clothes. I hoarded them and ripped pages out and stuck them on the cork wall in my bedroom. When I could spare time away from the puppet theatre, I began to sketch — to emulate my favorite photos from *Vogue* and *Harper's Bazaar.* There was a photo of a yellow Giorgio di Sant'Angelo sunburst-pleated chiffon dress, circa 1972, that I sketched from three different angles. I often sketched on scraps of paper, and I especially loved the cardboard sheets with a white laminate side that came in my father's shirts from the laundry and which he saved for me. The first sketches were for their own sake. Crude pictures of fancy women, severe faces, the hair and shoes obsessively rendered. After a short while, though, the sketches became about something else. By the time I was eleven I began to understand the very basic ideas of design. Lines. Shape.

In the remaining basement space, which

135

was considerable, I set up my atelier. There was a hand-me-down drafting table from my uncle Sam where I did sketches under the light of a red-enamel clamp-on architect's lamp that I bought with my allowance money. Next to that was a high console made of old lumber scraps that held all my painting and craft supplies. My father rigged an illegal telephone extension that hung on a two-by-four beam right near the stairs, for my mothers' use while doing laundry. I erected a little desk underneath that, which became my "office area," complete with Rolodex. In it I kept the numbers of the four fabric stores I went to, as well as Halston's office address and telephone number, which I'd looked up in the phone book. I had no need for the number, no intention of using it; I just loved the idea of having it. Nearby I had another cork wall full of tear sheets from *Women's Wear Daily* and *Vogue*. *WWD* was a staple in the household. My dad got his daily copy sent to the house so my mother could see it, too. My atelier was complete when eventually I took possession of the giant 1950s black-and-white console television that was retired from the family den, where it lived till it was replaced by a huge color console TV a few years after we moved in. Once I had that TV in that spot,

I was able to spend hours on end working while it created a kind of white noise in the background (I still rely a lot on the white noise of TV).

At that time in my life my mother was my most important critic and champion. I've often thought that whatever she lacked in "mothering the person" she made up for in "mothering the artist." There were times when she was more concerned with the mess I'd made than noticing the work, and times when I'd come up from the basement with a bunch of sketches that she would dismiss by saying she was too busy to look at them. But when she did pay focused attention to something I made, she treated me like a professional, not a child. Her cold-blooded assessments were the greatest form of encouragement because I knew they were honest and constructive. She'd say things like "that orange blouse would work better in white." Or "that dress would be 'dressier' if it were full length." She spoke to me like an adult and never sugarcoated her opinions.

I loved that basement atelier, and if I wasn't in the garage with my puppet shows, I was there. One day while I was finishing off one of my leading-lady puppets, I was confronted with a lot of extra purple "by-the-yard" fringe I had purchased a few days earlier. I got the idea to fancy up a red-and-white striped shirt of mine by adding the fringe onto the breast pocket and all the way down the sleeves and across the back along the yoke. I never had a particular inclination for dressing up, but that day I wanted to know how it felt to wear fringe. I still remember the moment of crossing over, sewing onto something other than a puppet. It was the first piece of clothing I ever manipulated with my hands. It was a magical sensation to wear that fringed shirt, something that one short hour before had been a mere figment of my imagination.

That same day, maybe because I felt so good about the creation of the shirt, I decided to take a bike ride. I also knew it would please my mother, who was constantly admonishing me to get some exercise and fresh air. Before I left I made sure to put on a shapeless grey-wool crewneck over the fancy fringed shirt, which completely concealed it. I made it all the way to the old-guard Syrian neighborhood of Avenue S, and then I did something really out of character: When I encountered some of the boys in my class playing basketball, they asked me to join the game, and I decided it would be good to make an effort to be less antisocial. Within a few minutes of playing I got hot and decided to take off my sweater. And there, underneath, was my fancy shirt with the fringed trim that I had forgotten all about. The horror that washed over me was like the anxiety dream in which you're walking down a New York City street and suddenly realize you're naked. I didn't even wait for the repercussions. Without uttering a word, I jumped on my bike and fled.

From the age of eight, I spent a lot of time in our windowed conservatory room taking piano lessons and practicing. The piano itself was distressed to look antique, a baby grand that felt and sounded more like a toy piano. Despite its flaws as an instrument, it was on this fake piano that I acquired genuine appreciation for music. Mozart, Bach, Bartók, Debussy, Scarlatti. My reading skills were bad and they never really developed, but I had a good ear. Soon I could pick out any tune and even make up accompanying chords and create full, dramatic — albeit cheesy — arrangements. This might have won me favor with some musicians, but it only added an edge to my already difficult relationship with our piano teacher, Miss Rivlin. She preferred a more rule-bound approach to playing piano. And since my sisters were always much better at following rules than I was — and were always much better prepared for lessons — she much preferred teaching them. In contrast, I relied on my ear and spent most of my time at that tinny piano making up schmaltzy arrangements of Gershwin tunes that I copied from Judy Garland and Streisand recordings.

Miss Rivlin was a sneery older lady with hard, small, judgmental eyes set beneath a dome of lacquered black hair. She wore cardigan sweaters draped on her shoulders and pearls, mostly to clutch in horror as I mangled passages of Muzio Clementi. Her tortoiseshell half-glasses hung from a chain around her neck and would get pinned onto her face like a dart when she was impatient or disdainful. She treated me like a hoodlum, and while I wasn't, the more she treated me like one, the more I became one. After about two years I finally gave in to her disdain. I stopped practicing altogether and spent most of the lessons making up dramatic excuses for why I hadn't practiced — injured fingers, wrist trouble, etc. I was fearless in my defiance. One day before my lesson I hid underneath the piano and watched as she settled in, waiting for me to appear. An awkward few minutes passed while she looked around the room for me. I let it go as long as I possibly could, and finally I jumped out from beneath the piano and yelled "BOO!" She leapt out of her chair and ran away. After that the atmosphere between me and Miss Rivlin became notably more hostile.

My days of traumatizing Miss Rivlin came to an end soon after, when my sisters announced that they no longer wanted to take piano lessons. Given my natural affinity, my parents decided that I should continue on, but with a new piano teacher. Alan Small was a middle-aged man with a good sense of humor who wore short-sleeved cotton-blend plaid shirts and smelled of pencil shavings and cigarettes. He had big, sensitive ears and a disproportionately large, round, bald head. We got along much better than I ever did with Miss Rivlin, and he taught me piano more in accordance with how I was naturally inclined to learn it. In addition to the classical pieces we studied together, each week on staff paper he would handwrite tunes — Gershwin, Burt Bacharach, anything he knew I liked — and leave the bass clef on the page empty so I could fill in the accompanying chords and create the arrangements myself. The drudgery of routine piano lessons became more like a happy musical collaboration, and I practiced constantly and looked forward to our weekly meetings.

My piano playing became a source of pride for my parents, who would encourage me to play for company. Most dinner parties or holiday gatherings culminated in me dazzling the group with an excerpt of Mozart or my schmaltzy new arrangement of the Gershwins' "The Man I Love" or a rendition of Sondheim's "Losing My Mind." Sometimes I felt a bit like a performing monkey, trotted out so my parents could seem like sophisticated culture mavens. Occasionally I resented this, but for the most part I was hammy enough to love the attention and would be slightly pissed off if the subject of playing for the assembled company *didn't* arise.

Other than my parents' insistence on piano lessons and showing me off at dinner parties, there wasn't much music in the house. When my father left music behind as a profession, he seemed to drop it altogether as a part of his life. We had one portable hi-fi stereo, a blue Naugahyde thing that looked like a suitcase, with speakers that flipped out on each side of the turntable. It was a family possession, but it was usually in my room. Streisand was always playing.

And Judy. And Liza. And Dusty Springfield and Dionne Warwick. I saved whatever money I could from my allowance to buy more records. There was a record store on Avenue J and East Sixteenth Street called Harnik's Happy House that I could walk to, and there I bought all my records. But Barbra was my favorite. I collected her records in whatever technology was prevalent. I began with the full collection on vinyl, then I moved through eight-track tape, cassette, CD, and digital. Sometime in the early 1970s I succumbed to a magazine circular I found: Columbia House Record and Tape Club, which offered fifteen cassette tapes for a dollar. I got so many of my favorite tapes from that club: Sergio Mendez & Brasil '66, the *West Side Story* movie soundtrack, a compilation of Stravinsky ballets, and most beloved, *Liza with a "Z."* My parents' bedroom was next door to mine, and my mother used to complain about the noise, often barging in and turning the volume down herself.

Ironically, the female impersonations that eventually became a source of shame and awkwardness for my parents originated with a gift from my mother. It was the *Funny Girl* soundtrack, which became my prized possession and which I listened to obsessively.

An unselfconscious transformation occurred in me as I sang along: I started impersonating Streisand. And the more I sang along, the more I could reproduce those sounds. As I added to my record collection, I also added to my repertoire of impersonations, which soon included Judy Garland, Dionne Warwick, Petula Clark, and Shirley Bassey. At that point I had no inclination toward drag; I was more interested in creating a vocal illusion. Before puberty I really could make my voice sound exactly like these women. I secretly bought a special lock for my bedroom door, a sort of stainless-steel plate that fit between the door and the jamb with a brass fob that slid into place and insured privacy. I spotted it in the window of a big hardware store called Doody (no kidding) a few doors down from Midwood Trimmings. I knew if I could have total privacy I'd feel more comfortable developing my abilities as a performer. And once I was alone, I started using my room to practice not only the vocals but the mannerisms of the singers, whom I'd seen in movies and on TV. I tried to bring whatever physicality I could to the performances — which was often crude. I never used clothes or makeup, just voice and mannerisms. Even at that age I knew I was copying these women not necessarily to become better as a female impersonator, but more to find my own voice, to find my own personal ideas and the ability to put a song across as myself.

When I was doing these impersonations I could fly up to the ceiling and observe myself. I looked like, sounded like — *became* — these women. I got lost in the volume of sound, some coming from the record, some from my body. I got lost in the lush arrangements, and in the passion of the singing. I felt gorgeous. I knew the impressions were good, and once I grew brazen (or foolhardy) enough to perform them outside my bedroom, I got the attention I needed — even if it was the wrong kind of attention. The impersonations were okay if I chose my audience wisely.

There were some strange mixed signals from my parents. When my mother's family visited, my female impersonations were okay, even encouraged. Aunt Adele — my mother's favorite and closest sister — seemed really entertained. But when my father's less broad-minded family was around, my whole personality had to be shut down. And though my mother and father never ridiculed me, they were terribly uncomfortable around certain aspects of my personality, and probably fearful of what was to come. They weren't wrong to be concerned. Not to apologize for their actions but, really, how do you tell a twelve-year-old boy in 1973 that it's okay to impersonate Streisand in public?

My flamboyance was always obvious: I was musical, I put on glittering puppet shows, I drew pictures in the pages of the religious books at school, I had a basement atelier. Many of those could be chalked up to being "artistic," but the impersonations risked exposing me on a whole other level that I didn't comprehend. It was somehow related to this mass of shame that followed me around like a stray dog. Whatever it was, it was getting closer.

7

The basement flooded the same year my father had his first heart attack, and I always thought of that flood as a kind of physical manifestation of our anxiety surrounding his illness. Any moment my mother wasn't at the hospital tending to him, she was bailing water. We all pitched in. As scared and exhausted as she was, I got the sense that the flood gave her something real to focus on, something to do — water to bail, a tangible physical challenge with an end in sight; the slow, steady progress of one bucket of water following another. A lot of the details about my father's first heart attack were kept from my sisters and me. I was twelve, and my sisters were fourteen and sixteen. We were old enough to know there was something terribly wrong, but we didn't know exactly what, which left a huge empty space to fill with conjecture.

The day it happened we heard the story

thirdhand from Aunt Adele, who came over and made us dinner and stayed with us while my mother remained at the hospital. She said my dad and my uncle Sam had just eaten dinner at his favorite restaurant in Midtown, called Bon Vivant, and while my uncle was hailing a taxi, my father fell in the street. An ambulance came and rushed him to the hospital. A day and a half later my mother came home looking like a total wreck, took off her shoes and stockings, and started bailing water. Her story was less complex; "Your father is just fine," she told us.

My sisters seemed paralyzed with fear. I remember feeling a certain guilty relief that my father wasn't in the house. At that point in my life his presence made me feel physically anxious. I was on the brink of realizing that my lifestyle had a name, and my sexual leanings weren't something I'd be able to hide forever. And if I couldn't hide them, then I'd be another of those fairies whom my father thought should be lined up and shot. I realize now that he most likely never would have confronted me, but at the time I was always terribly nervous about a confrontation I was not ready for. When he was in the house, I was on tenterhooks.

When my dad returned from the hospital

our lives changed. The food we ate as a result of my mother trying to cook healthier was bland to the point of being funny. She made a ridiculous celery and mushroom casserole that was so terrible, it tasted like a kind of medicine to *cure* heart disease. All fried and fatty foods were banned. My father was forced to quit smoking. This health regimen was something he did only within my mother's sight. Outside of it, he ate corned beef sandwiches and smoked, winking at me to not tell his secrets.

The family schedule was also affected by my father's new semi-invalid status. He was encouraged to rest and to sleep, and so he was around in the mornings until 11:00 A.M. or even noon. Of all the things my mother had to adjust to, that was the hardest. She wanted to seize her days, but was slowed down considerably by my father's long morning routine. He woke up around nine and dominated the bathroom for at least an hour with his morning toilette. Then he had special breakfast needs and a whole regimen of pills that needed administering. His work schedule, though shorter, was never less stressful. Business was difficult, and many was the time I witnessed my father in his office, red in the face, screaming at someone over the phone. It was a challenge for him to spend less time at the office. He felt his absence would affect business adversely, and it probably did. The heart disease added a whole layer of stress to his life, which was already stressful. He was the breadwinner for a family of five, with a bar mitzvah around the corner and two daughters who needed marrying off; two very expensive propositions.

My parents' lives as a couple changed after the heart attack, too. They didn't go out as much. And there were the weekly visits to the heart specialist, a man my father swore by ("the number-one heart doctor in the country"), Dr. Robert Dresdale. My mother had less faith in Dr. Dresdale, based on the fact that my father didn't seem to be getting much better under his care. They went to Dr. Dresdale once a week for a year after his first heart attack, and once a month thereafter. He became my father's friend and advisor. My mother struggled with my father's devotion to him, and they quarreled about it. He had two more heart attacks after that first, including one that went undetected for a while, which would make anyone waver in her faith. There was talk of heart surgery, but Dr. Dresdale overruled that in favor of putting a healthier lifestyle in place — a lifestyle that my father really never committed fully to. My mother wanted to get a second opinion, but my father held on to his idol worship of Dresdale.

My bar mitzvah was a confusing distraction from my father's illness. I recall it as one of the most troublesome times in my life. At the same time that I was excited about the pending festivities I felt an underlying dread, the sense that I was being initiated against my will into the wrong club.

I had bar mitzvah lessons with a man named Mickey Cairey, who taught all the boys in our community for decades. His presence made me uneasy. He was a gnomish, disheveled figure in suits two sizes too big and orthopedic shoes — rough-edged in general, a guy who according to my father was "the salt of the earth." He spoke in the same coarse, uneducated manner as my father's family, with a thick Brooklyn accent and aggressively bad grammar, representing all the things I was trying to escape. He was pitied for his unmarried status and vagabond mien, and he seemingly had no life other than teaching bar mitzvah boys and arranging funerals. The community was grateful to him for doing things they didn't want to do themselves — such as burying their kin and teaching me the words I needed to know for this meaningless rite that was about to take place.

Perhaps I shouldn't have taken it all so seriously. Bar mitzvahs in the Syrian community at that time were far less about boys becoming men and far more of an opportunity for families to showboat their wealth. Families prepared for their sons' bar mitzvahs years in advance. They reserved temple and venue dates, and saved up for the extravagant parties they'd be expected to host. It was a Byzantine undertaking that dominated the family of the bar mitzvah boy for as long as two years. The glamourous excess of the production was not lost on me, and I took a great interest in my mother's obsession with dresses and flower arrangements and catering. Had it not been for the religious aspect, I might have enjoyed the proceedings.

Instead, I felt deep uneasiness, fear, and skepticism about the whole concept of "becoming a man." I felt wrong about accepting or carrying out any of the things I was committing to. It was one thing to be swaying and mumbling in shul or pretending to daven in school. It was another thing entirely being in the spotlight, leading the ceremony proclaiming my devotion to god.

I felt like a terrible liar. And there weren't only religious repercussions. Passing from boyhood, where whatever sexuality I was inhabiting could be overlooked, into manhood, a time in one's life when sexuality would become almost the center of one's identity, was overwhelming and frightening in its implications. At a family gathering I once overheard my father talking to his sisters and a few of my older cousins about the fact that I was obviously still a virgin, a condition that would need to change in the coming years. The consensus among them was that when the time came, I should be indoctrinated into manhood by being taken to a brothel. I didn't know exactly what they were talking about — and I was too terrified to ask — but I could make a good guess. I remember my older cousins snickering and nudging each other. My father never followed through on this, but the very thought of it caused me panic for days.

At the time the standard bar mitzvah had many parts to it. There was the weekday event, usually a Tuesday or a Thursday during the morning prayers, when the ark of the Torah was opened and the bar mitzvah boy went up and read the parashah aloud — the paragraph in the Torah that relates to his birthday. That was usually followed by a

153

small breakfast held in the lobby of the shul before everyone went off to work. Then there was the Saturday "Shabbat" service where the whole thing was repeated in front of a much larger congregation and with considerably more ritualistic fanfare. On that same day, the bar mitzvah family was obligated to host something called a *sebbet.* The home was flung open for the entire community — usually about three hundred people showed up — for a casual, albeit uncomfortably tight, lunch served out of tinfoil bins on long, ungainly folding tables set up all over the house. The guests would stay all afternoon, praying and singing and eating.

The pièce de résistance of any bar mitzvah was the grand evening celebration, when the family got to really put on a show and spend a fortune. My dad's heart attack limited the possibilities. Instead of the evening party, which seemed a little too stressful and a bit out of our reach financially, we put the emphasis on an elegant luncheon, to be served at home, on the day of the actual bar mitzvah. Because of so many bar mitzvahs in the community, mine happened on a random Thursday in May, even though my birthday is in the middle of October.

My mother took the helm early. My parents went on a vacation to St. Thomas a year and a half in advance of the event and came back with a dozen Georg Jensen silver vases for the tables, which they got for a big discount in one of the island outlet stores. My mother started sourcing fabrics for tablecloths at least a year before the event, constantly nudging my father to bring home swatch books of fabrics that might work. Having not exactly finished the décor on the house, she borrowed paintings from Aunt Deanne, colorful abstract paintings done by her mother, which lent a wonderful, modern, finished look to the place. Tons of temporary and last-minute décor was decided on. They found a Lucite trolley with stainless-steel wheels, which they set in the living room as a bar. Also they found a wall-mirror sculpture, popular at the time, consisting of clear, smoked-, and black-mirrored slats that overlapped to form an abstract city skyline.

My mother was excited by some of the details and overwhelmed by others. In a community where status symbols were everything, she had a big task ahead. There was a story she told about a lunch hosted by her friend, a woman named Adelaide, considered a doyenne of beautiful china and crystal among the ladies of the community. Adelaide was tired of them snooping about her table, so at that lunch she set out her best Baccarat and Limoges, and on the flip side of every dish was a small sticker she'd had printed that said "none of your business." (I wondered how my mother knew about those stickers!)

There was definitely a greater need for my mother's afternoon lie-downs during this period. She would take to the sofa, or on bad days her bed, with reading materials you might expect of the times: novels by Saul Bellow and Philip Roth and nonfiction by Gore Vidal and Norman Mailer. These afternoon "rest periods" were a sign to the family that she was on shaky emotional ground.

Still, whatever social or financial pressures my mother felt over the bar mitzvah were more than compensated for by her passionate engagement with selecting the wardrobe. She scoured the usual places in order to dress my sisters, and bought and returned so many dresses. She finally settled on a silvery-blue satin flapper dress for Norma, accessorized with silver lamé tights and patent-leather Mary-Janes. Marilyn wore a patchwork-print flounced peasant dress with her hair partially braided. My father

156

was an elegant man despite being portly, and he dressed himself well. He had a weekly standing haircut-and-manicure appointment. He wore custom-made suits and a seasonal turnover of ties and shirts, all of which he had made at a place in New York City called Kohmer Marcus, where he took me on occasion to witness those fittings. He also had a great collection of pocket squares, a few of which I still have and carry.

My mother's wardrobe was given another level of attention entirely. Months and months in advance were spent studying magazine spreads, tearing out photos, combing the racks at every major store in the tristate area. Dinner table conversation was dominated by what would be most appropriate for her to wear. She would need one outfit for shul and another for hostessing the luncheon at home. She found a tailored off-white silk shantung suit at Loehmann's and splurged on Gucci accessories. Stacked-heeled sling-backs, a bone-leather clutch with the signature red and green ribbon trim, and a straw fedora. For the luncheon later at home she changed into Geoffrey Beene apple-green-and-white printed chiffon hostess pajamas, self-belted and finished at the waist with an oversized green-and-white silk poppy. There was no fudging this one. It was purchased full price at Saks Fifth Avenue. She paired it with strands of faceted emerald and white crystal beads that made it look even more stylish than the way it was originally shown.

My clothes were also a pressing concern — not out of a desire to outdo anyone's preconception of chic, but simply to find things that would fit. I guess all the stress I felt around the bar mitzvah caused me to eat my feelings a little more than usual. All the while I appeared to be dieting, I was actually eating in secret, which resulted in my getting even fatter. Evenings, after a miserable day at yeshiva, I broke away from the TV only long enough to raid the stock of Syrian pastries that my mother had labored over and stored between layers of waxed paper in shoe boxes hermetically sealed in plastic and neatly stacked in the basement freezer. Often before dinner I ate two or three portions from the pots containing the meal, and serving bowls at the table were mysteriously less full. Embarrassing, yes, but not enough to stop me from doing it again and again.

It was nearly impossible to find boys' clothes that fit me, even in the so-called "husky" departments. Shopping for clothes in my preteen years with my mother was hideous! I would look at something, and she would say in a loud voice that everyone could hear, "No, Isaac, no bell-bottoms for you." She'd continue with a choice piece of fashion advice: "Trendy clothes aren't for overweight people." Or: "Clunky shoes make heavy people look heavier." Or: "Wear neutrals." She told me flatly that I was too heavy to wear the loudly printed Qiana shirts that I desperately wanted and were so fashionable at the time. Sometimes she would look at something I held up and say only, "It's a travesty." She was protecting me, trying to make my clothing choices above reproach — inoculating me from ridicule by harshly criticizing me in advance. Utter disinterest in the subject of men's clothes only added to the beleaguered attitude she had toward her overweight son and the process of finding clothes that worked.

Dieting was the bane of my existence. I tried for months prior to my bar mitzvah, hoping to shrink myself into a standard size. I even accompanied my aunt Adele to Weigh In, which was the local version of Weight Watchers. That should've been mortifying, but I loved Adele. She and my mother were like two peas in a pod, so I actually found this weekly ritual kind of fun. Adele was an energetic blond ten years my mother's junior who was always dieting. "Adele is the real athlete of the family," my mother said lovingly about her over and over, and she was. She was always playing tennis or skiing or jogging. We all loved her, even my dad, who nicknamed her "Toots." Weigh In meant that I got to spend time with my favorite aunt. She and I had a secret society, with special foods such as Sealtest Ice Milk and skim-milk cottage cheese. There was also a sweet, chemical powder called Alba 77 that came in envelopes and that we mixed in a blender with skim milk and ice cubes to produce a questionable, yet sort of satisfying, diet malted.

In the end, Weigh In didn't work in time, and the hopes of me getting into an off-the-rack suit were nil. My father took it upon himself to have a suit made for me. A team from his factory in Philadelphia came to New York and took my measurements, and a few times that winter I accompanied my dad to Philly for the fittings. I changed into the suit in an empty office and stood on a fitting cube while they pinched and prodded and measured and smiled knowing smiles at me and at each other, which made me even more paranoid. The suit, which fit beautifully, was a two-button job in powder blue wool shantung with a huge notch lapel. Underneath I wore a kind of Liberty-print shirt and, if I remember correctly, a butter-yellow tie. My loafers were white patent leather with squared-off toes and big Pierre Cardin "PC" logo buckles. All the rules my mother had drummed into my head about what overweight people should wear were broken. Her attentions were scattered, and she assumed my father was handling it. By the time she focused on me, the deed was done. Ironically, I didn't feel particularly fat in that suit, I felt great. It lent me a kind of false confidence. When I look back at the pictures, I know she was right all along. I looked heavier than I would have in a dark grey or navy blue suit, but the powder-blue feeling was worth it.

On the day of the luncheon, we were awakened by the arrival of the caterers and waiters with crates and urns and rentals of all kinds. The house was unrecognizable. The furniture had been emptied out a day earlier and replaced with round tables covered in canary-yellow-and-white plaid organza tablecloths. Placed on each table were white lilies in the silver vases that my parents had purchased on vacation. It was an unusually beautiful cool and sunny spring day. The tulips on the front lawn were peaking. The original lead-crystal-paned doors in the front of the house were temperamental and attached to an equally temperamental alarm system. They mostly remained shut, but that day they were flung open, adding to the excitement and the feeling of vulnerability in having all these people come into our home to celebrate an event about which I had such ambivalence. This was supposed to be the social pinnacle, but I felt disdain for these people who made my life so difficult and were now entering my house under the false pretense of celebrating me.

Once the party was fully under way, my nervousness and a lot of my loathing for the whole elaborate charade flowed out of the house on the cool cross-breeze. Everyone seemed happy. Even the ritual of the bar mitzvah earlier that morning seemed light and airy compared to the nervousness I felt in advance. I was more hysterical about reading that parashah than anything I had ever done. I found my way to the podium on shaky legs, but a few seconds into it my inner ham emerged and my nerves disappeared. By the end I discovered I was as good at singing my parashah as I was at doing Streisand in the alley, and there wasn't much of a difference between the two. The only thing missing was applause at the end, which doesn't happen in shul.

The food and the clothes all made their impact, most of the guests were duly impressed, and my parents shone as hosts. But by the end of the day, the great irony revealed itself: What was supposed to be about me was much more about my parents and the obligation they felt to acknowledge their son becoming a man. I've always been good at gritting my teeth and making it through tense times with a smile. That day those skills were tested — I was seething on the inside, while on the outside grinning and bearing, aided by the aura of the custom-made powder-blue suit. Even now, people who know me well are astounded by my ability to appear content, even jolly, when in reality I'm spitting nails. Mostly it has to do with my fear of upsetting others, and my distaste for confrontation.

At the end of the day, when most of the crowd had gone and only a few stragglers remained, I channeled my feelings into my puppet show. I flung open the garage door and put on a rousing performance of my puppet *Follies.* The show that evening had an ominous, manic quality to it. The *Gypsy* overture played extra loud on the cassette player, and my Rockettes danced with a little too much enthusiasm.

8

The year I was born my family spent the summer in a charming cottage in Bradley Beach, New Jersey, which is a tiny town near Asbury Park that the Syrian Jews descended upon every year when the weather turned warm. The cottage was in a perfect spot, across the street from a lake and close to the beach. In old pictures and home movies it looks idyllic, with a small front porch and red-and-white striped awnings. There's footage of me in my playpen bouncing up and down. There's a happy photo of Maureen smiling broadly and holding me on her hip. There's a red convertible Thunderbird in slightly later pictures, too, which was my father's pride and joy. "If you close your eyes I can make the car fly," my dad would say to my sisters and me, seated in the back. We would close our eyes and he'd speed up, which really felt like taking off. "If you open your eyes the car can't fly anymore," he'd say, so we'd keep our eyes shut and swear we were really flying.

A few years later my father lost everything in the failed attempt to take his company public, and we spent summers in Brooklyn for a while. By the time we were ready to reenter the summer social fray, the Syrian Jews had shifted the scene up the Jersey Shore from the charming cottages of Bradley Beach to the oversized, ostentatious houses a few miles north in a town called Deal. There, starting at age eleven and lasting until my early adulthood, I spent summers in an ever-changing series of odd rentals.

I dreaded our summers there. During the winter months I had an easier time staving off depression — lost in my garage with my puppets, and sketching in my basement atelier. The summer was supposed to be a break, a vacation, but for me it meant being forced to confront all my worst fears. It's not that I avoided them entirely during the winter months, but they intensified and came to visible life during the long summers spent in that provincial beach town. To this day I experience my peccadillos, insecurities, and intense nervousness tenfold in the summertime. June and July get

166

progressively worse and every year, for a few days in August, the world comes to an end.

A very big part of my summer anxiety came from the necessity of appearing in a swimsuit. As early as I can remember I hated taking my shirt off at the beach, feeling too fat to be so undressed in public. All the bullying in the world about being effeminate doesn't hurt me nearly as much as one sly remark about being fat.

The town of Deal, New Jersey, like so many beach towns, had a lot going for it before it became overbuilt. There were about fifteen blocks of gorgeous old houses, mansions really, built at the turn of the century and occupied by people like F. Scott Fitzgerald and Norma Shearer. By 1972 those houses were almost exclusively owned by Syrian Jews, and early McMansions were being built on any available vacant lot. The community was growing, its affluence was growing, and so was the exclusivity of its borders. To this day the richest families still live within the original fifteen-block radius, with descending castes of other families living farther and farther from the middle.

Dead center of the daytime social scene was the beach club, which was called the Deal Casino. (Nothing to do with gambling.) It was located smack in the middle of the town, on the oceanfront. It sets me on edge to even write about it all these years later. As you walked into the Deal Casino you were confronted with a huge pool, like a vast kidney-shaped water-village. Around the pool were cabanas and lounges with the same kind of social significance as the layout of the town itself. Those blue-chip families that had been members of the casino for longer had cabanas closer to the pool. The girls sitting on the lounges in front of those cabanas were given special consideration by the eligible boys. The rest of us inhabited cabanas that were rows and rows back, which felt like a whole other town. Eligible girls were expected to remain pristine on their lounges, in big hair, full makeup, high heels that never came off, and the skimpiest bathing suits decency would allow. The thought of ever going near the water and ruining the effect was out of the question.

From the time I was eleven, my mother and sisters and I stayed put in Deal from July Fourth until Labor Day, while my father stayed in Brooklyn three nights a week and commuted the rest of the time. There wasn't much of anything for me to do in Deal. There was just me and my adolescent insecurities, with no change of subject. I tried day camp one year but discovered that was worse than being on my own. So I created diversions. One year I took it upon myself to organize a production of *Bye Bye Birdie* at the local Y. Another year I hand-painted T-shirts and sold them. And one year, encouraged by Uncle Sam, I made twenty paintings and took a booth at the local art fair at the end of that summer. Since I couldn't haul the garage or the basement atelier to Deal, these were the projects I clung to. While around me people were luxuriating in sun, ocean, and grand parties of all kinds, I was hiding in a dark location, away from the crowd, working.

Any fear disappeared along with good sense when my inner ham emerged. Two or three times each summer, an audience would assemble at the Deal Casino to watch me do my female impersonations like they would a kind of sideshow freak. It started one random Saturday, when someone — I was easily swayed — convinced me to do Barbra Streisand. I got up the nerve and belted out "My Man," which drew a huge crowd. At the end they cheered. And hearing that applause made me feel so great. It's an instinct, perhaps a warped one; even the people who hate me love me when they applaud. You can feel it. Like a big collective caress. No matter what they say about you in real life, or do to hurt you, you're being rewarded at that moment. They love you, and they're telling you so.

I did another number, and before I knew it I finished a full "set." Judy, Dionne, Liza, all the favorites. One day, at the climax of one of my shows, I noticed my father watching from the back of the crowd, a deeply puzzled look on his face. I didn't stop singing, but I kept one eye on him and watched him peel away. I ended the show abruptly and was afraid to go home. But my father never mentioned it. That kind of denial was how he dealt with a lot of things about me he didn't understand.

Like the time when I was nine and locked myself in the bathroom with my mother's makeup. For all the times I watched obsessively as she applied it, this one time I wanted to know what it would feel like on my skin. To me it was no different from painting the faces of my puppets. Still, I was sure this wouldn't go down well, so when I was called to dinner I panicked and quickly washed my face with soap and water, leaving behind smears of makeup on my face that wouldn't have been noticed by a child my age. I still remember the expression on my parents' faces — simultaneously noticing and refusing to notice. Dinner went on as usual; no one said a word. It was the same that day when my father watched me perform at the Deal Casino. He saw and refused to see. But from that point forward I think he couldn't deny the reality of who I was and why I was jeered at and bullied all the time. It had to be difficult for him having a son who did things like female impersonations in public, and I felt certain that he was ashamed of me. At shul or family functions, I found it harder and harder to be with him.

Behind the scenes, invisible to all but me and one other person, a true milestone occurred in Deal the summer right before my bar mitzvah: I not only became a man, but I lost my virginity. I had a friend who was almost exactly my age, with whom I had sleepovers. We got along on so many levels, something I'd never really experienced before with anyone. This boy and I spent days and days together, constantly in each other's company. We played all kinds of games, and rode our bikes, and had a really easy rapport. One weekend we were at the Deal Casino alone in my family's cabana, which was far away from the center of the beach club. We couldn't be heard, and the cabana door was locked with a hook-and-eye latch. Narrow stripes of bright sunlight slipped through the slatted doors, but otherwise the cabana was dark and cool, and the scents of salt and chlorine were edged out by the stronger scent of Bain de Soleil. We were undressing, changing into our swimsuits, and while I hadn't gone through puberty yet, I noticed that he had. He had a man's body. One thing led to another, and before I could even think about the significance of what was happening, we were fumbling through youthful sex. He instructed me on how to please him and he administered my first orgasm, which was like being let in on a great secret.

We went on having innocent sex for a few years, and I wasn't plagued by guilt or confusion. The sex had no political or social ramifications for me. It didn't feel dirty or have perverse connotations. It was beautiful. And purely physical. I never felt self-conscious, and he seemed as gratified by it as me. Our friendship was not altered in any way; the sex was merely something else we did together when we were completely alone. It didn't seem unnatural or wrong, yet it was something I knew we had to hide from everyone else.

When I look back on it now I'm grateful

that I was able to have something so sweet and uncomplicated. And illuminating. It ended when we were fourteen or fifteen and we both went our separate ways. When it was over we never referred to it again. There were certainly no expectations of becoming a legitimate couple — I was still so young I didn't really understand what this sort of thing even meant beyond feeling good.

Sex with him didn't feel like anything as serious as a lifestyle-defining choice, nor did I pine for him when it was over. I wasn't in denial about my preferential love for men, but I was still piecing together what it all meant. Now I knew, though, that there was an action I could associate with my longings. The taunting and bullying took on a new meaning, too. I started to understand the connections between my sexuality and the thing I was being ostracized for. All those years of being the outsider were tied to this one trait, which was as natural to me as my hair and eye color, and which was just starting to make itself felt for real.

9

A few months before my bar mitzvah, my dad bought me two pairs of professional scissors: one for fabric — a heavy, classic pair, about a foot in length — and another, equally long, for cutting paper patterns, although I didn't yet know what paper patterns were. The scissors looked crazily phallic — long blades and big round handles. In silhouette, basically male genitals. My father had my name, which was also my grandfather's name, etched into the enamel of both pairs. When he presented them he warned me to "never, ever use fabric shears for paper, or paper shears for fabric." He also gave me another gift, which I thought was a joke at first: the family's ubiquitous utility scissors. He said, "These were my father's" — something I never knew till that moment — "and now they're yours. Take very good care of them. You were named after my father, and you're like him. He had a lot of talent. He could make anything he wanted."

In a corner of our basement in Brooklyn, carefully covered in plastic, were two old industrial sewing machines that belonged to my father. One was a beautiful Singer straight-stitch machine made of polished wrought iron from the turn of the nineteenth century, which he referred to as "the old iron horse that built this country." The other was a temperamental and dangerous Merrow machine from the late 1920s, which had a heavy thick blade that cut as it overlocked and could easily have cut straight through my thumb. It was common knowledge in the house that a sewing machine made before the 1930s was better in every way than any new machine. These cast-iron machines were more solid, built to last, more reliable than any newer machines could be, and they were sought-after. These two machines were fitted into wooden tables and converted to modern electrical motors with switches underneath that when turned on would make the whole basement vibrate.

Until I was about thirteen, I sewed everything by hand — puppets and whatever backdrops or stage curtains required stitching. After the fringed shirt episode, the idea of sewing with a machine became more ap-

175

pealing to me. I had begun experimenting with the idea of sewing clothes, but doing it by hand was just too slow. To that point I thought of needle and thread as a means to an end. If there was something I envisioned it could be mine with ingenuity and patience. I had plenty of the former, but never much patience. Sewing by machine would be faster; also the quality and look of things might improve, I thought. Still, I was too terrified by the speed of my father's machines to learn how to use them. The summer before my thirteenth birthday I had my eye on a brand-new home-sewing machine at the Singer Sewing Center, which I'd gone to inspect at least four times. I saved up my money babysitting until I finally had the eighty dollars I needed to buy the machine.

Things between my father and me had always been strained, and as I got older the strain grew worse. Every so often in an effort to bond with me he'd involve me in the repair of something broken around the house, which was a kind of hobby for him. But I always had a hard time with it. Those household fixes felt more like he was lording some kind of fatherly dominance over me. "Hold this level," he'd say, and I'd hold the level in place for an eternity while he did the rest, my mind elsewhere. Mostly we didn't get along. A lifetime of being told how lucky I was not to grow up in the poverty he described as his childhood made me feel squeamish about accepting anything more from him than what I absolutely needed. Also it felt like we were always vying for my mother's affections. And whatever her motivation, she never did anything to diffuse that dynamic. Eventually great animosity grew between my father and me, and I was most comfortable staying out of his way.

I fantasized about buying that machine for the greater part of the summer. I wanted to go into the store, point to the one I'd picked, pay for it, and leave. I knew that if my father came it would turn into a big production. He'd schmooze the salesperson, it would take forever, and I would be mortified. My father dropped hints about being part of the process and I should have been grateful that he took an interest in my sewing, but this purchase was something I wanted to keep to myself. Also, I didn't want to indicate to him in any way that I was following in his footsteps. I did not want to work in the garment business, which seemed dreary and limiting to me. I knew I wanted to make things. Art. Puppets. The sewing machine was meant to be a tool for that. In fact, sewing clothes felt like a concession to my family history and, though I knew sewing machines were invented for the manufacture of clothes, for a short while I actively resisted doing so.

When the time came to pick up my new machine the only person available to drive me to the Singer store was my father. When we arrived he looked at the slick new machine I wanted to purchase and shook his head. Then he steered me toward an older and much better one. I hesitated — this was exactly what I didn't want to happen. But after a few minutes I knew he was right. The old machine was at least twice the weight of the new one, certainly more beautiful — it was curvy, polished, black wrought iron, like a small version of the iron horse, with Singer written in gilt, remounted into a new case veneered in grainy black Naugahyde. It was portable, though massively heavy, with a beautiful wooden dome that clamped onto the machine when it wasn't in use and, again, like the iron horse, it had been adapted from its original foot pedal to an electric motor with a leather strap that propelled the wheel. What I really loved about that machine was that it could backstitch — which the new machine couldn't do. Even before I knew how to sew,

I knew that a machine that could backstitch was far better than one that couldn't. My father's choice of the older machine prevailed. And he pitched in the additional twenty dollars.

I knew that I had something really great in that machine. I approached learning to sew with it methodically and respectfully, unlike my manic and risky approach to other tools. I taught myself to sew, but my father stayed involved from a safe distance. He and I reached a kind of détente over that machine. In this one case he could guide me without being overbearing. He taught me how to wind a bobbin, thread the machines, set the tension gauges properly. He'd bring me a new attachment for it every month or so, like a ruffler or a leather foot, or gauges that attached to the side of the needle and helped me stay within my seam allowances. He'd adjust the new piece for me, and off I'd go. All of that *now* strikes me as very dear.

I always loved sewing. Cutting cloth. Construction. Pins. The forward progression of sewing fast, like flying. But sometimes the plane fell out of the sky. I remember terrible fits of anger when something went wrong. I might destroy my latest project — pull a puppet or a backdrop completely apart. But I'd always get it back together, undo the damage, and finish.

On that beloved machine, I made the first piece of clothing I ever sewed from scratch. It was for my mother, made of double-faced wool, rust heather on one side and an autumnal horse-blanket plaid on the other. I made a straight skirt (rust face-out) and a matching shawl, the edges of which I finished by hand with a kind of naïve whip-stitch. I'd thought that a straight skirt would be easy, but they can be quite challenging even for a professional. This was before I understood the concept of darts, so I made the skirt without them. Luckily my mother's figure, though wonderful in clothes, was never too curvaceous, so darts weren't as necessary. The end result was a crude piece that she paired shrewdly with a white ribbed wool turtleneck sweater worn untucked, hiding the chewed-up waistband and horribly set-in zipper. She wore it to shul on Rosh Hashanah with the shawl dramatically tossed over her shoulders, and accessorized it with a gold-coin medallion necklace on a thick gold chain, a massive opaque jade cocktail ring, and rust stack-heeled suede boots.

When I think about that machine now, its importance in my life, I'm simultaneously touched and amused. Back then it wouldn't have occurred to me that my father bringing home a ruffler was a sign of love. But it was. And leave it to my mother to transform my first-ever attempt at making clothing into a fashion event. She knew I'd be crushed if she didn't wear it — and if she wore it, she was going to make sure it looked good.

Having lived through the ordeal of my bar mitzvah, I was faced with the much more life-altering choice of where I would go to high school. I'd humored my parents long enough; I was depressed, fatter than ever, and I had to get out. My choices were limited, though. There was the local public high school, and another in Coney Island named after John Dewey that my eldest sister went to. Neither of those appealed to me and Flatbush Yeshiva High School was out of the question. Then I got really lucky in the form of a great teacher who changed my life forever.

My eighth-grade English teacher at Yeshivah of Flatbush, a woman named Sheila Kanowitz, was modern and good-looking. She didn't wear a wig; instead she wore her own straightened, thick, dark hair knotted on top of her head or in a ponytail. She wore almost no makeup and had dark expressive eyes and, in general, a very expressive face that grimaced with opinions, acknowledgments of humor, exuberance, and sarcasm. She treated me like a peer; we made each other laugh.

She assigned a book report on the novel *To Sir, With Love,* and I decided rather than write another boring paper I would do a dramatization using the entire classroom as a set. And instead of having one of my adolescent classmates play the leading role, a black teacher named Mr. Braithwaite, I prerecorded the lines on a Panasonic cassette tape player, leaving his actual physical presence to the imagination. I knew there would be less disbelief to suspend and definitely more tension if the main protagonist was in some way abstracted, and it really paid off. The class loved it, and Ms. Kanowitz was impressed. It didn't escape her notice how out of place I was in the yeshiva, and sometime early that spring she approached me with the idea of auditioning for the Fiorello LaGuardia High School for the Performing Arts, which was the premier public school for the arts in all of New York City. The name alone was thrilling: *Performing Arts.*

Convincing my parents took a lot of doing. At first it appeared hopeless — my father added the word "unequivocally" to his "no" — a real ten-dollar word he used when he meant business. The fact that I'd have to ride two hours on the subway every day, a solid hour each way, didn't help my cause. In those days the subway wasn't nearly as clean and safe as it is now. And Performing Arts was located in the center of New York City, on West Forty-sixth Street between Broadway and Avenue of the Americas, right smack in the center of Times Square, which back then was a really seedy neighborhood. There were porn movie houses and prostitutes on every corner, junkies in plain sight, and streets filthy with uncollected garbage. Danger notwithstanding, my mother was amenable to the idea, and once she was on board I knew she could convince my father. I'm sure it wasn't easy for either of them, but I think they were so eager for me to find some kind of happiness that they ultimately overlooked all the possible dangers and agreed that I should try. My mother made a prophetic statement: "The day you start that school you're going to be so happy, you're going to drop all the extra weight."

Once my parents accepted the idea, it was decided I should audition for both the music and the drama departments. My piano teacher, Alan Small, was charged with preparing me for the music audition. We picked a Mozart sonata, which seemed to show off my capabilities to their best. One of my greatest assets was my ability to play very fast, and that really shone in that particular piece. I also prepared a schmaltzy arrangement that I wrote of the Gershwin song " 'S Wonderful."

My mother drove me to the audition that Saturday and waited in the lobby. More nervous than I'd ever been in my life, I walked up three or four flights of stairs to where the music department was located. It was a strange building, erected in the nineteenth century as an elementary school, proportioned for little children, not the growing teens who inhabited it during those later years. The water fountains were lower than usual and it had very shallow staircases that produced a trippy *Alice in Wonderland* effect. I waited in the hall for what seemed like an eternity, listening to snippets of music coming from other auditions. From what I could hear, I felt like I had a strong chance. Finally I was ushered into a small auditorium. I seated myself at the piano and after saying my name and introducing my music, I began the Mozart piece — and stumbled out of the gate. I was trying to show off my fast playing, which seemed easy at home but not so much in front of others. I paused. Breathed. Looked at the teachers who were running the audition, begged their patience, and started again a bit slower. And again I stumbled. And again I started and stumbled again. I held back my tears and finally I got going. At the end I received a round of applause, probably out of sympathy, but the applause made me more confident to play the Gershwin, which I did with a great flourish.

Ms. Kanowitz helped me prepare for the drama audition. We chose two monologues from a list of suggestions supplied by the school; one from a play by William Inge called *The Dark at the Top of the Stairs,* and another from a play about a morphine-addicted vet and his family called *A Hatful of Rain.* I navigated my way to the Drama Book Shop on the subway. It was located in the West Forties, up two flights of stairs. It's a place I got to know very well. Those rooms lined with shelves and all those thousands of plays became a kind of mecca for me and my classmates those years in Performing Arts. Ms. Kanowitz helped me plumb some of the more mysterious depths of the characters, staying late and meeting me one weekend. I felt apprehensive about memorizing all the words, but once I was able to concentrate on the character and think his thoughts, I found that remembering wasn't the issue. It was about making it real, and convincing myself it *was* real.

I never thought I would come close to getting into the drama department — my talent, I'd always told myself, was for music, and so I wasn't nearly as nervous. A senior student volunteer who was enlisted to read with the auditionees met me and brought me to a smaller room than the one used for the music audition. She had long dirty-blond hair that she switched dramatically from side to side. This was a girl who already, as a senior in high school, understood something about sex and being sexy. This sense of style extended to the drama teachers who judged me that day, all of whom seemed more attractive than the ones from the music department. Their hair and clothes made sense, even if it wasn't, in all cases, chic. The attractiveness of everyone else in that room further convinced me that I didn't belong among them, and I was resigned to the inevitability of being rejected.

First, I performed the Inge monologue, which was sad without being self-pitying.

Then I began the second monologue, and I was able to lose myself in it. A hush lingered in the room after I finished. (Actors do that for one another in class — they fall silent and speechless, as a way of overstating how good you were, also to make their reaction as or more important than your performance). I entertained guilty fantasies of leaving my torturous career as a pianist aside for what seemed like a more fun career as an actor but, as it turned out, the choice was not mine to make. About two months after those fateful auditions, two letters came in the mail from Fiorello LaGuardia High School for the Performing Arts; one letter telling me that I was *not* accepted into the music department, and one saying I *was* accepted into the drama department. I suppose the music faculty who auditioned me thought the stumbling and performance anxiety bode poorly for my chances to succeed as a professional musician — and they were right. Whatever the cause, the outcome worked in my favor. I didn't realize it, but fate was smiling.

10

Things went topsy-turvy those first few months at Performing Arts high school. Being sequestered at yeshiva for the first eight years of my school life then rushing head-on into this exposed, modern, libertine environment was like eating a main course of culture shock with a large side order of guilt. The main objective of the rabbis in my life was to prove what a fuckup I was. Meanwhile they drummed it into my head not to trust anyone but other Jews. So no matter how difficult life among the religion was, they made it impossible to accept any other, happier life among people I could relate to. The mostly sad, repressed world around me had suddenly transformed into a wonderful, vibrant one, and it was only with a good deal of fear and anxiety that I was able to start letting go of the past. The object now was to assimilate to a place where I actually belonged — despite the fact that I'd been brainwashed to believe that assimilation was the root of all evil. For at least the first year I felt like an impostor. I was convinced I had entered a dream and would wake and be deported back to the horrible world I had come from. Everyone at my new school seemed so glamourous and worldly, and there I was, this fat, overly sheltered yeshiva boy. During my first year at Performing Arts, while all this joy and excitement was going on in the foreground, there was a background hum of fear and skepticism.

Still, I realized that this new world set before me could be my salvation. There were people of color, whom I was drawn to as a reaction to my father's racism. I was eager to have diverse friends just to prove him wrong. There was a transgender person named Ro with whom I spent hours in the library. There were homosexuals — mostly closeted — but also out ones like Wallace Jenkins, a classmate who would become a great role model. And Alan Reiff, also in my class, who seemed so much like me: chubby and effeminate and from a Jewish home. He wasn't out yet either, but that wasn't the point. It was good to know I wasn't the only one with that exact set of attributes.

For a long time the other kids seemed to

be having a lot more fun than I was. For that first year I only let myself put a toe in the waters of this new society. These other kids fit in so much better and they looked better, too. I was fat and pimply and had a Jew-fro while they were (for the most part) thin and good-looking, and their ethnicity always seemed to add cachet while mine seemed like a draggy old thing that needed to be shed. Being black or Hispanic was so much sexier. For the first few months, whenever I made inroads with a friendship, something always reeled me back in. For a while kashruth — Jewish dietary laws — was an issue. I was afraid to eat things that weren't kosher for fear of being found out. Also, most of the cool parties took place on Friday nights, which were out of the question for me because of my obligation to be home for Shabbat. And when boys and girls paired off I was completely stumped. I never lied, but I was also too scared to claim my sexuality just yet. Eventually I figured out how to put the subject off with self-deprecating fat jokes, and I functioned as a kind of asexual jester.

Just like in the movie *Fame,* every day at lunch there was a deejay who played disco music in the cafeteria, and everyone danced with everyone else. For the first year, while that dance party was going on I would quietly slip out and take walks by myself. I would stop at a deli on Sixth Avenue, buy lunch, and walk across Forty-seventh Street, the block referred to as the Diamond District, which is lined with jewelry stores owned and operated by Orthodox Jews. I'd ogle jewelry, then I'd sit on the steps at St. Patrick's Cathedral and eat my lunch. On the way I would pass Saks Fifth Avenue and peek at the windows. Eventually lunch became less important and studying the clothes in the windows at Saks became my obsession. Geoffrey Beene. Calvin Klein. Bill Blass. Sometimes I would go inside and look. At the time Yves Saint Laurent was the reigning fashion god and an inspirational figure in my life. Two years prior he designed his great Russian Peasant Collection, which I studied on the pages of *W* and *Vogue,* and the collection in Saks that fall still reflected that influence. Fabulous paisley prints, fur-trimmed hats and gauntlet gloves, and suede Cossack jackets.

Sometimes I went to Rockefeller Center, which since my early childhood had been one of my favorite places. I had happy memories of skating there around the holidays with my uncle Sam and his family. Another walk was into the nearby theatre district, where I would loiter in front of one or other of the great Broadway theatres. My classmates and I were completely obsessed with *A Chorus Line,* which had opened on Broadway four months before I started at PA. I had already seen it with my family as a birthday treat for Norma's birthday, and I saw it roughly seven or eight more times that first year at PA via standing room tickets. I would venture to say the entire drama department had seen it as many times as I had and, like me, had the original soundtrack recording down cold. Once a week during my lunch walk I would get to the Shubert Theatre on West Forty-fourth Street and stare at that marquee and hope to see one or two of the stars entering the building.

One of my first assignments at school was a dream opportunity for a theatre-obsessed kid like me. We were instructed to locate and meet someone who worked in show business and interview them. It could be anyone who worked in any capacity in the theatre. An actor, a stagehand, even an usher. I had a big idea. Having been with my family to see the original stage production of *Chicago* the spring before, I became obsessed with Gwen Verdon, and I got it into my head that I had to interview her. I stood outside the theatre one Wednesday between the matinee and the evening shows, waiting. I was a nervous wreck. One of the other stars of the show came out and noticed me standing around.

"Waiting for someone?" It was Chita Rivera.

I told her about the assignment to interview someone in the theatre.

"I'm in the theatre," she said. "I'll do it."

"Oh. I know. Um. I was waiting for Gwen Verdon. But thank you very much," I said and walked off a few feet, not aware for a second how disrespectful this was. And the same thing happened with Jerry Orbach when he came out a few minutes later! When I look back, I wonder why those great performers even noticed me, let alone offered to be interviewed. Finally Gwen Verdon emerged, and not only did she agree to do the interview, she linked arms with me and walked me to Joe Allen and bought me a cup of coffee. She was wearing a short fur coat, high-heeled boots, and a shoulder bag. She was sweet and solicitous and full of motherly advice about the ins and outs of show business. She spoke lovingly about her association with and marriage to Bob Fosse, another person I was obsessed with. Her advice was to try not to be involved personally with people you work with, which sounded like good advice even coming from someone who so blatantly did not heed it. She told me how she got started, how hard she worked to get a break. She told me that she considered herself first and foremost a dancer.

That conversation with Gwen Verdon is one of the great memories of my life. It feels like something out of some showbiz novel. The information she imparted was great, but the idea that she would take the time and shower me with attention that way was more than I could have dreamt. I was determined. I reached for a star at a moment of change in my life. I was met with kindness and love. It was a lesson in perseverance and humanity. But more than anything, that meeting was the proof I needed that I was safely en route to the right life.

There wasn't a locker room at PA so we were supposed to change into tights, which were required in first year acting and dance classes, in the boys' bathroom. I was too self-conscious and felt too fat to take my clothes off in the presence of the other boys. As a matter of fact, for the entire four years of high school I only saw the inside of the boys' bathroom a handful of times. Every day I found a deserted back stairwell in that labyrinthine building, and I'd change in a manic fit, all the while hoping no one would pass by. I prepared everything in advance, undoing all the buttons and zippers before I took anything off and I was undressed for only seconds between dropping my pants and shimmying into my tights. If I heard someone coming I would cover myself up or sit on the stairs and throw my coat over myself till they passed. Tights-wearing was a huge concession — almost a deal-breaker. I actually considered dropping out of school based on the mortification of wearing them. There were days when I thought I might pass out or throw up from embarrassment at how fat my legs and thighs were. Even if I had been at my thinnest, I still would never have been able to compare myself to those gorgeous boys and girls in the dance department who lived in their tights from morning till night and did nothing but dance and work out all day long. (Even later in my life, when I was at my thinnest, compared to models and dancers, I was a monster.) When I put those tights on I felt like the butt of some terrible joke. Eventually I managed to find compromises. Instead of the required white T-shirts, the teachers allowed me to wear big white shirts that concealed my huge stomach and cottage cheese thighs and by year two the rules relaxed and we were allowed to wear a broad variety of things to classes.

We had ballet classes and modern dance classes every day, and yoga on Fridays, all taught by the same teacher, Charles McGraw, who was a prototypical 1970s gay man. He had a thick Southern drawl and liked to call his students *kindelah.* He also liked to quote Nietzsche and other German or French existential philosophers. I was never any good in dance classes except in teaching myself the way to physicalize comedy. I figured out how funny I looked in my attempts to assume fifth position or downward dog, and I milked it for laughs. I hadn't watched that many reruns of *I Love Lucy* for nothing. If I was going to be the class clown, I was going to do a good job of it.

Like a lot of my classmates, if I lagged slightly in my grasp of method acting, I made up for it in hamminess. I was an ace in my favorite class, which was Voice and Diction. I saw that class as my ticket to a new identity. Coming from Brooklyn, I was marked by an accent that I was painfully aware of, one I associated with the community and that I was committed to leaving behind. Within the first two months at school we had a master lecture by the wonderful actor Raul Julia, who demonstrated for us the thick Puerto Rican accent he naturally spoke with and the beautiful diction he was able to call upon for the stage. He went in and out of that stage diction with ease, and that illuminated an issue that was pretty common among my classmates who were facing similar changes in their lives. He spoke about the family and friends he grew up with and how they saw this ability of his to speak beautifully as an affectation. A lot of eye-rolling took place in Brooklyn in those first months of my studying these new sounds. It was Raul Julia's advice in that talk that made it easier for me to progress and ignore what my old friends and family were implying about the refinement of my speech. At first I was sorely conscious of dropping in and out of good diction. After a time it no longer felt fake, and after an even longer time I only remembered those horrible old sounds when I heard others speak them.

More inspiring than anything at PA was the drama faculty. In contrast to the rabbis I was used to — even in contrast to the adults I knew — these were people I could look up to, people I wanted to grow up to be exactly like. They were sophisticated and authoritative when it came to the arts. They were caught up on current events, they were funny, they had political viewpoints that agreed with their lives. A society of thin, good-looking, more than a little vain middle-aged people who did not judge me or threaten me because I was creative. They knew nothing of Sephardic versus Ashkenazic Jews. They didn't tolerate racism or sexism. They were irresistible characters right out of a Sondheim musical, full of neuroses, which related more to the situation of being an artist. They were role models, and my inspiration for transforming my body and my speech. They influenced our every move and taught us lessons not just about the craft of performing, but also about life.

It was because I had these wonderful role models that I was finally able to lose weight. Another factor was that my parents had purchased a stationary bike the year before, and they were ready to admit defeat and move it out of their bedroom and into the basement. I volunteered to keep it in my bedroom, and just the nearness of it became a kind of inspiration. I rode it every night for hours, listening to Juliette Gréco records.

I went on the Scarsdale Diet for six months and ultimately lost seventy-five pounds. I bought one pair of tight jeans, a size 32, which was the greatest victory of my life. I wore those jeans most every day with over-sized shirts; I wore my fat clothes on my new thin body. Baggy, frayed clothes were stylish then, but in my case they had a double meaning. If my pants were worn paper-bag style, held up at the waist with a belt, it wasn't merely an ironic fashionable look — it rang with a certain truth.

On my first day in school I met Robin Leopold, a girl who was at the center of a popular clique of kids who seemed to know one another from their past lives together in Kew Gardens, Queens. Robin was my first close friend at PA, and it turned out we were in the same drama class. She was the opposite of the people I grew up around. I envied Robin the freedom she had to come and go as she pleased, with no commitments to her family. Another revelation: Parents outside of the Syrian community clung to their kids way less than mine clung to me. Robin's mother was a glamourous divorcée with huge white-blond, cotton candy hair. She wore tight, see-through blouses over lacy lingerie; matching, tight gabardine bell-bottom trousers; and always,

always, huge dark glasses and a cigarette dangling from the corner of her mouth. Robin seemed full of a healthy disregard, almost disrespect, for things like family and religion. This both scared me and inspired me. On December 2, 1975 — just three months after I met Robin — her father was killed in a fire at a famous nightclub in New York City called the Blue Angel. There was all sorts of speculation about the fire, inferences made that Robin's father was a gangster, a target of the mob who started the fire that killed him. I got the impression her parents' divorce was bitter, and Robin hadn't been at all close to her father. This suspicion was confirmed a day later, when she decided to go ahead with her birthday party, which had been scheduled earlier that month. I remember how simultaneously scandalized and delighted my friends and I were that she didn't cancel the party. She didn't bother explaining, either. I respected her so much for not succumbing to any pretense about the need to mourn an estranged father based on outmoded social mores. (And the party was pretty good, too.)

Another absolutely fabulous thing about Robin was her older brother, Guy. He worked as a waiter at a restaurant called Serendipity, which was a favorite of mine.

The mere fact of him working at Serendipity was proof that he was an actual, living, breathing, out homosexual, because everyone who worked there in those days, I learned, had to be gay. The owners themselves were gay, and it was a policy set in stone that they hired only other gay men. My friends and I used to go there at least twice a month, not merely because we loved frozen hot chocolates, but also to observe Guy and the other gays in their natural habitat. Those were some of the most thrilling evenings of my life — eating Zen hash and knowing that I was in the company of many gay men, and that it was okay.

During those years the Upper West Side became a second home for me. So many of my friends lived there. Kevin Ryan. Ted Lambert. Francesca Rollins. Gina Belafonte's apartment on Seventy-fourth and West End Avenue served as a meeting place and sometimes a crash pad after long nights out. When my parents asked where I had been the night before, if I told them I was at Harry's house, it rationalized my racy new life, and they almost encouraged my independence. The Belafonte place was a gigantic floor-through prewar apartment all done in tones of beige, with luscious upholstery, draperies, more bedrooms and wonderful old prewar bathrooms than in most huge three-story houses in Brooklyn. Even more than the John Banter interiors of my childhood, I formed my ideas about what a chic cosmopolitan interior looked like from that place. There was a separate, smaller apartment in the back, with a recording studio and a guest room where I learned about the glories of prewar plumbing — a good hard shower.

My one degree away from Harry Belafonte was more than a celebrity association. He legitimized my new life in my parents' eyes. My mother talked endlessly about her girlhood dancing to Harry's records. My father's worship of Harry as a musician trumped any racism. All the parents and faculty kept their eyes peeled on open school events where they might catch a glimpse of him. The first few times I met him I couldn't speak for awe. He always made a point of welcoming us into his home. He'd walk in, Handsome Harry with the glow of starlight, and knock us all out with his gorgeous smile and easy manner. Overcompensating perhaps, so he might be perceived like other dads, who ironically never showed their faces to us. Gina's mother, Julie, was also quite gorgeous. Always dressed in Saint Laurent or Giorgio di Sant'Angelo, she had a great face that I always assumed was Native American, which is the look she worked, never breaking her glamourous character. Her olive complexion, braided hair, high cheekbones, and almond eyes, made more extreme with contour and eyeliner. It wasn't till recently that Gina laughingly set me straight: "No, darling. Julie is a nice Jewish girl from Brooklyn."

But it wasn't just a gorgeous physical reality chez Belafonte. Harry was always at the center of things politically. He was exemplary as an artist and an activist. Photographs on the walls in his study ranged from the very chic — Julie in a Dior couture evening gown circa 1955 at the White House — to documents of historical importance, such as pictures of Harry at the side of Martin Luther King, Jr. The stories about Harry's fight for equality were inspirational. One legendary story involved the co-op board where they lived, which had initially rejected him in his bid to buy the apartment. His revenge was to buy the whole building.

Gina had a good-looking boyfriend named Hector, and by the end of the second year I nurtured a vicarious fantasy that they were having sex. The issue of sex became more

and more important at school as I got more
and more terrified of it. A lot of the girls in
my class seemed sexually advanced compared to the boys. For some reason the
young women at school didn't feel bound
by provincial ideas, even in the late 1970s.
The more I observed my girlfriends fulfilling their sexual desires with seeming abandon, the more I pitied the Syrian girls their
prudery, and the more I was able to justify
my own sexual feelings. I was officially
closeted, but I started to open up to my
nearest and dearest friends. Most of my gay
friends handled their sexuality the same
way: by denying it. My best friend, Kevin
Ryan, and I were out to each other early
on, but it wasn't something we talked about
openly with others.

Kevin was another very lucky relationship
that I fell into. He and I shared a genuine
lust for knowledge, an insatiable need to
know about art of all kinds, but especially
movies. We went constantly to the Thalia,
the Regency, the Carnegie Hall Cinema,
Cinema Village and saw all kinds of life-
altering movies. Kevin and I shared books
back and forth. We also assumed each
other's sense of humor. What made him
laugh made me laugh, and we gave each
other permission to tell each other's stories

in the first person. Our friendship was like a long meeting of comedy writers for some esoteric version of *Saturday Night Live.* We coined the phrase "Adonis Goldfarb" which described a sexy-looking Jewish boy made even sexier by the presence of a yarmulke. The catchphrase was: "Teach me the Talmud, baby." In the late 1970s, Liza Minnelli and Chita Rivera were in a bomb of a musical called *The Rink,* which had to do with competitive ice skaters. Kevin and I thought it was hilarious that someone might mistakenly wander into the show expecting a performance of *The Ring,* the Wagner operas. We did a miniversion alternating as Liza and Chita belting out bits from *Das Rheingold,* with Fosse-like choreography.

Kevin and I clung together, and it was that bond that made it feel okay to come out. We were never lovers; there was no physical chemistry between us. Like my earlier relationship with Jackie Gindy and one or two other great friendships after that, it was a kind of romance with everything but sex. In the early years after I came out, I was always complaining that I didn't have a boyfriend. I thought there was something wrong with me. I wasn't exactly sure what I wanted of men, but my specific sexual desire was starting to merge with my idea

205

of an object of love, love being the primary objective. I watched as my girlfriends paired off with boys, and hoped I'd meet someone who would pull me out of my misery, be my secret lover, validate my feelings. But ultimately I think these close, chaste friendships were the most valuable of my life. In the greater scheme of things, friendship is more important to me. It went on like that for a number of years to come. For the time being love, love between two men, was the motivating factor, the reason I was gay — sex, not as much. That would come later.

11

Like any New York teenager, I owed my independence to the New York City mass transit system — notably, the subway. I loved it — it filled me with a sense of freedom, and finally I grew to hate it. I was always late in the morning and would run all the way to the D train or in the opposite direction to the F train, both a long ten blocks away. I'd see the elevated train pulling into the station above me, and I'd speed up, running up the stairs, then jam myself in without thinking. Ten minutes later my claustrophobia would kick in and I'd start hyperventilating. A few times I blacked out. I never made an issue of this or told my parents because I was so afraid that if they found out, they would forbid me from going back on the subway and it would ruin my chances of staying at PA.

The subway was a total mess in those days. A chaotic, claustrophobic, lawless place. On good days it felt like a place where anything could happen. Occasionally the filth and noise of the subway wore thin. A lot of evenings, to avoid one more hour on the subway, I would meet my father at his office for his drive home, which happened daily at about 6:30 P.M. Although I was now farther from my father emotionally, we made small talk in the car, and his office became a place for me to hang out while I waited for him to leave. His business was making children's clothes under the labels "Little Ruffy Togs," which were infant and children's sizes, and "Big Guy," teen sizes. (I could never fit into any of those clothes. Not when I was an infant, not when I was a teen — I was always too fat.)

My father had a secretary, Evelyn Glick, a middle-aged woman with a heart-shaped face, fluffy black hair, and crazy bright-red lipstick, which she was constantly adjusting in a compact mirror. She wore washable white knit gloves all day to protect her hands, a lot of white collars, bows at the neck, and half-glasses that hung from a chain. She had a sour streak and complained bitterly about my father and his temper. He'd slam the phone down in a rage, grunt, and violently crumple a piece of paper. She would lock eyes with me, gently float an *un-*

crumpled piece of paper in her wastebasket, and say with a deadpan reading, "There's more room in the basket if you don't crumple." Then she would wait a beat and add: "And so much quieter."

There was a younger woman in the office named Stephanie who assisted Evelyn. Stephanie was big-boned, lethargic, and sexy — a poor man's Peggy Moffitt crossed with Kim Novak. She dressed in clingy printed knits and colorful scarves that she wore as headbands in her streaked brown lacquer bangs, which touched the tips of her fake top lashes. Stephanie was not such a perfectionist in her office work, and when she was in the ladies' room, which was often, Evelyn would complain aloud about everything from her typing to her bagged lunches, and would pose the question: "Is Stephanie more of an asset or more of an ass?" Evelyn was full of phrases such as "Don't talk, chum, chew Topps gum." When my father criticized her work she'd say "Kiss my ass in Macy's window . . . at high noon." Some of those phrases imbedded themselves in my memory forever.

If there was anything I picked up from my mother, it was how to listen to women. Evelyn and Stephanie were my first willing test subjects. It's unclear who sought out whom;

they took more of an interest in me than you might imagine full-grown women would take in their boss's fourteen-year-old son. These women told me everything, and not just about clothes and shoes and hair and makeup. Evelyn talked about being single at her age and living with her kid brother in Brooklyn. Stephanie talked about her dating life and how "men are pigs!" That was one remark I heard again and again.

When people talk about me and my clothes they say "Isaac loves women." Which is a great piece of flattery. But I think what they mean to say is that I'm actually interested in women's stories — which is true almost to the exclusion of any other kind. I never was into men's stories: survival stories, war stories. Love stories, though, Cinderella stories — which tend to be categorized as women's stories — I take to naturally. I'm interested in the social aspects of these stories, but I think it's the shallow side I love more. I love the clothes. The gowns. The hair and makeup. And I just think women's bodies, the architecture of them, are far more beautiful than men's bodies, comparing them side by side. Which is a ridiculous thing to do. The funny thing is, I don't really make an effort to have more women friends than men. It just works out that way.

When I wasn't hanging out with my friends or listening to Evelyn's and Stephanie's snarking while waiting for my lift home, I wandered the department stores in the area. B. Altman, which had a rambling, under-stocked, lonely quality about it; and Lord & Taylor, which had a great luncheon counter on the seventh floor called the Bird Cage. I got to know these stores like the back of my hand, but none as well as Macy's, which was right across the street from my father's office. I went up and down the noisy wooden escalators, looking at all sorts of clothes, accessories, housewares. My parents gave me a Macy's credit card (I think largely to avoid the always-stressful task of taking me clothing shopping), but I didn't buy much, I mostly looked. Still I had a great feeling of power knowing that I could whip out my charge card at any moment and buy something if it seemed appropriate. This made the shopping more compelling. And the idea that I could fit into clothes any-where in the store and not just the husky departments was also at first a little unreal.
Some of the memorable things I bought on my own:

- An olive-green velvet YSL blazer (on sale).
- A navy-blue cotton poplin YSL military shirt jacket (which I wore well into my early adulthood and if I had it now I'd still wear it).
- An ankle-length, yellow, rubberized, Ralph Lauren rain slicker with a khaki corduroy collar.
- A rust herringbone cotton shirt with a flanged button placket by a designer named Jeffrey Sayre. (A really important European designer in the late seventies and early eighties. I passed his shop on the rue du Faubourg Saint-Honoré in Paris on my first trip and felt so international that I already owned something of his.)
- A teal-green tweed Jhane Barnes crew-neck sweater (another really important American menswear designer in the day).
- A rust-and-Naples-yellow herringbone-patterned thick cotton terry cloth Geoffrey Beene robe, which was chicer than your average licensed robe. Also more expensive. I think it was originally something like $300 marked down to $70, which was still hugely expensive for a robe at the time.

- My favorite polo shirt ever, a thin-striped, long-sleeved Gant number in celadon green, taupe, oyster, and navy blue.
- A cream, red, and blue broken-pinstripe Calvin Klein Viyella flannel shirt.
- A Calvin Klein denim jacket that I still have and wear.
- About three pounds of multicolored paper from Paper by the Pound in The Cellar at Macy's. It was stationery meant for letters, but I didn't write many letters so I used it for other purposes. I remember cutting it up like construction paper, using it to make holiday cards and various school presentations for years after. I swear I still have some of the blue paper somewhere, a gorgeous Wedgwood blue in that heavy, linen-finish stock.

By this point I had taken full control of how I dressed myself, and neither of my parents involved themselves at all. As long as I looked presentable — meaning I wore a sport jacket to shul and had a good winter coat — I was taken off the list of sartorial priorities. I had known for a long time that my looks weren't going to be my fortune, so

I approached dressing myself as an act of expression rather than anything that approached elegance. A few years prior, when my family was in the car headed home from a visit to see relatives, my mother remarked proudly about what a good-looking family we were, especially her kids. My father caught my eye in the rearview mirror and said, "Well, Isaac knows looks aren't his strongest point. He knows he has other qualities." My mother shot a killing look across the front seat. She tried to backpedal for him, but the harder she tried, the more he dug in his heels. "I'm doing you a favor, Isaac. You know that looks aren't everything. Especially for a man. They're not nearly as important as other qualities." It was almost as if he were talking to himself about himself. For me at the time, even more meaningful than his statement that I wasn't good-looking was the fact that he was equating the two of us. He was not good-looking, and I was his son, so therefore I wasn't good-looking either. He thought he was helping me by saying what he did. And no matter how hard my mother tried to bolster my confidence, she got nowhere. Though my lack of self-confidence on the issue of my looks was not formulated that day, it was confirmed.

But my father's statement, however poorly put, accomplished one really good thing: It deemphasized the importance of physical appearance. I was able to think of myself not as a subject but as an arbiter: someone who could stand on the sidelines in basic black and give an honest opinion with absolutely no axe to grind. I backed into the role of family stylist without knowing I wanted the job, but I embraced all the power that came with it. It was one thing when I was a child innocently opining about which dress I liked better. Now the responsibility became almost professional. The pressure on my sisters to compete in the over-the-top arena of that social scene was increasingly intense, and almost every time they left the house, I would weigh in. A shoe would get changed, or hair would be put up in a pony tail — and I can't count the number of times my mother stood before me in a cloud of cigarette smoke and Fracas challenging my opinion.

I was so young and so confident as a style arbiter. Three things combined to give me that confidence so young: The first was my increasingly sophisticated understanding of what motivated women, what inspired them (and not just on the subject of clothes). For as long as I could remember, I'd absorbed thoughts and ideas from my mother, and increasingly I had the voices of my sisters and other women, like Evelyn and Stephanie, in my head, too. These were real women with real goals and concerns — something I got on a deep level. The second thing was my ability to erase myself from the equation — for which I can partly thank my father. Unconcerned about how I looked or by my own aesthetics, I didn't try to impose them on a woman. So I dressed the *woman* and not who I thought she *should* be. The third was my love of costumes and glamour. This would seem to contradict my strong sense of who women really are, undistracted by some idealized view of them. But it never felt contradictory to me at all. It seemed the most natural thing in the world, that a person — like a character onstage — would decide what message she wanted to communicate and would dress herself accordingly. Whether consciously or unconsciously. I naturally took to the task of translating those messages into clothing.

My first professional fashion commission came to me courtesy of a classmate of mine, Ted Lambert, who had been cast in Andrei Serban's production of *The Trojan Women,* which toured Europe the summer before.

He appeared in it with another child actor, Diane Lane, who had just completed a movie with Laurence Olivier called *A Little Romance* and needed something to wear for either the New York City opening or some other related event. Ted got her measurements from the wardrobe department at La MaMa, which produced *The Trojan Women,* and we agreed on a fee of sixty dollars for the whole job, start to finish. I bought a beautiful, bright-peach silk broadcloth and matched it to silk rattail cord that I used to make a crisscross torsotie belt that looked like something out of one of the Grecian sculptures I had seen at the Metropolitan Museum of Art. We had nowhere to fit the dress, so we snuck into a fitting room at Alexander's, a discount department store on Third Avenue and Fifty-eighth Street, across from Bloomingdale's, which closed, taking its place in history some time in the early 1990s. The fitting room was big and bright, and I smoked incessantly through the fittings and held pins in my teeth, emulating photos and movies I'd seen of fashion designers. I wore my favorite scarf, a striped ochre-and-navy knitted thing that I'd bought at Macy's. It was about a foot wide and six feet long, very fashionable at the time. I kept it on for most of the fitting just for effect, and finally I was just too hot, so I took it off and flung it on the bench. Midway through the fitting an attendant knocked on the door and threatened to call security. We finished the fitting and sped out of there. I was so nervous that I left behind that scarf, the loss of which I never quite got over.

Diane Lane was about twelve years old, and I was fifteen. I remember thinking of her as the luckiest girl in the world to be so beautiful. Her skin was luminous, and she had a long, beautiful body, not at all gawky like other girls her age. Her hair was already colored, which at first struck me as something perverse, that someone at her tender age should be held to that level of perfection. I could sense that her star was on the ascent. It seemed right that a girl who looked like that, who had been groomed — literally — for stardom, had a bright future ahead of her. I was still weighing careers and still nursed some hope that maybe I could be the one wearing the costumes and not just the one making them. But increasingly, between my exposure at PA and what my dad had pointed out about my chances of making it in show business, I knew I wasn't good-looking enough. I thought: *Who would ever believe me as a movie star?*

About twenty-five years later I hired Diane to be the image of my secondary line. On the first day of the shoot with Diane, I was in her trailer as she was being made up by Pat McGrath. It was with great trepidation that I brought up the story of the peach dress. I was so afraid she wouldn't remember. But she did! She said she remembered the dress and remembered that day in Alexander's. I would love to come face-to-face with that dress now, not only to see the crazy way it was assembled; this was before I understood anything about dressmaking or construction. The dress, for all its idiosyncrasies, was rather beautiful when it was finished, and it fit Diane well. But more than anything, that dress was a symbol of a big corner being turned. As I made that dress, with a mixture of despair and relief, I relinquished my dreams of a career in show business. I had the idea that only beautiful people could dream of things like starring in movies, and I could only imagine a lifetime of rejection ahead. I told myself I'd be happy with any nearness to show business at all, even if it meant making costumes or dresses, like this one, for movie stars like Diane Lane. I went into the dressing room at Alexander's that day and left behind not only my scarf, but also my dearest dreams.

■ ■ ■ ■

My fascination with ballet began in my second year at PA. I became close friends with a beautiful, statuesque ballerina named Suzie Goldman who came from a ballet-obsessed family. Suzie was trained at home till the age of seven, when she entered the School of American Ballet. She was accepted into the corps at American Ballet Theatre when she was a junior at PA, and I went to see her dance a lot. Her sisters were both dancers, and her mother, Phyllis, was a ballet teacher who gave classes in their apartment on Park Avenue and Ninety-fifth Street. (I'm going to pause here for a moment while you imagine an apartment with a ballet studio where the living room ought to be. There was almost no furniture, only wooden floors, mirrors, and a barre that had originally belonged to Natalia Makarova.)

There was a kind of body dysmorphia that was nurtured in us at that time, one that was already lodged in our brains. All we thought about was how to get thinner or how to stay thin. Suzie's mother didn't help; before we went out Phyllis would pull me aside and say good-naturedly, "If she eats anything out of line, you call me." Suzie and

I went out dancing together constantly. No dinner. Just mineral water and dancing and sweating, a punishing, yet fun, aerobic workout. We'd start at one club and go to the next and the next and just dance for hours. We might wake up the following morning slightly sick, but three pounds thinner. Though I may have ruined my intestines for life, I was never happier than when I was at my goal weight. Even today, no matter what goes wrong — the world could come to an end — if I'm thin, everything is hunky-dory.

The Goldman family had a friend named Elaine who had a fabulous apartment at the El Dorado and who adored ABT. She had a box in the grand tier at the Met every ballet season, and she often invited me to join her. Other nights I would tag along with Suzie and watch performances from backstage — where I witnessed some pretty glamourous goings-on: Gelsey Kirkland, wasted on cocaine, making her entrance flawlessly, as though nothing were amiss; Jessica Lange holding their baby as Baryshnikov kissed her good night then turned on a dime for the grand pas de deux; visions of ballerinas in footlights stepping in resin boxes then lining up as swans or Wilis, it was something out of Degas. Also the beautiful male dancers backstage — it was with a mixture of inferiority and desire that I regarded them. Anyone would have felt like a different, less-important species being in such close proximity to those beauties.

I became a member of an exclusive bunch of people, a society I've never left, whose priority is seeing all kinds of dance; ballet companies from all over the world. (Another reason to live in New York City, one of the few cities that hosts such a large number of yearly dance shows and events.) The Royal Ballet, the Bolshoi, the Grand Canadian Ballet (where I got my first glimpse of the great Rudolf Nureyev), the Danish Ballet, San Francisco Ballet, The Joffrey. I learned the differences between these companies, their specialties, their styles, their strengths and weaknesses. I went to modern dance performances, too. To see Martha Graham whenever I could at City Center. And Twyla Tharp. And Trisha Brown. And my absolute favorite, Merce Cunningham, whose shows influenced me well into my middle age. (Once my friend Mark Morris and I went to see Merce Cunningham and half the audience walked out. We wondered aloud what we were doing wrong that people were *not* walking out of our shows in droves.) One of the great nights of my life was when

I saw *Tango Argentino* in 1985. I sat there in tears of joy most of the night and I was led into another dance obsession that included lessons and a whole trove of tango clubs in New York City which I fear have since closed. Looking at dance became a lifelong occupation. It's with a certain comfort and pleasure that I go to shows now, to theatres, so familiar they feel like my living room, where I see so many of the same faces in the audience, balletomanes, like myself, who have been returning again and again all these years, some friends, others I know only to exchange a nod of recognition.

When Suzie wasn't onstage I went, often with her, to see New York City Ballet across Lincoln Center Plaza at what was then known as the New York State Theater. The more ballet I saw, the more engrossed I became. Engrossed with the bodies and engrossed with the art form — the structure of it. Shortly after I started my clothing company I was asked in an interview to identify the greatest design influence in my life, and without batting an eye I said "George Balanchine." The way he solved problems, the elegance, and the way he pared things down. The perfect, logical patterns on the stage — the aesthetic, the *thinking* influenced me more than anything I'd seen in my young life.

I went to ballet classes outside of school to learn more about what I was looking at onstage. I discovered my love of dance was boundless. I took jazz classes. African dance. In order to learn more about the Fred Astaire and Eleanor Powell movies that I was becoming increasingly obsessed with, I took tap dancing classes upstairs at Carnegie Hall with an old vaudevillian who has long since passed away, and whose name I can't remember. He worked in a studio that was more like an office, full of pictures of him in his heyday with all the greats of vaudeville, most of whom I didn't recognize. His wife accompanied the class on an upright piano. Classes consisted of no more than four people at a time. He sat behind his desk, which was piled with papers, chewing on a cigar, instructing us, shouting "Hop!" and "Again!" and "Brush out!"

My interest in dance resulted in a very developed, very critical eye for the subject of costumes. More than any other performing endeavor, dance requires a real editing of excess when it comes to costumes. The more I look at dance, the less I want costumes to draw attention away from the dancers' bodies, and the less I want to distort the shapes and patterns the choreographer is trying to create. For that matter, why should a costume distract from the effect an actor is trying to make? Costumes have to add to the picture, add to the emotional content onstage. I developed a distinct opinion in those years about costuming for the theatre. With the exception of a big revue, or a pageant, or a tableau vivant, less is definitely more.

Midway through my third year at Performing Arts, I was approached by a senior acting teacher to help make costumes for *A Midsummer Night's Dream,* the Shakespeare play that would be presented in the Spring Drama Festival that year. The costume shop at Performing Arts was a large square room with massively framed wire-mesh windows, which were impossible to open, looking out on Forty-sixth Street. The edges of the room were loaded with racks and cabinets full of old costumes and hats. The costumes for *Midsummer* consisted of simple togas and floral wreaths and such. At some point I had a total inspiration for Nick Bottom, who is meant to transform into a donkey onstage. My idea was to weave the donkey head out of twigs, like a basket, thereby revealing glimpses of the actor's face beneath. The idea (which, to this day, I think was really good) got shot down by the costume designer, and instead we used the stock papier mâché donkey head they kept in a closet for just such productions.

My interest in design was growing, but it was creating a subtle rift between me and my classmates. It felt like my friends now identified me not as a fellow actor but as something else. That decision I'd made in the dressing room with Diane Lane was beginning to solidify, and for all the excitement I was experiencing in discovering fashion there was also some remorse. I was relinquishing my dreams of becoming a performer. I watched my other friends get accepted into the drama and dance departments at Juilliard and Purchase, which seemed like a simple, natural progression. For me it wasn't as simple.

At that time my priority was to find a way out of the house — getting away from that repressive community and protecting myself from the horrors that lay ahead, when my true self would be revealed. If I was going to live my adult life honestly, fashion seemed like the easiest way to make the money I'd need to escape. At that point my teachers made it clear that pursuing two careers was impossible. They insisted I choose; and fantasies of a life in show business didn't seem to solve the problem of how I'd free myself from my current environment, one that threatened to suffocate me.

Once I made the decision, I threw myself into a more practical approach to life. My puppet shows, which had been a way to express myself artistically, were now a means to an end: Making things became about making money. I came up with the idea to create a mobile puppet show that I could take to children's birthday parties. I worked my hands to the bone on that puppet theatre for months. I mimeographed flyers at my dad's office and put them in the lobbies of the two shuls. Weird how I had no hesitation about advertising to these people who I felt such anger toward. But they were willing to pay, and I needed the money for the purpose of buying my own freedom.

Making those puppet shows took an enormous amount of energy. On top of the physical exertion of setting up the complicated puppet theatre I had constructed in the basement atelier, the very thing I was doing was evidence of how different I was: a kid myself entertaining other kids. The puppets also made me an easy target for harassment. I heard the word "faggot" more and more.

Toward the end of my second year in high school, Robin Leopold introduced me to a friend of her family's, who managed the small Madison Avenue shop for Lederer, the wonderful German handbag maker. By that point sketching was becoming important to me. My sketches were no longer just dramatic expressions of women in makeup with big hairdos. I was beginning to love the power of bringing my thoughts about design to life in the form of a sketch. When Robin's friend asked for handbag sketches I obliged, and she bought two and paid me seventy-five dollars, which was a fortune to me at the time. Sketching was a dream occupation. Think a thought, draw it out, sell it, move on. No execution. No heavy lifting. Later in my career sketching would be the basis for massive amounts of the aforementioned heavy lifting, but at the time I never imagined I could make so much money doing something so interesting. And needless to say it was a lot less backbreaking and emotionally exhausting than schlepping those puppets around Brooklyn. As soon as I found an easier way to make money, I was thrilled to put the puppet-show days behind me.

By my third year in high school my atelier in the basement became more important as a place where I made clothes and sketches. I began selling sketches of shoes to a company located in the Empire State Building called Shoe Biz. It was also run by Syrian Jews. I felt that familiar disdain of working with the very people I was making great strides in leaving behind. But it was good money, and I was good at it, so I was able to separate my love of the work from my feelings about the people I was working for. I remember one group of shoe designs I presented had cone heels, (which were trendy at the time) decorated with leather florettes. It was thrilling to walk into the showroom three months later and see the actual shoes that had been made from those sketches. They were exact replicas in exactly the same colors. A life-altering moment. From that point on I was a goner for design.

In my senior year in high school, I met Haim Dabah, the owner of Gitano, who started purchasing my sketches. I applied the same principles. They needed tops, so I sketched tops. They needed ideas for jean pockets, so I focused there. They were launching handbags, so I sketched those. Whatever was needed, I was willing to try dreaming it up.

The money I made in high school meant I

didn't have to ask permission from my parents to do things they might have disapproved of. A huge portion of the money I made went to paying for taxis, something few others my age even considered. If the subway was my ticket to freedom, then a taxi was a first-class passage.

More than once I worried about the great amount of money I was spending on taxis; I was afraid I'd get "spoiled" for mass transit. "Spoiling" was something horrible — a fate worse than death in the house growing up. What would happen if I stopped making money and had to readjust to a regular diet of subways and buses? Both my parents constantly warned my sisters and me about getting too used to luxuries. Aside from being the pat explanation that accompanied a "no" when we wanted something my parents couldn't afford, "spoiling" was generally seen as something to be wary of in life. The Kennedy children, who were my mother's preferred examples, were not spoiled. "Do you think the Kennedys just give their kids anything they want?" my mother would say, as though Jackie Kennedy were our next-door neighbor. "John-John has to work if he wants a car. Caroline doesn't get money for a taxi whenever she wants. She has to earn it!" And my father talked about one of his friends who lost so much money when his company went bankrupt that he threw himself out a window rather than live his life without the luxuries that "spoiled" him.

For all my good intentions of being punctual, sometimes I would run very late, and my only alternative was a speeding taxi. It was difficult when I was a kid getting taxis in Brooklyn, but they were my saving grace on so many mornings. I'd run to Ocean Parkway and though it was dangerous — traffic moved fast, it was a major highway — I would hail the first taxi I saw, which would barely come to a full stop before I'd jump in, and we'd speed forth, seconds before being rear-ended. As necessary as taxis were, it was their luxury that appealed to me. The old Checker taxis were especially grand. They were the size of tanks, with backseats like small sofas, ashtrays, actual jump-seats, and never a seat belt in sight. You could fit eight people in the backseat of one of those old cars — two wearing ball gowns.

I took taxis whenever I felt the slightest bit of danger. If there was a dicey situation happening on the street, I could hail a taxi and speed off. Once Kevin and I were sitting at an outdoor restaurant on the Upper

West Side when a car stopped with a screech half a block away and two guys came out, one with a baseball bat and another with a gun he shot into the car behind him. Everyone ran for cover while Kevin and I dashed into a nearby taxi and sped away. I have memory after memory of being ill in the backseat of a taxi, holding on just long enough to get home or to an emergency room. If I was coming down with something, had too much to drink, or had eaten something bad, I felt safer in a taxi than an ambulance. Because I lived so much of my life out of the house as a kid, I saw taxis as a kind of moveable shelter. I even thought of them as places to entertain my friends. I couldn't host parties at home the way some of my friends did, so I felt really good about squiring them around in taxis. When I was a senior in high school, one night I picked up a boy at Studio 54, gave him a lift home in a taxi, and we made out in the backseat. When I got to college I had a boyfriend named Eric and we went as far as two people could in the backseat of a Checker taxi. Later, on dates, the only way to know if someone was into you was to make a pass in a shared taxi home.

My new friends. My ability to make money. These things helped transform me from terrified yeshiva boy to street-smart New York who could support the lifestyle I envisioned, with no apologies or explanations. If there were one physical thing to express the best part — the most romantic part of my young adulthood — it would be a Checker taxi speeding through New York City in the rain. And the more I sped forth, the less I looked back at the community I was leaving in the dust.

12

When I was sixteen I met another muse, also named Sarah. Sarah Haddad was a very beautiful and glamourous woman of about thirty, a dead ringer for Catherine Deneuve, with heavy-lidded eyes and glamourous strawberry-blond hair. I knew my mother approved of her as the leader of a bunch of young women in the community, often referred to as the Jet Set because they seemed to travel out into the world a lot more than the average Syrian. Their racy edge, their glamour and worldly ways, were accepted because they mostly upheld the community traditions and kept mum about the ones they didn't. My mother was anxious for me to transition away from what she thought of as an unstable life in the theatre to a more navigable career in fashion. After all, my father's business was childrenswear, which seemed to everyone, me included, like a short jump away from fashion. On top of my sketching abilities, I suppose my reputation in the community as an outsider made me edgy and interesting to Sarah Haddad, and so after my mother made the introductions, she invited me for coffee. We sat in her dinette and talked about clothes — not as a teenager talking to a thirty-year-old but as equals. She showed me some fabulous clothes she had recently bought in Europe, and I remember feeling torn because they were things I didn't like. She asked if I would design something for her to wear to an upcoming event, and I was thrilled. Imagine a full-grown woman, such a good-looking one, paying you to design clothes for her! On top of everything else, she offered to engage a seamstress to make the dress. This was a dream job.

Even among the Jet-Setters Sarah was exceptional. According to the Syrians in Brooklyn, business was for men only, an idea that Sarah never challenged except in her actions. She did exactly as she pleased and was good at secrets. She never made a big deal about things she did, some of which were against the traditions. She ran her own life, often with no explanation and never any apologies, and in so doing stayed out of the fray of criticism and resistance. She stood as a leader in the community and always had the best parties, the best clothes, and had an edge of worldliness that made even the most conservative members adore her and look up to her. She had grand personal style — that beautiful head, long legs, broad shoulders and an ability to look sexy — racy even — without succumbing to the overtly objectifying sexiness that was prevalent in the community among those women who wanted to appeal to their men.

On the Saturday morning that Sarah was supposed to pick me up to go fabric shopping there was a huge snowstorm. I thought for sure she would cancel, but at exactly the appointed time she drove up in her forest-green Jaguar wearing furs and high-heeled boots. In the car she explained her theory about people who canceled because of silly things like weather conditions. "You know, people like that will never get anything done." She had absolutely no professional experience to that point, but I knew when she showed up that I could rely on her. The car swerved on the ice a few times, but once we got to the city we had the fabric stores to ourselves.

Jerry Brown was located across the street from Carnegie Hall and up the block from Steinway Hall, which lent it an air of cultured exclusivity. It was a shrine. Nothing like the garment-district fabric shops we bypassed that afternoon, and it made Midwood Trimmings look like a garage sale. It had a serene atmosphere, almost like a temple, radiating a devotion to quality that few would understand today. You wouldn't go there on a whim. Nowadays if a fabric doesn't sell, it's considered passé regardless of its quality. At Jerry Brown good fabrics were considered more fabulous the older they got. Often Mr. Brown bought fabrics and put them away for a while, until they became examples of bygone luxury. He was a collector of textiles in the way other people collected paintings, and he handled the fabrics the way art gallerists handle art: as commodities, with extreme care. Most of the inventory was on the first floor, housed in locked wooden cases with recessed lights that spotlit the fabrics in otherwise moodily lit rooms.

You would never dream of calling Mr. Brown "Jerry." He was small and impeccably dressed, usually wearing light-colored neutrals, fleshy tones that accentuated his colorless complexion and balding head. He was an intimidating gentleman who rarely spoke and mostly stood in the shadows of the store and watched. His gaze was such that anyone without a distinct purpose and a thorough devotion to textiles felt like an interloper. One didn't want to be dressed too casually in that shop. Later, on the few occasions when I had business with him, I would wear a suit and tie, and it tickled me that his mostly dour mien changed a bit. He'd smile from time to time and treat me like an equal.

Then there was *upstairs* at Jerry Brown. If you couldn't find what you were looking for anywhere else in the world (and I mean the world), you would make an appointment to meet Mr. Brown upstairs, in what was referred to as "the vault." Here he kept the most beautiful stock of special textiles ever amassed anywhere. Ancient, precious things. Things that hadn't been made for decades, woven in places that were once known for excellence in textile manufacture. Mr. Brown sold fabrics from Lyon well into the 1980s, as though it were the 1950s and Lyon were still a textile capital. He had large stocks of those fabrics, which you can't describe in terms that anyone would relate to today; their beauty, lightness, excellence in handling are from a whole other realm. (This is definitely a personal preference, but I think the best fabrics, no matter how warm they're meant to keep you, are light in weight. Even a nice heavy flannel, coating, brocade, or an embroidered textile is at its best when kept as light as possible. It's a lot like a cake. Who wants a heavy cake?)

I still remember some of the fabrics I got up there. One I remember in particular was a sheer, matte, silk velvet that I wish I could have today, just to prove to myself that I'm not insane and that there ever was anything as beautiful and perishable as that. It was like the wing of a butterfly turned into liquid. It had a silk crepe back with a matte velvet face, the whole thing slightly, miraculously sheer. The kind of thing you'd imagine Isadora Duncan wore to bed. And if you wanted lace . . . Mr. Brown had one of the greatest stores of it up in that vaultlike room. Nineteenth-century laces. Nineteen-sixties laces. Hand-tatted lace from Belgium that cost two or three thousand dollars a meter, which in today's marketplace would be unpriceable. Reembroidered lace. Lace in the most exquisite colors, which makes the idea of colored lace okay (colored lace usually makes me slightly sick). I got so many laces from him for some of the most beautiful wedding dresses and evening dresses in my career.

Swatching was out of the question at Jerry Brown. Usually a young designer would go out looking for textiles and take cuttings of things that caught his eye in order to either match something to it, or to make a more sound decision later, after a short consideration. And at places like Poli (another wonderful fabric store on West Fifty-seventh Street that is long gone) or B&J, one of the better garment district shops, "swatching" is their stock-in-trade. But not so at Jerry Brown. Even when I became quite successful I would have to put a deposit down and borrow the entire bolt of fabric on memo rather than take a tiny swatch.

From the time I was extremely young I had an ability to see almost everything in a store with one glance. I can go to a flea market and tell you in thirty seconds whether it's worth staying. Not so at Jerry Brown. You could look for hours and always find something fresh. That day with Sarah, as I was looking through the venerable cases, a shade of mauve caught my eye. The color of dead roses, the fabric had a kind of textureless face, with an exquisite dull sheen like a common silk lawn, only with the mystique and movement of a heavy crepe. It was rich and light, something I had never seen before. So plain and so expensive. I knew the fabric would be perfect for the design I had in mind. Then the salesperson called it "peau d'ange" — angel skin —

which made me love it more.

Sarah got a recommendation for someone who wanted extra work as a patternmaker and dressmaker, a Filipino lady named Lupe. A week later we went to visit her in her small one-bedroom garden apartment on the Upper West Side. This was before that area underwent its big gentrification, and she forsook a living room in favor of a small workroom with mannequins, a cutting table, three sewing machines, and an ironing station. She spoke little English, but that never stood in the way of our work, and she was the first in a long line of people I would have to communicate with without a common language between us. As anyone in the fashion business can vouch for, sewing rooms all over the world tend to be real melting pots of languages, and yet there are rarely any communication problems. We speak "the language of the pins," as I call it. Rather than talk, we show each other. It's something I applied from dance-class methods. In sewing rooms and dance classes, reading and speaking are not nearly as productive as demonstration.

The dress — a simple sack design with drawstring shoulders and a sash — made "a big hit" when Sarah wore it. A plunging *V* revealed her back, one of her most beautiful

241

assets that you wouldn't have known about. I went to her house to help her dress that night, and when we were finished she looked truly beautiful. The dress was just below the knee, and not a spangle in sight. Just that mauve against Sarah's beautiful young body. It had a kind of sex appeal that was closer to ancient Greece than to the standard disco-era schmaltz. I convinced her to keep her hair and makeup simple that night, and she looked young and sophisticated. Some-one named Cookie Cohen, the wife of Joe Cohen, who owned and ran the fabulous M&J Trimmings (one of the greatest trim-ming resources in the world), was a big fan of Sarah's dress and asked if I would make her a gown for her son's bar mitzvah. This was a big compliment, seeing as how Cookie had ins with all the fashion houses on Seventh Avenue and could easily have got-ten a dress from anywhere. A bar mitzvah dress was a huge opportunity, and I under-stood the implications of that commission. I left the salesmanship to Sarah and took on the mantle of designer. I always left busi-ness to the people who seemed to know what they were doing, and in the case of Sarah at that time, if there was anything she knew about, it was how to influence other Syrian women and their clothing choices. If this went well it could solidify a business for Sarah and me. If Cookie's dress was a "hit," Sarah and I would be on our way, whichever way — still unclear.

For Cookie's dress I selected a brown and gold lamé floral damask fabric and combined it with lilac and pink chiffon. It was a fishtail-shaped gown built on one shoulder and it had a multitier handkerchief hem and a train. The dress looked great on Cookie, and within weeks after that bar mitzvah I was approached to make clothes for a number of Syrian women. Without knowing exactly what was happening Sarah and I were forming a little business. I was the designer and she was the business liaison. Before the end of my third year at PA, Sarah and I created a label for our venture called IS New York. "I" for Isaac and "S" for Sarah. We split the bill because she took financial responsibility for the company, but I couldn't help wondering why I accepted the fifty-fifty deal. I thought there should've been some major distinction for being the actual designer but I was too polite and conflict-averse to raise it as an issue. Mostly I was scared to lose her patronage if I asked for what seemed rightfully mine. Another instance of a familiar irony; what drove me to make money was my determination to get away from the community — and yet here I was using a community connection as backing. I adored Sarah, but it's something that to this day I wish I could go back in time and correct. If only I'd waited to see what the wide world would bring me — the world *outside* of the community.

Ricky Haddad, Sarah's husband, was a partner in Haddad Brothers, a big family firm that made childrenswear and is still in business. Haddad Brothers had a factory on McDonald Avenue in Brooklyn with a big cutting facility, and another larger factory in Ossining, New York. Ricky agreed to let us use those factories for a nominal fee in their off seasons. In the actual world this makes no sense at all because factories that specialize in childrenswear don't know the first thing about making women's clothes, and vice versa. We learned a lot about those things those first few months, but aside from a few horrible setbacks — a whole range of appliqué blouses that had to be recut and remade — for the most part, it worked.

I set to the task of designing a tiny first collection, which began with the sourcing of fabrics — two of which I remember as though they were hanging on a rack in front of me now. One was a crimson sequined georgette from Sequins International. With that I made a round-yoked top with a revere collar and leg-o'-mutton sleeves tucked into a matching high-waisted, floor-length, side-slit skirt with a red satin sash. Then I did something very audacious for a fifteen-year-old: I made an appointment with a fabric company I had seen an ad for in *Vogue,* an Italian firm called Cugnasca that made gorgeous silks and prints. I went up to their New York office with Sarah, looked through the racks, and picked out a pale celadon-green crepe printed with what looked like multicolored graffiti tags. I ordered a "piece" (fifty yards) and designed a very simple tank top in the print with a pair of matching pegged pants.

When the first samples were made I invited some of the girls in my high-school class to model the clothes at a shoot at Sarah's house in Brooklyn. One of the girls had a boyfriend who was a budding photographer, and he agreed to take the pictures. At the time Henri Bendel was the greatest, most exclusive store in New York City, so once we had the portfolio, we attended one of their Thursday evening open calls for new labels. Sarah and I set up our things on a rack in the middle of the floor among the ten or twelve others who showed up. Finally the buyer appeared. She was a short, dark-haired woman in her midforties, with enormous round glasses, and dressed in black jersey. She never questioned my age — it was generally assumed I was in my early twenties because I was tall and overdressed. The buyer spared the time for Sarah to change into an outfit or two as she considered our tiny collection and our hopes were set high, but we were rejected after a week of intense waiting. We did land an order from another very glamourous store on the Upper West Side called Charivari. We took the clothes there one night just as the store was closing, and one of the owners — a guy with a big mustache, dressed in head-to-toe leather — gave us ten minutes to show him the line. He ordered three or four pieces, including a fabulous red silk taffeta blouse that was cut like something out of the nineteenth century with a high collar and pearls for buttons. We took our clothes to a number of small, exclusive clothing shops in New York City at the time and showed them to any buyer who would look.

We traveled back and forth from Mc-Donald Avenue to Ossining delivering fabrics, patterns, zippers, picking up samples, overseeing the cutting and sewing of different pieces. It was my first taste of the designer clothing business. All six pieces that we shipped to Charivari sold out quickly, and they reordered — a word which came to mean "success" in my vocabulary. Another shop that sold our clothes was called Lonia on East Fifty-fifth Street, down the block from the newly opened Manolo Blahnik. We expanded downtown to a store called Yuri Marchesi on the corner of Prince and Mercer. It was run by a devastatingly sexy guy (at least to an awkward teenager like me), the eponymous Yuri, who lived in a loft above the selling floor — his disheveled bed was visible above the proceedings. He was tall and overly tan and had thinning dirty-blond hair and a Russian accent, and he wore seriously tight leather pants. (Leather pants were the go-to look for garmentos then). I suspect there were drugs around because the store was always filled with loud disco music, half-empty champagne flutes, and a retinue of jittery, talkative people who were in and out all day and night.

It wasn't spoken of, but my parents breathed a distinct sigh of relief when my female impersonations, my puppet obsession, all my dreams of show business seemed to be phasing out in favor of a business that could be understood by the family and the community at large. No doubt there were ugly, scary things about the garment business — sex scandals, drugs, etc. — but these were nowhere near as prevalent nor as public as in show business. In those days world-famous designers hid behind their brand names. My mother was thrilled by the idea that her son might actually go into the same business as Norman Norell and Geoffrey Beene. Instead of pressuring me, she inspired me. She talked only of clothes. She encouraged me to look at *Vogue* and *Bazaar*, which didn't take much encouragement. At our Saturday-morning breakfasts, which continued well into my late teens, she would tell me things about the glamour of the fashion business and about her days as a young woman, when clothes were her biggest priority. She was so proud of her reputation in the community as a stylish dresser, and of her wily sartorial ways: buying inexpensive things and doctoring them up with trim, wearing clothes back-to-front to give necklines extra drama, wearing little boys' clothes, and men's silk pajamas to the beach. It was my mother's dream I was fulfilling by becoming a fashion designer, even more than my own. Which isn't to say that she dreamed of becoming a fashion designer herself — more, she wanted to be the mother of one.

In my last year at PA my mother got the idea that my father should introduce me to an acquaintance who occupied the showroom next to his. Ellie Fishman designed a line of little girls' dresses under the label Youngland, which was acknowledged as the leading childrenswear label of the time. She was an acclaimed designer responsible for bringing elements of high fashion to children's clothes. The day we met she walked into my father's showroom like a visiting religious dignitary and was received by his salespeople with a bowing reverence. She was a tiny lady in early middle age with a large majestic head and bluish chestnut-colored hair carefully arranged, so as not to look overly coiffed. She was understated and modern, dressed in a rust-and-white-striped blouse by Gil Aimbez, a blouse I had noticed in the window of Saks the week before. At first she had an icy mien and I felt ashamed to even suggest I might want to be in the same industry as her, someone so refined, with such exquisite taste. She sensed my unease and in barefaced New Yorkese said, "Don't be nervous, I won't bite!" Then she looked at my sketches. This wasn't the fickle eye of my mother or the untrained eye of Sarah Haddad. This was the professional eye of someone who seemed adept at noticing good ideas and spotting talent.

She won me right away with praise: "I'm glad I came over here," she said to my father, "your son is very talented." Then she gave me some harsh, necessary criticism. Making clothes, advising others who seek your advice — it doesn't do to lie. People sense you're lying and you lose their trust. There's a way to mix charm and criticism in order to get the result you want, whether it's from a sample maker you're guiding to remake a piece with a finer hand, or someone who's asked your advice about what to wear. Ellie was my first example of this sort of charm offensive — a kind of fashion tact that those in positions of authority seemed to know a lot about. I was open to her because she seemed really to care about me, and not just as a favor to my father. At the end of the first meeting she advised me to take adult design classes at Parsons in the evenings, and to apply full time to the Parsons design program when I finished high school. At that time Parsons was one of the finest design educations available. Although I still think of fashion as a light-hearted endeavor, Ellie Fishman approached it like it was a noble profession —

an art form. It wasn't just about what women wore to temple and dressed their daughters in to marry them off. Ellie spoke of designers like they were prophets. She advised me to stop what I was doing with Sarah immediately, which came as a great relief. As much fun as I was having with Sarah, there was something impure about it. I was ready to say goodbye to garment bags in the forest-green Jaguar trunk and schlepping to factories in Ossining. What Ellie was suggesting seemed bigger and more exciting than where I was headed with that little side business. If I was going to knuckle down and be a designer I would do it the right way. What she was suggesting was a direct line from me to the big time, to the world of Halston and Bill Blass. The things she said echoed what I had been thinking and hoping — that there was something greater and more dignified to hold out for.

Ellie Fishman made a few calls and sent me to meet some of her designer friends, including the great Mollie Parnis, who was known for her strictly tailored suits and dresses. She advised me to learn all I could about construction and mourned the fact that she didn't know how to instruct seamstresses to make her designs through demonstration. She claimed she was "at the mercy of pattern makers."

Ellie also called her friend Anthony Muto. He had a very successful collection called A.M./P.M., which made smart dresses that a woman could wear for day into cocktails. His atelier was the most glamourous place I had been to yet — a far cry from my motley basement atelier and the depressing factories on McDonald Avenue. Great natural light streamed in through big industrial windows, emphasizing the high loft ceilings and the soaring shelf units that held endless bolts of fabrics organized by color and weight. But the crucial elements hung on the wall in the form of his sketches, and on the mannequins — the fascinating half-finished clothes that represented all the possibilities on Earth and seemed to be sewn by the hands of angels.

He looked through my sketches, which I accompanied with a running commentary of self-disparaging remarks. I didn't think much of my work, especially after seeing his. And whatever I wore that day felt wrong from the moment I set foot in that office. Especially compared to his loose-fitting silk shirt and triple-pleated leather trousers. (Yes, he wore leather trousers, too. It was an epidemic.) I was just too young and too inexperienced to feel anything but awkward. He was austere both in appearance and personality. Friendly but formal. He didn't say much. He also praised me right away and then went on to criticize me in that fashion-tactful way. He treated me like an equal, which tempered the spate of criticism that followed. I wasn't really aware yet of the pervading homosexual culture in fashion, and I'm still not sure if he was gay. It didn't matter. Even the straightest man in the fashion business has an honorary gay status in my book. (Especially if he's wearing triple-pleated leather trousers.) I aspired to his look because he was thin and well-styled and talented and sphinxlike.

He eyed me up and down in a way I wasn't used to being looked at. "How old are you?"

"Sixteen."

"Oh god," he said. "And what made you start sketching?"

"I don't know. I like clothes."

He went through each sketch with me and revealed what was good, what was right, and what was wrong.

I wasn't sure why, but I was very drawn to this man. Not sexually attracted. More as a role model. A man functioning in an identity that was close to one I dreamed of for myself. I knew exactly what I needed to know about him, no more, no less. He wasn't flamboyant like Michael Sherman or an intimidating tastemaker like John Banter. I came away from the meeting inspired — mixed with my signature touch of depression and languor. I committed to the idea that there was a world where I would be accepted, but I felt the huge distance between where I was and that future location. Anthony Muto was the ambassador for the place where I wanted to go. The fashion world appeared to be a rarified environment where people like me were accepted and even, at times, exalted.

When I got back home to Brooklyn that night, I sulked. Maybe for too long. My father, sensing something was wrong, took me aside and asked me "if anything fishy happened" in the meeting that afternoon. He told me he thought Anthony Muto was one of those "fairies" and that if I was going into the fashion business I would have to be careful of them because they were everywhere. *Right,* I thought to myself. *One big one right under your nose.*

I was getting closer. I was still too scared to call myself gay, and it felt like I'd have to roll a boulder up a hill to reach my goal of living as a gay man. Part of that great burden came from the fact that in order to find real acceptance I'd have to leave the past behind once and for all. I made up my mind to do exactly that.

13

My senior year in high school I was cast as Touchstone in our production of *As You Like It,* and the choice of that part for me was far more meaningful than my drama teachers could have known. I was enthralled by the definition when I looked up the word: "a fine piece of jasper that is employed to tell the value of gold; a standard or criterion by which something is judged or recognized." The issue of authenticity was especially big for me right at that time. I might not have fully come out until my first year in college, but the major reckoning, the confrontation, the admission of it to those of my friends closest to me, took place in my senior year, and it was all very tied up in that Shakespeare production. Integrity regarding the subject of my homosexuality was the motivating idea in my life; reckoning with it, digesting it, and ultimately tying that identity to the making of art that reflected who I was.

The only person I could discuss any of this with was Kevin, who was cast as Jacques in the production. In theory we were gay, but we sat on the sidelines of it for the entire four years of high school. It was around that time that Kevin and I coined the phrase "Jewish affair," named thus because of the overthinking and lack of action-taking Judaism seemed to teach. A Jewish affair is when you make eye contact with someone in a restaurant or a theatre from across a room but never follow through, never actually meet them or speak to them. It ends when you leave the room and never see each other again. We had our Jewish affairs every day, but never actual affairs.

Death in Venice, which Kevin and I passed back and forth in our senior year, is a tragedy about the ultimate Jewish affair. It's a novella by Thomas Mann, a beautifully wrought story about a homosexual attraction that occurs between a young boy and an older man, so delicate and subtly shaded that it's easy to miss the implications. The characters eye each other for weeks; one even dies before meeting the other. We talked about that story for months, its subtleties allowing for broad interpretations and bold skirtings around the subject of its relevance in our lives. Then, finally in the dead of winter 1978, at the Fairway Deli across the street from PA, eating powdered sugar donuts, we touched on the subject. Wondering aloud about the straight couples at school — "How far do you think John and Amy have gone? You think they actually *did it*?" Then a long silence. Ironic stares exchanged. Finally, nervous laughter, and Kevin said, "I'm pretty sure neither of us will be dating girls anytime in the near future."

In the 1970s and '80s Manhattan was a wicked place. It had many more lurid, burned-out neighborhoods than posh, trendy ones. SoHo was a deserted, dark place with mostly broken street lamps. The thirty blocks north of Lincoln Center, the Upper West Side of Manhattan, was the definition of urban blight. There was a sliver of a bourgeois residential neighborhood where Gina and Kevin lived on West End Avenue, but that was bordered on all sides by a depraved, charred cityscape. Hell's Kitchen wasn't full of restaurants and luxury high-rises then. It was called Hell's Kitchen because it was *the* hottest, filthiest place in hell and on Earth. It extended into Times Square and the theatre district, where my school was located. You risked great danger if you set foot into certain parts of Central Park in broad daylight, and you'd be nuts to venture there after dark. On a daily basis my friends and I witnessed lurid things — things you'd think I'm making up. Dead bodies. People being chased down and slapped into handcuffs. It was a real-life cop show that played out inches from the noses of New Yorkers, and we were completely unperturbed. For every example of glamour there was twice as much decay, decay that sometimes dominated the scene. Grand Central Terminal was in ruins, while two doors down a sleek new skyscraper had just gone up. This kind of high contrast defined New York City at that time and was a big part of what informed my aesthetic as a kid — the juxtaposition of beautiful new things among squalor. Always something rotting next to something fresh. You can't trust something handsome unless it's laid alongside something really ugly. This idea, this contrast that existed in New York City, was a central influence on me and a whole generation of postmodernists.

I learned to drive in 1977 when I was sixteen. I drove a huge, brown, hand-me-down Cadillac that my father gave to my sisters and me, which made me feel completely omnipotent, completely exempt from any danger. The same year I enrolled in two evening classes at Parsons, and on the nights I wasn't at night school, I was driving that car, circling for eternity to find parking on my way to any number of nightclubs. If my time at Performing Arts left me with anything, it was a superb appreciation of disco music. "We Are Family." "Ring My Bell." "The Hustle." Learning to dance the Spank and the Rock were part of my initiation into society. Donna Summer was a goddess. "Bad Girls" was a defining part of my last two years at PA. It's funny now to consider the fact that underage kids all over the city were dancing and singing along to songs about hookers.

Hearing that same music at full volume on the massive speakers in a club made it all the more heady. There were so many clubs, intimate ones, arena-sized ones, and each with its own personality. One on the Upper East Side called Hippopotamus, filled with reserved, rich white people. In Midtown, in the bowels of Port Authority was GG's Barnum Room, which had a trapeze above the bar and a clientele made up exclusively of transsexual hookers and johns. There was Escuelita in a basement on Eighth Avenue and Thirty-eighth Street, which felt the most dangerous and fun. I remember descending the stairs and having to be frisked at the door before entering. Inside were Latina drag queens doing shows into the wee hours, competing for attention on a runway lined with tinfoil and colored Christmas lights, while their families, their old mothers and wives and babies, sat at long tables drinking and cheering them on amidst the gangsters.

No teenager would make it past the front door of nightclubs like those today. But way back then there were no such discriminations. Nothing like "carding" had yet been invented. My friends and I looked a lot older than we were, and we dressed like freaks. We loved thrift shops like Canal Jean Co. and Reminiscence, and we wore our strange, beat-up remade secondhand pieces like they were haute couture. I made a bright-purple leather bubble jacket with matching pants and brightly colored jumpsuits out of tablecloths that I bought cheap from a small housewares store that was going out of business in Brooklyn. A fluorescent-yellow jumpsuit was a standout. So was a metallic silver leather vest and pants that I wore under a thrift jean jacket, BeDazzled within an inch of its life. I wore everything with high-top sneakers and lots of pins and bracelets, all concealed from my mother and father under a big loden-green coat, which I ditched in the car.

The center of the world at that time was Studio 54. It was an abandoned theatre that had been remade into a massive disco with soaring ceilings and a dance floor right below the fly-space of the original stage. It had a wonderful theatrical lighting grid overhead that emanated mind-blowing lighting effects before anyone was used to that sort of thing. At climactic points in the music, scenic flats would fly down just above the heads of the dancers. A neon skyline. A desertscape with a horse. A half-moon with a twinkle in his eye flew down from one side of the dance floor and was met from the other side by a spoonful of cocaine that sent chaser lights up his nose — it was known as "the moon and the spoon."

Marc, a good-looking guy with fringy blond hair wearing a huge Norma Kamali sleeping-bag coat, ran the door. He would see me and my motley group — a mix of my high-school friends and my new friends from Parsons, and would part the sea of people and welcome us into the club. On the off nights when that didn't happen for whatever reason — Marc was too distracted, or worse, not working the door — I would squeeze my way through the crowd and mention Jack Dushey's name to one of the bouncers. Jack Dushey was one of Sarah Haddad's best friends; he and his wife, Sonia, were charter members of the Sephardic community Jet Set, but also, one of the three main investors in Studio 54, with Steve Rubell and Ian Schrager.

I was enthralled by the scene at Studio 54. Extravagantly dressed and undressed people from every aspect of society. All kinds of boys. All kinds of models and celebrity sightings. Halston. Andy Warhol. Cher. Lauren Hutton. A fabulous drag queen called Rollerina, who worked as an accountant by day; on weekends he put on flouncy dresses, loads of makeup, jeweled cat-eye glasses, roller skates, and glided around Studio 54 till the wee hours. Other flamboyant people like sports stars, writers, socialites.

Up the carpeted stairs in the front of the house was a landing where there were bathrooms that acted more as dimly lit lounges with all sorts of louche goings-on. Farther up the stairs was the balcony, where people went to sit on carpeted platforms and watch the crowd dancing and partying below. Things went on in that balcony. All sorts of making out, and more. When I was finally through dancing I would separate from my friends and make my way upstairs alone to stand around and pose and watch others standing and posing, or I'd watch those seated together passionately making out, groping each other. I had a drink or two and smoked a lot. I wasn't there to participate, I was there to watch.

The one time I did partake of anything close to sex at Studio 54 was when I was standing by myself at the rail in the balcony. Like a miracle, a tall blond guy in jeans and no shirt, smelling of poppers, approached and started kissing me. It seemed like he was mistaking me for someone else. But his lips felt like heaven, and his hands roamed my body. I followed him out that night but didn't go home with him. We shared a taxi and made out in the backseat till he got off in the Village and I continued on to Brooklyn in a dream that evaporated the next morning.

Studio 54 has been depicted and described so many times as a magical place where the elite met the street, celebrities hobnobbed with common folk, nights would be whiled away in an energized, sexy, druggie haze. The Studio 54 that I observed as a teenager wasn't as carefree as that. Drugs were a big part of the scene; what I witnessed was a kind of desperation to be high. Or higher. People dancing in frenzies, not wanting to come down, disappearing into the bathrooms on the mezzanine to find others with cocaine or Quaaludes in an effort to tweak and prolong the synthetic ecstasy.

It was a glorified "boy market." It seemed the only people in the whole club that anyone paid any sexual attention to were the young, shirtless boys. There was certainly diva worship — gay men hunting for fabulous women to either emulate, gossip about, or fawn over. Jerry Hall or Bianca Jagger walked in and all action and time stopped dead. But for the most part it was sexy bartenders in booty shorts on roller skates, or boys trying to further their social ambitions who got all the libidinous attention. Recently I was talking to a friend, about fifteen years older than me, who, as a fashion editor, spent a lot of time at Studio 54 in its heyday, and she vehemently agreed that it was a desperate, sweaty meat market where girls were "sexual persona non grata." Lecherous older men eyed the boys, who objectified themselves in order to move up the food chain. And as eager as I was to get in the front door, and for as many times as I returned, a lot of times the scene there made me sad. I would never be one of those beautiful boys who seemed to have the world by the balls. And I would never want to be a lecherous old man. Admittedly, I wish I could have been wanted for my body. To be one of those boys dancing on the speakers in booty shorts. And yet I was the furthest thing from that.

We stayed out till all hours of the morning. There were dinners or parties, then discos, then after-hours clubs. Sometime in the spring of that year, when my parents were away on a trip to the Bahamas, I was out for the night. Around 4:00 A.M., after dropping off Ted and Francesca, two of my closest friends from high school who lived on the Upper West Side, I was all alone in my Caddy, and it was raining hard. I was on Riverside Drive, about to make a right onto the West Side Highway, when suddenly the car just stopped. Right in the middle of the intersection. Kaput. I tried a few times to restart it, but it wouldn't budge. I sat there for a minute, not too anxious, wondering what to do, when I noticed a free taxi in my rearview mirror. I got out of the car, locked it, hailed the taxi, and without so much as getting wet, I was on my way home to Brooklyn, thinking of myself as very clever to figure out such a great solution. The next day I called my uncle who lived near us in Brooklyn. He and I went to collect the car, which was still there intact, in broad daylight, not a hubcap missing. He gave it a jump and we were on our way without even a fine.

That story is only remarkable for how it illuminates the way the world has changed. Things like that could never happen in New York City now. I guess every generation feels that way about their own past.

If I wasn't at school or out dancing, loath to go back to Brooklyn, I found places to spend off-hours. The Museum of Modern Art was a place I loved to go. You could be alone for hours in that garden with your thoughts and the Rodins. I also loved the Guggenheim. But I loved the Met especially. There were some afternoons in those days when it was empty. And it felt fuller with work that I didn't understand. Gallery after gallery with art I was desperate to know more about. Going back again and again, with no agenda except to pass time. I studied the permanent collections, especially the painting galleries, which seemed to get bigger and more complex every time

I revisited them. I sat alone at the wonderful Dorothy Draper cafeteria with curlicue chandeliers and drank coffee that came out of portly carafes with crimped wax paper lids. That spring of 1978, when I was seventeen, wandering around the Met with no specific destination, I came across an exhibit, at the entrance of which was a huge black-and-white photograph of a woman named Marella Agnelli. I had noticed images like this but never realized they all came from one source. A sign on the wall said RICHARD AVEDON PHOTOGRAPHS, 1946–1976.

A picture of Dorian Leigh in an evening dress by someone called Robert Piguet, standing in a powder room in a place called the *Île Saint-Louis*. An emaciated, elegant woman wearing a dress by someone I'd never heard of, in profile, looking in the mirror at her own perfection, posing but not pretentious. There was no question of her belonging in that grandeur. The huge, square bottle of perfume on the edge of the marble sink, the dress, the hair, the enormous jewels, all seemed to be a secure part of her life. There was a picture of Dovima in a Balenciaga cloche seated next to a large Afghan dog named Sacha at Les Deux Magots. What was more affecting, the image or the words on the wall describing it? What is a cloche? Who were Dovima and Balenciaga? And what was the social significance of Les Deux Magots? From what I could tell it was a world that existed in Paris, a world where women were thin and had pointed, arched eyebrows and heavily glossed lips. There were some good-looking people I came across in my daily life, but none on this level, or at least none that affected me the way these old Avedon pictures did.

Maybe because I was so young, the pictures felt to me like facts, not contrivances — truthful, not pretentious for a minute. Physical manifestations of my own fantasies — refined to a point I had not yet dreamt was possible. But even when they were at their grandest, they had a touch of reality to them, a way in, a kind of grit that made them even better. It had to do with the women. Always a reserve or mystery in their expressions. No bimbos. They weren't exactly "pretty" as much as "exquisite." The backlit *pointe d'esprit* Lanvin-Castillo hat sitting on Carmen Dell'Orefice's head would have no reason for being were it not for the angle, the length of her neck, the knowing, almost sad look on her face. Avedon made sure that no matter how

269

grand or frilly the subject, there was a greater thought contained somewhere in the photograph — in the eyes of the subject, in the background full of dirty French acrobats or elephants. For every ruffle there was something rough, for every stroke of eyeliner there was a stroke of reality.

Inspiration presented its usual double-edged sword. The Avedon exhibit filled me with inspiration, ideas, and an impulse to get to work, followed again by the familiar tinge of spiritual nausea. I floated among the beauty in that gallery. But I also sensed that the level of greatness could never be equaled. Contemplating the arduous road ahead trying to get anywhere near that level of perfection, I felt defeat. I went back to that exhibit many times, and I walked back and forth, pondering how beautiful the world could be and wishing I had been born at another time. I longed to be alive in 1957, there in the streets of Paris, when Carmen jumped over a puddle in a fabulous Pierre Cardin coat. A little later that year my sister Marilyn gave me the book from the exhibit for my birthday, and I spent most of that year studying it the way I think my rabbis, years earlier, hoped I would study the Talmud.

■ ■ ■ ■

I had a strong work ethic from birth. Nothing ever mattered to me except what I was making or performing. Nothing was going to come between me and my artistic accomplishments. Not my family. Not my love life, whatever that was to become. My sexuality and my creativity were always strongly intertwined, even before I was a practicing homosexual. Kevin and I sat for hours every day at the Fairway Deli, amidst the crumbs of powdered sugar donuts, speaking of our artistic ambitions, equating our budding sexuality with art, convincing each other that being gay was a privilege reserved for the great. Every day we thought of five new examples of great gay artists. Not just obvious ones like Oscar Wilde or Truman Capote. It seemed the more we learned of the great thinkers and artists of history, the more encouraged we were to enter their ranks.

But as strong as we were in our convictions, we were intimidated by the times we lived in. It took months for me to confide to my closest circle of friends that I was gay, and I was slightly annoyed at the unanimous response: "Duh!" It didn't seem like anyone at school was surprised at all, and in retrospect, it's funny that I thought they might be. My classmates were all facing similar situations, difficult admissions about entering adulthood: teen pregnancy, alcohol and drug abuse. Mostly they were caught up in their own dramas, so I was met with understanding and love. The closest thing to a bully that I encountered at school was an actor in my class who went on to achieve a kind of middling fame. He solicited other boys in the class to side with him. But the bullying consisted mostly of a series of snide remarks, name-calling, and dark, tasteless jokes; after all, we're talking about a drama-school bully. Those of us who came out at that time tried our best to be honest and do the right thing, even though we had no idea what that meant. The closest things to role models we had were slightly older kids, graduates we learned who had come out, closeted gay adults, a few teachers we suspected but who kept their identities hidden. I was very careful about who I told and didn't tell — it was a matter of great trust, because even though my family was a world away in Brooklyn, I didn't want it to get back to them. But I was also having difficulty *not* telling everyone I passed on the street. Once the process of coming out was started, it was harder to pretend at being straight.

If I had ideas about who I was to become, how I would integrate myself into society, those ideas changed and morphed over the years. It's the plight of the minority. No matter how much integrity one dreams of maintaining, the times dictate otherwise; it's a matter of a certain amount of conforming or perishing, the typecasting of history. If you were gay in those days you were a loner, a crazy serial killer, or the zany, shallow-yet-understanding best friend, who is full of styling advice and says "you go, girl" a lot. I'm guilty of giving in to those expectations, taking on some of those attributes after years of fighting against them.

About fifteen years ago I was on *Hollywood Squares,* which was a dream come true for me, having been a devoted fan since childhood. Just the idea of climbing those stairs and sitting in a box with eight other *zany* celebrities was a thrill. There were joke writers who helped the celebrities if they got caught without a witty response — something I saw as superfluous. One of the answers they wrote for me ended in *you go, girl!* But I thought of a better answer that was much funnier, and the first time I was called on I told *my* joke, which got a lukewarm laugh, if not a sort of groan. The next time I was called on I used *their* joke, practically shouting "you go, girl!!" at the end. I got a huge raucous laugh and a cheap, disillusioning lesson in what plays.

Things have changed somewhat since then, but being a half-out gay teenager in the 1970s, I understood even then what might be tolerable. I knew in order to be true to myself and integrate myself into the world I'd have to comply somewhat, even exaggerate. All of this informed my approach to playing Touchstone in the Spring Drama Festival. Ironic that Touchstone is written as a sex maniac who pursues women relentlessly. Instead I identified with the role of the clown who calls out fakery — another acceptable gay stereotype — and I focused on that. I made my own costume, something no one else did. It consisted of a motley coat, assembled from remnants of fabrics I'd collected. I wore it with bicolor tights I made — even though I was as insecure as ever about my thighs, which no matter how thin I got, I still perceived as hugely fat. And I made a jester hat with bells on the ends, and a staff wrapped with ribbons like a maypole, onto which I fastened a papier mâché likeness I made of my own head wearing the same hat.

Not long before our rehearsals started, a rumor circulated that the film director Alan Parker was making a movie about our school, and that he would be casting some of us in it. It turned out to be true, and it was the most exciting news any of us could dream of. Originally it was supposed to be called *Hot Lunch,* but that turned out to be the name of a popular porn movie, so the name was changed to *Fame.* I read for the part of Montgomery, the sensitive acting student who ultimately realizes he's gay, but I had no illusions that I'd be cast. When I went on the audition, I shrugged and then read the character description aloud: "Montgomery is a skinny, red-headed boy of fourteen." I looked straight at Alan Parker and said, "That's none for three," which made him chuckle. But Alan Parker did come to all of our Spring Drama Festival productions looking for bits and pieces to include in the movie. When he saw *As You Like It,* he decided to include me, wearing my jester hat, carrying my jester staff, and reciting one of the Touchstone monologues.

The movie was largely shot in an old high school on Tenth Avenue whose interiors looked exactly like those of PA. The experience was mostly about waiting for shots to be set up. It was good practice for anyone getting into the movie business, most of which is about waiting. That day on the set — a small classroom with a stage — there was a huge camera and a lot of technical people crammed into the room. There was a smoke machine generating smoke (I'm not sure to what effect, because there was never any appearance of smoke in the scene). Alan Parker called "action" a few times, and I proceeded with my monologue: "Now I'll stand to it. The pancakes were naught but the mustard was good . . ." went the monologue that no matter how hard I ever tried, I could never make funny. I did it three or four times. That took half an hour, after waiting for two days. The footage was cut into the montage at the start of the movie depicting kids auditioning for PA, and it was my big moment. A lot of my classmates and I were extras in the crowd scenes. We got paid for our working days, and we got our SAG cards, something beginner actors dream about. Altogether, I worked five or six days over the course of that summer after graduation, and I ended up in the movie for a total of about three minutes.

I went to the opening screening with Kevin, whom I remained close with for years. It was the late fall of the following year, a big day at the Ziegfeld Theatre, at that time the last real movie palace standing. I reconvened with some friends I hadn't seen since graduation, more than a year before. That movie was an immortalization of the time we spent at Performing Arts. A manifestation of our dreams and expectations. And though we were secretly so proud to have gone to such a school, thrilled that our story was preserved forever, we acted very blasé about the movie, as teenagers are wont to do. But seeing the old gang, we couldn't hide our enthusiasm — hugging each other, declaiming how much we missed each other and really meaning it. It was a validation for me. These were people I loved who loved me back. No delusion. I'd made real friends in the real world, independent of my family and the community, and no one could take that away from me. We sat in the back of the house and smoked (yes, in those days everyone smoked in movie theatres) careful not to seem too enthusiastic, overly critical of the tiny details about PA that the movie got wrong.

Two or three students from our class remained together at Juilliard, and there was a bigger group of about six or seven at Purchase who stayed together, but by the time of that movie premiere, most of us were already flung to the far reaches of our destinies. I had moved into another realm, and I acknowledged, sadly, that those years, maybe even the best of my life, were in the past.

14

In June of 1978, just after graduating high school, I took a taxi to Kennedy Airport with way too much luggage, and boarded an overnight plane for Paris. I got it into my head that I had to see Europe. The Avedon exhibit had convinced me that Paris was heaven on Earth, and there were constant references made in my evening classes at Parsons to the art abroad, the galleries in Florence and Rome, and especially the Louvre. In that year, between puppet shows, selling sketches, and whatever money I made from IS New York, I managed to amass a little over two thousand dollars, which was more like seven thousand dollars today. The plan was to fly to Paris, spend a month there, spend three weeks traveling by rail to destinations in Italy and Spain, then fly to London. Two months abroad. I made one reservation at a cheap Paris hotel on the Left Bank, and I bought a Eurail Pass that would get me anywhere I wanted to go on the Continent. I had no other plans or reservations. I had it in my head that I would let the spirit move me. I went entirely on my own. No tour, no group, no friends. I was seventeen.

I made very little of the goodbyes to my family. I was afraid my mother would try to stop me if she had more than a minute to consider what I was embarking on. Determined to be chic in Paris, I packed two enormous suitcases with all the clothes I'd made for the trip — a grey suede jacket, jumpsuits, and paper-bag pants, a Be-Dazzled jean jacket. On the plane I wore a massive, taupe gabardine thrift-shop trench coat, which I thought was the perfect attire for the mystery and drama I might encounter on the night flight to Paris. I had no fear. I sat in the back of that plane full of excitement, thinking of what a glamourous time I had in store. I had more than enough money for the two months away, having also budgeted to buy myself some new clothes.

About an hour into the flight out of JFK, terrible dread set in. The old falling backwards feeling came over me even as I hurtled forward at an amazing speed through the dark of night. The magic plans for adventure were replaced by panic that grew and grew to the size of the very continent I was heading toward — the huge, lonely mass of unknown: Europe. I was terrified about finding my way, about speaking foreign languages, but mostly about being alone for that length of time with no one to talk to. It seemed like a great idea in the planning — I love being alone — but suddenly the prospect, when it was upon me, was harrowing. I made it through the flight only by telling myself I'd turn right around the minute we landed and take the next flight back to New York.

When we landed my better self prevailed, and the daylight eased my panic a little. I ventured from Charles de Gaulle and then on the Métro to the center of Paris to find my hotel. I misread something and I got out at the wrong stop. I emerged from underground up to the banks of the Seine on that hot, sunny morning, drenched in sweat, my luggage and baggy layers of wool weighing heavily on my back and my spirit. I schlepped up the banks of the Seine through a marketplace. Everything was for sale: mattresses, paintings, postcards, wicker baskets, birds and chickens in thin wire cages. On I trudged, desperately trying to recapture the bravery I had when I left New York, stopping in my tracks every fifteen minutes in a panic to frisk myself for my passport and my American Express Travelers Cheques. The map I got from the airport diagrammed a jumbled maze. I walked and walked for what felt like hours till I found rue Saint-André des Arts in the Sixth Arrondissement. I couldn't be too far from the Hôtel Saint-André des Arts, but for some reason I could not find it. Welcome to Paris! I walked up and down the block at least three times. Finally in desperation, I piled myself and my bags into a taxi and said in my best French accent: "Hôtel Saint-André des Arts, *s'il vous plaît.*" The driver chuckled. Then he launched into a torrent of rude foreign syllables, destroying whatever confidence I had in my sad high-school French, which I'd been boning up on those weeks in advance. Without moving the car an inch he pointed to a shabby brown edifice with gold letters, right in front of the taxi: HOTEL ST ANDRE DES ARTS.

I checked in and was led up steep, narrow stairs that felt like they'd give way under the weight of my luggage, to a room that possessed a Zola-esque rawness, with slanting floors and an austerity that filled me with even more dread. It was dingy in a way that a JAP from Brooklyn, who had only stayed in bourgeois luxury hotels for family vacations to the Bahamas and the like, had never experienced before. It was a stifling little room located in the back of the building, no window, lit solely by a single sconce above the bed. The walls that weren't filthy exposed brick were painted a soul-crushing brown. The bed was a tiny damp cot made up with old linens that were sheer with wear. The bathroom was a dingy shared concern down the hall. Worse, my room didn't have a lock on the door, which I only discovered that night, when I tried to get to sleep. I jammed a chair up to the door in order to keep it shut. I fell asleep at midnight as though bludgeoned on the head, and I awoke a little after 2:00 A.M. in more of a panic than on the plane the night before. It was a dread that had actual physical attributes: My arms and legs ached and my stomach churned. I was all alone in a dark city where I was sure that everyone else was sleeping peacefully through the night. I called my mother and cried.

At 3:30 A.M. I left the hotel and started to walk through the dark city. And something incredible happened. As I walked I noticed the lights of a storefront where the shadows of bustling activity played on the drawn curtains. Then a few blocks later I noticed another such place. And a few blocks later,

I came upon a third, this one with a lit sign: PÂTISSERIE. I braced myself and went in. I stood for a long while at the counter, enraptured by the sugary smells of baking. After a long contemplation, I pointed at a small strawberry tart. A baker with greasy black hair sneered at me. My attempt to smile was not reciprocated. With the tart in my possession I stepped back into the street and took a bite. Sweet, but not overwhelmingly, the freshness of the strawberries came through. After the third bite I let myself believe how good it was; the most delicious thing I'd ever eaten in my young life. As I backtracked to my hotel I stopped into another pastry shop and bought what looked like a large éclair that was filled with hazelnut pastry cream — the *second most delicious* thing I'd ever eaten. From that moment I felt I could at least try to handle whatever new depths of fear and dread I would encounter in Paris. Knowing those pastry shops were open in the middle of the night soothed my nerves to the extent that I was able to continue.

The next day I purchased a small red book of arrondissements from a *tabac* nearby, another thing that made me feel a bit more secure, and I set out to see the Louvre, which was the reason I took the trip in the first place. I arrived on foot at the museum, which in those days created an entirely different impression than it does today. It was before the I.M. Pei pyramid, and before the travel and tourism boom of the 1980s and '90s. The Louvre was so elegant then. The entrance was through the front door, a very grand front door, not a descent on an escalator into the basement of a glass prism, as it is now. Before the relentless throngs of people started showing up in the 1990s, desperate to get a glimpse of the *Mona Lisa,* the Louvre had a dusty, deserted quality. It was an intimate experience and, paradoxically, it felt grander for that. There were pictures hung on walls, enough lights to see, and a few other people meandering through the deserted galleries. Looking at art there seemed more an individual experience, just you and the pictures. It was easier to form a real opinion, as easy to *not like* something as it was to love it. Now in most museums all over the world, there's a lot of design and glass and stanchions and guards and so much wall text telling you what to think.

I wandered the galleries of the Louvre filled with awe and my usual growing sense of dread. I didn't really know what I was looking at, and I felt defeated as I progressed. I was a museum habitué back home, but this was different; this was a deluge. It was *my trip to the Louvre.* So much to see and not nearly enough time. So much iconography and symbolism — so much history to grasp. It was too much for me — which I realized after returning three or four times that week. So enigmatic and unconquerable, the Louvre. I cried a lot on that trip. I was ripped in half between hate and love. Inspired by the Manets and Degas, tortured by the Renaissance, confused by the neoclassicals. This ambivalence fit perfectly into my overall impression of the city. I wrote the following lines in my sketchbook: *"Feeling inspired and angry. I promise to conquer the Louvre if I live through this trip. And I might come back permanently!"*

The trip was never meant as a fashion pilgrimage. What I really wanted was to learn about art; my focus was on museums. But I did manage to see a few of the famous shops like Hermès on the rue du Faubourg Saint-Honoré and Dior on the avenue Montaigne where I caught a glimpse of a lady who, in the middle of July, was dressed in dove-grey flannel, the tightest midcalf-length skirt I'd yet seen, seamed stockings, high-heeled grey suede shoes, and a small pigeon-colored hat with a pom-pom. She was being waited on, while holding a leash with a curly grey poodle on the other end that matched her suit. Straight out of Avedon.

The great pleasures of food were impossible to escape in Paris then. No matter how unfriendly a place, the subject of food aggressively reached out to even those with no interest. It lent a false feeling of security and well-being that offset a little of the disdain I was met with those weeks. For every rude encounter there was a soothing pastry or cassoulet. It seemed that any little place one wandered into from the street had some perfect dish of food that was brought to the table with very little ceremony and a sneer. There was no such thing as bad food, whether it was in a proper restaurant or the most insignificant café. Perhaps because of my very limited culinary exposure at that time, and because food in the United States was so middling by comparison, every bite seemed revelatory. Even the breakfast at the scary hotel was sublime. Each morning, aching from sleeplessness and the culture shock that came in the night, I'd stumble down the stairs, greeted by that sublime café au lait, bread, and butter.

On my second night in Paris, in an unremarkable bistro near my hotel, I ordered the first thing on the indecipherable menu. Something called "vol-au-vent." A small puff-pastry cylinder arrived at the table filled with a mysterious seafood, my first taste of crab — made better by the breaking of the rules of kashruth. It had the special flavor of tarragon, which I had never tasted before — another revelation. It was probably meant as a first course, but I was too scared to order anything else; it had gone so well to that point, I decided not to press my luck, I paid and left.

On one of my last evenings in Paris, as I wandered the quai des Grand Augustins, I came upon a restaurant called Lapérouse. It seemed way too fancy for me, but I was starving, and I felt brave, so I walked in. Right from the start I was treated with politesse, and having been exposed only to incredible rudeness for most of the trip, this made me even more paranoid than usual for the first half hour, sure the waiter was setting me up for a great embarrassment. He spoke a little English, and he indulged me with a few friendly words. He even described the dishes on the menu and made recommendations. And in that wonderful, plush belle époque décor, facing Notre-Dame Cathedral as the sun was setting, everything eased. It was a small oasis of pleasure where there was no work involved. No studying or analyzing. No fear of misunderstanding, no hostility. Nothing to do but sit there and soak up the luxury and eat the incredible food. I remember the price of the dinner was probably equal to the cost of all the food I'd eaten those entire two weeks in Paris, but it was worth it. What I learned at that moment was that I would never enjoy touring Europe in youth hostels, waiting for kindness to show itself. Those weeks I learned that ease of travel abroad — comfort, good food, and a sense of safety — is expensive. Travel might be fun, but on my terms. Terms that had more to do with restaurants like Lapérouse and less to do with the Paris Métro.

A month in Paris wasn't in the cards for me. What was supposed to be a fun adventure turned into an angsty taking of emotional inventory. Even doing my best to adjust, there's something sad about being alone abroad for great stretches of time. And insomnia is especially less fun in a foreign place. After two weeks in Paris I proceeded to Rome for a week and Florence for a few days. Then another week in London. There were benefits to seeing the Vatican and Westminster Abbey by myself for the first time. The Uffizi Gallery was there to be soaked up in my own way. There was no one else to wait for or accommodate — no other opinions to process.

But after a full month away, depression took its hold. In the past I had chosen to be alone, which is all the difference between solitude and loneliness. A month later I returned to New York, thankful to be in one piece, having learned a lesson: I wasn't the world traveler I thought I might be. In the years that followed, I did a lot of traveling to far-flung places, which brought me great satisfaction and a lot of inspiration coupled with a great deal of angst and hardship. I smile when I think back on that first trip abroad, or any travel for that matter. Yet another case of looking back fondly on something that's really such a pain in the ass.

15

In the fashion business, being too early is just as bad as being too late. Timing is everything. Often I'd introduce something and then abandon it before people got through buying it, leaving it for others to cash in on. A quote of mine has made the rounds over the years: "Good designers bore very easily." In fact, the minute something is established as *fashion,* I literally hate it. When skirts are long I want them short, and vice versa. And this is not limited to clothes. Anything really popular — a show, a novel, a restaurant — seems to suffer in my estimation from being "fashionable." It's been that way since I can remember. When bell-bottoms first happened in the late 1960s I wasn't even a fully formed person and I remember hating them after only six months. When my parents took us to see *The Godfather* in 1972 I remember all the advance hype made me skeptical of it. In my estimation a good designer is through with something as soon as he does it, and then is on to the next thing. In its own crazy way, this might be considered a form of anti-fashion. I wish there were another word to capture what I strive for. Call it *surprise.* I like surprise much better than fashion.

Learning who you are is about learning who you're not and learning who came before you. To me, one of the most important things is learning to make clothes and accessories. If you have style and taste you can make a go of things, but by knowing how to drape, how to construct clothes, how to sew, you stand a better chance of bringing it all to a higher level. If you make the clothes yourself, you're capable of creating something "inventive." After my interviews with Mollie Parnis and Anthony Muto, I was inspired to not skip any steps. I had already begun teaching myself to sew and was taking draping classes at Parsons in the evenings, but I knew if my clothes were to be on the level with Norell or Geoffrey Beene, I had an enormous amount to learn about the craft of making clothes.

The night before I officially started at Parsons I went out to the Mudd Club, one of my favorites at the time in TriBeCa (back then a burned-out, seedy neighborhood).

The Mudd Club had a modern, "new wave" energy, and there was no scene at the door, you just walked in. The music was less disco, more rock and roll. It didn't thud and pulse like a lot of the other discos I frequented. It felt chic and not as sex crazed. It was a Sunday night, and I got there rather early, and it felt brighter than usual that night, like someone had turned all the lights on. I noticed a girl smoking a cigarette alone on a bench opposite me. She was beautiful, with brass-colored hair; thick, beautifully arched eyebrows; a smile full of great white teeth; high cheekbones; and big dark-brown eyes. Part Doris Day, part Julie Christie. We started talking. She told me she was there with the designer Zoran, whom I had admired. She came off as slightly older than me, and I assumed that she and Zoran were dating, because when she introduced me to him later he glared at me and seemed to intentionally step on my foot. Later we said good night, and that was the last I thought I'd see of Zoran or the beautiful girl.

The next morning I arrived for the first day at Parsons School of Design and there was the girl. Jackie Spaniel. She was sitting at the pattern-making table next to me. She came from the outer reaches of Pennsylvania and had none of the wiseass jaded ways of the rest of my New York City friends. She had a purity, a freshness, an endless reserve of optimism and smiles, and it was a wonderful change of pace. That same day I met Peter Speliopoulos — dark-haired, sharp-featured, brought up Greek Orthodox middle-class in Springfield, Massachusetts — who also considered himself an outsider in his family, which included three younger, straight brothers. Peter and I had so much in common. We were both gay, from religious homes, and we had huge expectations of life and big ambitions in the fashion business. Peter, like Jackie, had that attractive, out-of-town sunniness that fed on curiosity.

Learning about fashion will always be tied up with the pursuit of society and nightlife tinged with immorality. We had as many opportunities to learn about sketching and sewing as we did staying up late and partying. But it wasn't the typical dorm-room partying with coeds chug-a-lugging from kegs. New York City was our campus, and our partying ran the gamut from chic Upper East Side clubs to strip clubs in Times Square. We plunged into the night scene of the city with the same energy we gave to our classes in draping and sketching.

The school was run by a woman named

Ann Keagy, who for over thirty years was known on Seventh Avenue as a perfectionist with an eye for talent. She cultivated relationships with people like Calvin Klein and Bill Blass, and had pull in every design room from Seventh Avenue to the avenue Montaigne. She ran that place like an army barracks, and the teachers under her were drill sergeants. Every stitch we made was scrutinized and harshly graded. Almost nothing was perfect enough. Every piece of muslin we picked up to drape with had to be blocked, a process of straightening out the grain by pulling and steaming. Then, in order to know what direction that grain was going when we draped, each panel had a length and width grain thread that had to be identified. There were many simpler ways of doing it, but we were taught to pull these threads. That meant hours of delicate work with a straight pin for no other reason than to confirm what was abundantly obvious already. It was the way our ancestors did it, and Ann Keagy thought it was best, so we did it. And I never regretted it — except while I was doing it. I remember sitting in the smokers' lounge with my classmates and someone wondering aloud if Brooke Shields, a girl slightly younger than us who was making millions in the fashion business, ever had to pick grain threads.

We had all kinds of immersion-type classes. We had eight-hour drawing classes with a beautiful older model named Victoria who looked like the Klimt paintings of Adele Bloch-Bauer. She would dress up in old clothes — tailored suits, grand ball gown skirts, feather stoles, mannish coats — and would do different poses lasting anywhere from one minute "gestures" to twenty minutes. We had other drawing classes with the great Steven Meisel who began his career as a fashion illustrator. His favorite model was a transsexual named Teri Toye, who was also the muse of Stephen Sprouse. Meisel would make us draw Teri in the flash-intervals of a strobe light, or in complete darkness.

We had rigorous textile-design classes where we learned the different properties of silk, wool, cotton, and synthetics. How they grew and where. The difference between one filament and another. How yarns were finished and spun, and woven or knitted. We learned to administer "the burn test"; burning cloth to determine whether it's silk or wool or cotton from the way it smelled when it burned, notes which are imbedded in my nose to this day. (I still quote my textile teacher: "Wool is god.")

The most influential teacher at Parsons was Frank Rizzo, who went slightly against Ann Keagy's brand of tyranny in favor of a more freewheeling, glamourous approach. He was a small man with grey hair, aviator eyeglasses, and a mouth that was built in a natural upturn, so that even when he was angry or hurt, he looked happy. He taught design when I was a junior and senior, and later he succeeded Ann Keagy as dean of fashion design. He knew and taught everyone from Donna Karan to Marc Jacobs and Zac Posen.

Rizzo and I had a special rapport from the start. He was someone who seemed interested in my happiness and really amused by me as a person. And I felt the same about him. He was the only one of my teachers who ever encouraged my diverse range of talents and never advised me to narrow the field. He knew of my interest in the theatre arts and said on more than one occasion, "If they can't catch up to you — fuck 'em!" I knew that he lived half the time in Tennessee with his boyfriend, Richard, a tall handsome guy with a drawl, who owned and ran a flower shop in Crossville, a heroic idea to me. I loved that Frank kept himself so separate from the rat race and would traverse the country once a week to be home. He was a wonderful design teacher, but he was also a magnificent and fearless role model for the many young gay men and women that crossed his path.

Even having all that background at Parsons evening school and more technical skill than most people in my class, I still didn't get the full essence of fashion as a subject — the object of the game — until second-year design classes. Our sketches were open to class critiques, and I noted that the focus was on flashier sketches, which seemed antithetical to my ideas about ingrained quality that wasn't made too obvious. In a world saturated with images, one had to do clothes that wouldn't be a bore, but that also weren't only exaggerations. They needed to be clothes that caught the attention, the right kind of attention — noticed for being smarter than the average designer blouse or pantsuit.

I started knowing what I wanted and didn't want. Organically, I hate overtly sexy clothes. I observed — I guess with all the going out at night — that the least sexy thing was someone trying to be sexy. If a young woman or man is beautiful, they look less so when they call attention to it. Also at that point I discovered that I liked even the dressiest clothes — ball gowns, tuxedos —

to look as casual and functional as ski gear. My mother encouraged these thoughts about sporty clothes. We met for our Saturday morning breakfasts only rarely by that point, but during one of them she pointed out that great American style was much more casual than European. She told me I took after my grandfather, her father, Alfred Esses, who was nicknamed "The Sport" and "The Prince of Wales" because of his great ability to make everything he wore at once elegant and casual.

I began to think more and more about the message a woman sends forth with her clothing. The social and political reflection of who she is. How flashy is she? How reserved? How big is her hair and how high are her heels? Does she have a sense of humor? This messaging is a big part of anyone's identity, and it became my job to help people send the message they wanted, and that I valued. It was a subject I had a lot of background in, having grown up with a mother and sisters who definitely dressed for end results.

The first major design assignment in my junior year was a swimsuit ensemble. Star fashion designers were brought in to critique our work, and mine was the great American

299

designer Charles Suppon. He had a celebrated collection called Intre Sport, which
was an early take on athleisure. You could
wear those clothes to the office, then to
cocktails, and maybe even to the gym the
next day. One of the more fabulous things
he did was a shaggy, knitted-mohair sweat
suit that was photographed a lot that year.
Having him as a critic cemented my awe for
this irreverent mixing of genres. He also
worked in the theatre, not just as a costume
designer, but as a writing collaborator with
Peter Allen, among others. His clothes were
great, but the idea of his diversity, his work
in the theatre, was what most impressed me.
He seemed like he had a fun social life, too.
He often walked into class disheveled and
bleary-eyed. One morning Peter leaned in
and whispered, "He smells like sex."

One of the major inspirations that I took
from working with Suppon was the idea of
doing *exactly* the clothes you wanted without worrying about what was expected of
you. For this project my idea was a white,
strapless, one-piece swimsuit with sage-
green-striped insets on the thigh, creating
the illusion of striped swim trunks beneath
the strapless maillot. Over that was a box-
quilted coat of an ordinary, but very pure
and beautiful, white sheeting fabric quilted

with white cotton terry cloth on the reverse, all edged in sage-green webbing that looked like it came off a sneaker. The whole appeal of the coat had to do with the glorious white freshness of two different textures and the subtlety of the light lamb's-wool padding in between. The quilting was a straight three-inch grid that came across as industrial — like the softest, coziest elevator pad imaginable. The coat stopped right below the hip line and had a boxy, oversized shape. I love the luxury of over-sized clothes, a taste I developed in high school. With my self-image, I always felt sexier in fuller, more covered-up clothes.

Charles Suppon picked my design as his Gold Thimble Award winner that semester, which meant my design would be singled out as the winner in the midterm fashion show. This was a huge surprise for me and everyone else in the class. My design seemed so plain compared to some of the flashier projects. To my second-year draping and sewing teacher, whose instructions I always ignored, this was an affront. It was a huge boost to my creative ego, though, and suddenly I was being noticed in class and in the school itself. It was a different thing now to walk the halls or sit in the smokers' lounge.

I got the sketch back from Suppon with a red Magic Marker star and a big note that said: "Show this with goggles and swim flippers." I hated that note. It negated all the good that came from being awarded the Gold Thimble. I didn't understand at the time what an amusing idea it was to style it like that. I had imagined the model with braided hair and bare feet, and his vision of it as a joke about sports clothes was too edgy even for me. Like any self-absorbed college art student, I couldn't accept such a radical revision of my work, so I devised a plan to get Suppon to change his mind. I thought if I could only talk to him he would understand my position. How could it hurt to call the guy and at least try? In those days directory assistance was a powerful thing. He was listed, and he answered the phone.

"Who is this?"

"Isaac Mizrahi. The student you gave the Gold Thimble to. Listen. I'm not sure I agree with the idea of showing my swimsuit with goggles and swim flippers."

"What is this? Who —"

"I thought if I called and explained —"

Dial tone.

The next day I was summoned to the teachers' lounge, a windowless room that felt like a big prefabricated closet with wall-to-wall industrial carpet that smelled of synthetics. The entire design faculty was assembled there, all of them scowling at me, Frank Rizzo at the head. I was warned that if anything like that ever happened again I would be thrown out of school.

In the end I got my way. The girl walked in the show with braided hair and bare feet. And to this day, I regret it.

My favorite class was one called "Museum," which convened every Wednesday morning in the costume archive of the Metropolitan Museum of Art, where we were shown some of the great clothes of history up close and were able to inspect and handle them while wearing white cotton gloves. One advantage I had living at home was my mother's encyclopedic, anecdotal knowledge of mid-century designers — American and otherwise. She told me stories about Norman Norell's alliances with Marilyn Monroe and Lauren Bacall, which weren't covered in those classes. She told me about Norell's love of theatre and his abilities as a costume designer, which often gets passed over in historical documents about him. He had a distant friendship, a kind of aesthetic dialogue, with Balenciaga. For instance, my mother told me there was a time when both would only show their austere and modernistic clothes on Asian models with high stiff coiffures, huge butterfly eyelashes, and erased lips. My mother would fill my head with fabulous facts and ideas about clothes that I would then use in class, amazing the faculty with the things I knew.

A few of my mother's choice proclamations:

"Norma Kamali is the Claire McCardell of her age. Racy, inexpensive."

About a Pauline Trigère coat she acquired at Loehmann's: "It was so beautifully made that when it got dirty it took itself to the cleaners."

And:

"Chester Weinberg is a designer's designer. He's the brains behind American sportswear."

On the virtues of Norell:

"The reason Norman Norell is so great is because he understands two things: textiles and women."

Rizzo was enchanted by these stories and proclamations. He practically invited himself to my house to meet the woman he called Sarah, never referring to her as my mother, which lent a kind of sophistication to our mother/son relationship. So with much trepidation I got "Sarah" to cook dinner one

Thursday night, and I invited Rizzo and my new friends Peter and Jackie. I was anxious about it, but the evening went off smoothly, in large part thanks to Rizzo's charm and great discretion. He was the same size and stature as my father, and he seemed to have great respect for my dad's stories about working his way up in the garment trade. And the fact that Frank was not obviously gay — at least not as obviously as some of the other faculty at Parsons — made the evening easier.

After that, there were a few more dinners in Brooklyn with Rizzo and various others, all at my mother's invitation. She liked Frank. She liked cooking exotic Syrian dishes and promising to send him the recipes. She loved that he knew all these famous, fabulous designers, and yet he chose to dine with her. It was my mother's way of involving herself in my life. She was coming to terms with the fact that I was not headed back to the fold after graduation, so she made it her business to get to know the world I was trying to root myself in. If she couldn't go with me into that world, she would do all she could to bring it to her.

16

Without exactly meaning to, I came out to Sarah Haddad, with whom I'd remained friends after we closed IS New York. One evening in the spring of 1979 we were having a late dinner after seeing *Evita* on Broadway. I was describing a new club downtown called The Underground, which had taken over the old Andy Warhol Factory, and I got carried away with the telling.

"I'm standing there waiting for my coat. It was sort of crowded at the coat check. Suddenly I feel someone pressed up against me. This guy was feeling me up. He was humping me from behind."

"And what was that like?"

A long pause and then I burst into tears right there in the restaurant, and I blurted out, "I loved it!"

Sarah understood the modern world, but was also firmly embedded in the Syrian community, so she got the darker implications of what I was telling her. In those days being gay wasn't merely alternative, it was truly dangerous. One night in the early 1980s Peter and I were walking together to a restaurant on West Eighteenth Street called Joanna, which has since closed — what you might consider a gay-ish restaurant with a gay-ish scene in a gay-ish neighborhood, if there was any such thing at that time — when we heard a screeching car coming straight at us at high speed, jumping the curb and onto the sidewalk. I leapt up onto a fire hydrant and Peter just made it out of the path of the speeding car that was coming at us with the intention of heaven knows what kind of gay bashing.

I was living a double life those years at Parsons. There wasn't a question of me living anywhere but home — one of my parents' reasons for endorsing Parsons at all was its close proximity to Brooklyn. Living in a dorm was out of the question. But the more I became comfortable in the world as a gay man, the less authentic I felt at home. I was already out of the closet at school, while concealing my true identity from my family. Revealing that I was homosexual to them felt like suicide.

It's hard to put into perspective in this

modern day when things are so much easier. Back then being gay was seen as a terrible fate for anyone. Factoring in the Syrian community made it worse. The enormous shame brought on me was something I might be able to handle, but the shame brought on my family would be intolerable. So while my friends at Parsons were whooping it up in their dorms, I was awake nights worrying and keeping my mouth shut at home. No matter how hard it was living within that family structure, it was harder to think about bombing it to smithereens by coming out at the wrong time.

And the longer I went without having sex, the more dangerous and mysterious being gay felt. Sarah suggested that I see her shrink, Dr. David Kahn. I had money coming in from selling sketches, so I made an appointment with him without saying anything to my parents. Dr. Kahn was a good-looking older man with thick white hair and thick white dentures. I told him about the sex in the cabana with my best friend those years earlier, which he assured me was completely natural. He eliminated any question that what I was feeling was in any way wrong, which did so much to ease my stress at that time. He zeroed in on my fear of coming out to my family, which was exacerbating my fear of sleeping with men. It was a kind of vicious circle. I couldn't bring myself to go through with sex without admitting to the world that I was gay — starting with my own family.

The anxiety was making my sleeping issues worse than they'd ever been. It was around this time I became aware that other people were sleeping a lot better than me, and that I felt tired all the time. Dr. Kahn recommended I go to a sleep clinic, where they offered me sleeping pills and told me to stop drinking coffee and alcohol. But nothing helped any more than a tiny bit. One night just after my seventeenth birthday, at 3:00 A.M., after hours of tossing and turning, I rose from my bed and thudded downstairs to the kitchen, where I went about making a cup of tea as noisily as possible. After about ten minutes of this racket my mother appeared, bleary-eyed, in the kitchen doorway.

"What's wrong?"

"Nothing."

"What is it? Why are you not asleep?"

I started in on the speech I'd prepared with Dr. Kahn's help, about how I was different from others and how this wasn't as strange or abhorrent as she might think. Finally I blurted out that I was gay. A few seconds of silence. Then my mother cried, out of melodramatic obligation more than anything else. She said she hadn't suspected a thing, which I didn't believe for a minute. For her not to have noticed would have been either neglectful or delusional. Perhaps as a way of reassuring her, I told her about how I had sought professional help with a psychiatrist and paid for it on my own. That didn't console her until I mentioned Dr. Kahn's name, and suddenly she perked up, "Dr. *David* Kahn? Really? I took a class with him at The New School!"

The first thing she said upon drying her tears was "Don't tell your father!" I had no great desire to tell him, but I also suspected that on some level he already knew. One day late that summer, my father and I were driving home to Brooklyn while the rest of the family stayed on the Jersey Shore. I brought up my plan to move out when I finished college, something he had previously agreed to. He said that after thinking it through, he would only allow me to move out if I married. A blowup fight ensued, and when we got home I confronted him in his dressing room. Determined to tell him everything, I shouted, "I am never going to get married!" He stood in front of me in his boxer shorts with a sad, knowing look on

310

his face. Then he turned pale green and staggered, as though he couldn't bear his own weight. He sank to the floor and sat there looking up at me. I thought he would die on the spot. I was ready to call an ambulance, but after a minute, he recovered. He said, "I know you don't mean that." But I did mean it. I didn't force the subject, and we never really spoke of that scene again. My better judgment told me not to mention the encounter to my mother. I knew I'd made myself clear that day about who I was *not;* still, it dawned on me that not telling him who I *was,* explicitly, was a good idea.

A few years later, after I moved out, I was home for Friday-night dinner and talking about how much I liked to cook and how it was taking on a bigger part in my life. Rather than allude to a future with a nice Sephardic Jewish wife occupying my kitchen, my father said, "Well, if you like to cook so much you better find a good cleaning lady who will do the dishes." I'm not sure my mother or my sisters even noticed the implications of that remark. Maybe I was desperate to read a kind of acceptance into those words, but I took them as a confirmation that he knew more than he let on.

Dr. Kahn agreed with my mother that it was a good decision not to tell my father. That surprised and disappointed me. It seemed there was less available love, more conditions placed on a human heart than I thought. Also, needless to say, I felt great relief. I was off the hook! The dreadful chore of telling my father was no longer necessary; the decision not to do so had been made by a professional — suggested in the first place by my own mother.

Technically I still had the problem of being a virgin. In therapy with Dr. Kahn I was repeating myself again and again about the same issues. About how intimidated I was by *real* gay men, about how they wouldn't pay attention to me, about my feelings of sexual inferiority — any number of problems having to do with the subject of being gay. Finally he did something dangerous that still shocks me today: He forbade me from coming back to therapy until I had some sort of practical experience with sex. Basically he told me I was unwelcome there until I got laid.

So I made it my business.

About two months later I was giving Sarah a lift into the city where she had rented a room at the Hilton Hotel on Sixth Avenue and Fifty-third Street in order to get dressed for a party she was invited to in Midtown. I told her about Dr. Kahn's ultimatum, and without coming out and suggesting anything specific, she informed me that the room would be empty after she left for the party and might come in handy for whatever purposes. . . . "What a shame for the room to go to waste!" Winking and smiling, she said she would leave the room key for my use if the need arose. I was baffled as to how I was supposed to execute this plan on such short notice, but I left my car in the garage at the Hilton with the plan to use the room even if alone. Later I took a taxi to meet a friend, Ginger, for dinner.

Ginger, about ten years older than me, was always coming on to me so that night on our way home from dinner I came out to her. There in the backseat of the taxi, baffling as it might sound, she professed a great love for me and leaned over to kiss me. I recoiled and explained again that I was gay. Ten minutes later, in a total about-face, she insisted we go to this gay bar close to where she lived on the Upper West Side called Cahoots. No stranger to a gay bar, Ginger took some kind of odd pleasure in pimping for me that night. She instructed me on how to make eye contact, how to make small talk — basically, how to pick up a man. Under Ginger's direction, while she remained in back, I made a foray into the busiest part of the bar, where a handsome guy smiled at me and struck up a conversation. He was a tall guy named Paul, with a prominent moustache, tight jeans, and cowboy boots, the gay uniform of the time. He was quite sweet and very gentlemanly and smelled good. After about fifteen minutes, Ginger approached the bar with her coat on and, with a wink, said good night. Paul and I were now at liberty to pursue our next course of action. I told him about the room at the Hilton, and within minutes we were in a taxi, one of the longest rides of my life, from West Seventy-ninth Street to West Fifty-third.

When we were finally alone in the hotel room, one thing quickly led to another, clothes were shed and within a few heart-stopping minutes we were in each other's arms. I think Paul got a kick out of being my first. I was lucky he was so nice — not a moment's feeling of remorse or rejection or pain. My body, even at its thinnest, is paunchy and hairless and green-white to the point of looking ill. Not very attractive. Paul's body was tanned, toned, and perfect. But the few self-conscious moments gave

314

way to the fascination of sex — especially because Paul seemed to be entirely engrossed. All through the experience I understood how important these sensations and emotions were, and I knew how lucky I was to be having my first real adult sexual encounter with such a nice guy. When we were finished and had our clothes back on, saying our goodbyes, I knew I would never see him again, and that was fine.

I pulled the big brown Cadillac into a spot in front of the house in Brooklyn and sat in it for a good forty minutes with the windows open as daylight broke. I listened to the birds chirping and thought about all those months of fear and loathing that had preceded this, and the ironic contrast with how natural and pleasant sex actually was. It seemed all those months of worry were completely unrelated to the simplicity, the organic joy of the night before.

By the time I finished Parsons I was officially out as a gay man — except in the old neighborhood. There, the only people who knew my secret were the two Sarahs and my sisters, whom I came out to in a fit of rebellion. I'm sure my mother would have liked it better had I not told them; I think she was waiting for me to grow out of some phase, for this ugly truth to somehow go away. One evening my sister Marilyn and I were alone in the house, and I blurted it out. She seemed physically jolted, as if by a damaging electrical current. But after a beat she understood. A few days later I told Norma, who had a similar reaction. Like sentries, they guarded my secret from my father and the community at large. But I couldn't live much longer with a huge part of me tucked away under lock and key. It wasn't enough for a select few to know. I wanted the world to know.

Everything happened with great speed around that time. Both of my sisters got married within two years. Those weddings became the center of the family story, and I diverted my own drama as the dress designer for all the festivities. (Some of those dresses were quite fabulous. My sister Norma's engagement dress was a highlight: a strapless lavender-suede bodice embroidered with pearls, attached at the waist to a full, multitier white organza knee-length circle skirt. The wedding dresses were fabulous, too, both the epitome of 1980s wedding dresses, complete with huge white lace leg-o'-mutton sleeves; Cinderella skirts; and big, floppy, satin bows.) Then I graduated from Parsons. And the minute that happened I started looking for a place of my own. It was the deal my father agreed to, and it couldn't happen soon enough for me, though it took a great while — almost a full year — for me to find a place I could afford. It was a large sunny studio on West End Avenue and Seventy-first Street that cost four hundred dollars a month. It was one spacious room with great views, a two-by-four separate kitchen, and a five-by-seven bathroom with a window. Enough room for what I needed and no room for much else. And it was in my old stomping grounds on the Upper West Side, close to Kevin and Gina and even closer to Lincoln Center.

I had bought a new Sony Trinitron TV a few months earlier in expectation of my new life. My affection for that set was outsize — TV played such a big, weird part in my sleeping disorder — it was more like my best friend than an appliance. I couldn't trust it to the moving men, so I hand carried it in a taxi the day before my move when I went to paint the place. That night I sat in the apartment, shafts of light slanting in from the street, the scent of fresh paint, the newness of the environment affecting my equilibrium. I was never one to acknowledge joy in the present. Worry and second-guessing are my stock-in-trade and have always affected my ability to feel happiness in the moment. But for that winter night in 1982 I allowed myself to feel blissful. I knew that it was to be the best night of my life — that the anticipation I felt would be better than anything to come after. And to a great extent, I was right.

The day I moved there was a snowstorm that threatened to delay me another week, but I convinced the movers to work in the ice and snow. With very little drama otherwise, almost unnoticed, and with no goodbyes, I slipped out of my parents' home. It felt more like an escape than a moving day.

17

Way before there were what we now call internships, there were things called *summer jobs*. Toward the close of my junior year at Parsons, Ann Keagy sent me to interview for a job at the Public Theater costume shop, which was run by a wonderful guy named Milo Morrow. Walking into that workroom was like being struck on the head by a brick of glitter. It was a huge ground-floor space in an old cast-iron building across the street from the Public. It had thirty-foot ceilings and was filled with sewing machinery, miles of fabrics on industrial shelves, and sketches of over-the-top costumes strewn among the work tables and pinned to corkboards. And when you looked up, a literal heaven of costumes. Stored hanging from the ceiling were hundreds of fabulous old costumes showing their undersides: eighteenth-century panniers, Elizabethan doublets, suits of armor, friars' dresses, clown costumes, sparkly fairy dresses, all hanging from the rafters. I knew if I took that job I'd never be bored. When I got back to Parsons, a satisfied-looking Mrs. Keagy told me I got the job. But that same day she also sent me on an interview with Perry Ellis, who was looking for another assistant. I was told he had not found anyone in the graduating class and wanted to hire one of the juniors for the summer and perhaps ongoing after graduation.

The interview was late that day and very last minute. The first thing I did when I walked in was apologize for the clothes I was wearing, which made him smile. I had on what I wore to school that morning, a pair of exaggerated, striped, pegged linen pants I had made. It was the fashion for linens to be slightly wrinkled, but by the time of the interview my wrinkles were way past the fashionable limit and I looked a mess. Perry Ellis had straight, shoulder-length brown hair and features that seemed too big for his head, including almond-shaped eyes and huge, horsey white teeth. His physique was sylphlike, as though he would fall over if you exhaled on him. I'm scared of skinny people in general, and everything about him was intimidating. He had an enigmatic, reserved way; an off-putting, WASPy demeanor that he used to his advantage. His generosity and humor only became apparent over time, and I was terribly uneasy around him for months.

He was wearing his signature blue oxford shirt with "dimple" sleeves (his term for a pleat in the shoulder which he invented and I always found a bit insipid) and khaki pants, which he wore almost every day I knew him. Behind him on a console were the most beautiful flowers I had ever seen, a massive bundle of marled pink peonies, his favorite flower, which were always kept around the studio, perfuming the days and looking like they were about to shed their petals in ecstasy. Leaning up against the walls of the conference room were photographs and illustrations of models in his clothes. Hanging in the reception area there was a beautiful Avedon portrait of him, which was commissioned by *Vogue,* and had him glancing impishly at the lens in mischievous contemplation.

Another consequence of the last-minute interview was that I didn't have any sketches to show him other than the ones from my final project, which I had made triple-sized. There was a visual comedy to this skinny man manipulating that huge, heavy stack of sketches. I'm not sure he knew what to make of them, and a few months later, when I was firmly entrenched in the studio, he said, "Darling, I knew from those sketches that you were crazy and that you'd fit right in here." Whatever it was that motivated him, he offered me the job on the spot and didn't flinch when I asked for the salary Mrs. Keagy suggested, which was higher than the usual summer-job salary.

While the interview was taking place I had the strong feeling that I was being scrutinized. First a tiny woman with boyish black hair and bright red lips and wearing a fox-hunt-scene printed bouffant skirt and black patent leather mules walked by slowly, craning her neck to look in. Then a tall chubby man with thinning light-brown hair and wearing coral pants and cordovan loafers peered in and asked a question of Perry, nodding cordially at me. Finally the most captivating, glamourous figure glided by, sneaking looks on her way to the Xerox machine in the next room. She was wearing a striped fisherman's T-shirt, men's trousers, and boat shoes, and she had chin-length curly brown hair. After my interview with Perry I was asked to wait to meet a few others in the studio, which is when I met Patricia, Jed, and Laura, the three who'd spied on me earlier. Patricia Pastor was the design director. She and Jed Krascella worked predominantly on the designer collection, while Laura Santisi handled all the licenses. I immediately apologized again about my last-minute attire, and I think that endeared me to them.

Having two summer-job offers created a conflict. Even though Perry Ellis was the most important American fashion designer of that moment, I wasn't his greatest fan yet. His clothes were less grown-up than I might have liked. And, truthfully, I was holding out for a job with Geoffrey Beene or Pauline Trigère, or one of the more established designers. And on the surface, the Perry Ellis studio paled against the job at the fabulous costume shop at the Public Theater, that colorful room full of costumes all hung from the ceiling — a glorious reward for a garage puppeteer. Should I follow my theatrical bent or hunker down and stick to the responsible plan I made to succeed in the fashion world? I felt the road distinctly forking beneath my feet. Never one to give in to the easy, attractive option, I decided it was almost a regression to take a job working at a costume shop — glittery and fun as it seemed. I had set out to conquer the fashion world and nothing was going to take me off course.

■ ■ ■ ■

That summer job at Perry Ellis transformed my attitude toward what working in fashion could mean. Perry made the pursuit of excellence seem as important in fashion as it was in medicine or law. Lives might not have been at stake, but it was evident that even something as superficial as fashion required first, the desire to make something of quality; and second, the necessity of sacrificing almost everything else to hard work. I'd arrive early in the morning and was usually met by Nina Santisi, (Laura's sister), who would have already been there for an hour. She was in charge of public relations and had the busiest job at that place in those days, coordinating magazines' requests to photograph Perry's clothes. She had the exacting efficiency of a school-teacher and the look of a beautiful English aristocrat, with peachy, poreless skin.

Patricia and Jed would show up sometime around 10:00 A.M. and at 11:00 A.M., the fitting model would arrive for the daily production fitting, which is when clothes from the most recent fashion show are adopted onto the line, scrutinized for fit, and adapted to the figures of real women.

Perry arrived just before noon for the end of the fitting. He would begin his day by answering to Peggy Lee, his personal assistant, a wry, quiet, good-looking woman who kept all his affairs in order. After Perry conducted numerous phone interviews and business calls, a late lunch was brought in. Then we would proceed with a design meeting that would last into the night, till at least 8:00 or 9:00 P.M., with breaks only to take care of studio and salesroom demands. Around show times our workloads increased triplefold. We worked most Saturdays and a lot of Sundays, and no one seemed to mind or even notice. As a result of all that time spent together, the lines between the personal and the professional blurred — we were more like family than coworkers.

My mother was only too happy to assist in blurring those lines. She came to the showroom more than a few times to order clothes wholesale for herself and my sisters, and was delighted to meet the people I worked with. She came up one day wearing an original pony-skin box jacket with huge leather-covered buttons and bound buttonholes that she'd kept from the 1960s, knowing it was just like something Perry had revived for one of his recent collections. Recognizing the wink, Perry was amused.

He said, "You have a stylish mother." And then, "She never throws anything away, does she?" After that, they carried on sporadic communications via me. He'd say something that he knew I'd say to her, and vice versa. Once she sent him chicken soup. I almost didn't give it to him, but she called Peggy Lee to make sure he got it. It was packaged in one of the round plastic Carvel ice-cream containers she used for freezing her monthly batches of chicken soup, and I was mortified when she demanded I get the container back afterwards.

I developed a lot of close relationships in those years, but the most important was with Jed, who became like a brother to me. Jed was a bit overweight, and he did the same thing I had always done — deflect attention away from more personal aspects of himself by becoming a kind of jester. I was his sidekick jester. After a while he learned that I did outrageous impersonations of Aretha Franklin and Streisand and Polly Mellen, and he'd ask for them regularly. He had a great sense of humor and would stop everything for a joke. After days and days of pressured work late into the night, Jed would find the perfectly timed comic moment to stop what he was doing and let out a random, ear-shattering, bloodcurdling

SCREAM. It was a release that everyone adored, it made us laugh and laugh. You could hear people in different rooms, upstairs, across halls, just laughing.

A lot of the humor in the design room made fun of the casual racism, sexism, and homophobia that had terrified me as a child. I was now surrounded by people who mocked it in a way that neutralized it. Perry's threshold for this sort of humor was high. He was such a WASP, and yet when he freely referred to the rest of us as "Kikes" and "Wops," etc., clearly in jest, we screamed with laughter. He was fond of saying things like "Mary, today I think I'll have one of those delicious Jewish rolls for lunch . . . What are they called?" And someone would say, "Really, Mary? It's called a bagel."

The offices at Perry Ellis were salonlike. Glamourous, influential people were in and out all day. I think the reason editors liked being there so much was because not only were the clothes great, but there was a sense of ease and humor about the place, so different from the other houses on Seventh Avenue, which took themselves very seriously. Aside from the model fittings, entertainment luminaries were constantly coming up for clothes. Within the first week I worked at Perry Ellis I encountered a number of celebrities — people like Glenn Close and Lauren Hutton, who were big fans of Perry's. On my third day on the job, as a joke, Perry sent me into the little fitting room (really a closet) with Tommy Tune's suit for him to try on, and he was standing there stark naked, a sight that made me blush. Perry ribbed me about it for weeks. Within the first month I was assigned the job of dressing Mariel Hemingway, who was to be Perry's date for the Met Gala that year. She was staying at the Stanhope, across the street from the Met, and I dressed her in a "gown," which to Perry meant a floor-length, black, hand-knit, Shetland cardigan sweater.

Early one morning that summer, the public relations department called to tell us Lauren Bacall was on her way up to look at clothes. Perry was away and Jed knew what an old-movie freak I was, so he made sure I was assigned to that detail. It wasn't until I saw her walking toward me in that showroom that I believed what was happening. I'd seen all of her movies in revival, but I had also pored over old issues of *Harper's BAZAAR* containing portfolios of pictures taken of her by the great Louise Dahl-

328

Wolfe. To my mother she was a goddess — a beautiful Jewish girl from Brooklyn who hit it big. "If anyone in Hollywood knows clothes, it's Lauren Bacall," my mother said again and again. She told me stories about Norell making couture clothes for Bacall in the 1950s, and in the 1970s Halston doing the same. I hung on every word of my mother's stories, which represented a fashion past that had to do with quality and vision more than sensationalism or flash.

It was early in the morning for Bacall when she came up those marble stairs to the showroom, and evidently before her morning coffee. She was grumpy, wore dark sunglasses, a trench coat, a bucket hat, and she had a Band-Aid on her face as though she'd cut herself shaving. Our meeting was polite and after about fifteen minutes of restraint I finally said: "Miss Bacall. You have to know how much I adore you. As an actress, but also as a fashion icon. *Designing Woman* alone. I mean . . ." From that moment I think she understood that she had an adoring audience, and as the morning wore on and the coffee took effect, she thawed. Two hours later she was still gambolling round that huge marble showroom in her pantyhose, throwing clothes on and off, laughing and enjoying herself. At the end of the appointment she was descending the stairs to leave, and I said to her, "If you ever need anything, please call. Actually. Just whistle. You know how to whistle?" We both groaned, but then she paused and gave me that big wonderful smile.

There was an extravagance that went with fashion in those days. Veronica Webb and I were talking recently about what it used to be like compared to what it's become in the industry, and she said, "Darling, we were raised in *Versailles*. The kids today can't imagine the grandeur!" It was the luxury business, and we were steeped in luxury amidst all the hard work and long hours. Samples were remade three and four times in the pursuit of perfection, no expense spared. *Vogue* was known to reshoot most of their stories at least once, for the slightest change of an eyebrow or the gloss of a lip. There were private cars, seaplanes to shootings at Perry's house on Water Island, fabulous dinners and parties, and the most beautiful flowers appearing in the office and sent to our apartments.

The real extravagances were the materials. Mad amounts of the most beautiful, luxurious textiles were ordered each season. "Sampling fabrics" means to order between fifteen and thirty yards of something in order to give it a try. Ideally the sample fabrics would arrive in New York a month or so after the fabric shows, to give the designers a chance to try them out — to make a skirt or jacket or evening gown, figure out how to manipulate the fabrics and decide which they liked the best. It never really worked that way, though, because mostly the Italian mills were late to deliver. So you hedged your bets and got into the practice of ordering much more than you needed so as to have backup fabrics at the ready. Sample cuts were pyramided on the floor of the studio because the shelves were stuffed to their limits. Before a collection there was hardly room to walk for the piles of sample cuts.

There were also stacks and stacks — literally *walls* — of shoe boxes full of sample shoes. In the same bet-hedging way, a designer would order excesses of accessories for his fashion shows. Looking at early prototypes of shoes one could never tell if the corrections would be made satisfactorily, so you'd order twenty times as many shoes as was needed for the average fashion show (which, in those days could go on for 150-plus looks — today, twenty or thirty looks in a show would be deemed lengthy and boring). The footwear and handbag makers would be responsible for sending hundreds and hundreds of samples, which sometimes arrived a day before the shows. Once, Perry decided he wanted one particular crocodile pump shown with everything. Crocodile was and still is a difficult thing to bring into the country, and those shoes languished in customs for days. They were released to us hours before the show and arrived on the premises as the crowd was assembling. The memory is burned in my head forever of Patricia Pastor tearing open boxes, throwing shoes across to me, and shouting, "Give these to Lynn Kohlman! And these to Nancy Donahue!"

Dining out in groups after work was just as regular an occurrence as working late. Jed and I went to dinner at Café Un Deux Trois, or Anita's Chili Parlor, or any number of places that have since closed. Perry sometimes took us out to lavish dinners at Elio's or Café des Artistes. One of his best friends was Tina Chow, and all of us in that studio were in awe of her. Talk about intimidating exotic beauty. She would drop in to visit Perry, not knowing I was alive, while I would study her every inch. Her moonlight skin. Her painstakingly buffed nails. Her short black-lacquer hair and bright red lips. The cashmere cardigan worn over a Hanes

T-shirt with mannish grey-flannel trousers. Nothing ostentatious, only discreet quality from the bones out. The first time Perry took us to Mr Chow, the fabulously chic restaurant owned by her husband, Michael Chow, my head exploded. It was the most elegant room I'd ever been to. The Lalique doors. The ivory lacquer walls. The Thonet chairs. The menus contained in Hermès leather binders. The scene was fabulous in a way I couldn't yet fathom. Fashion editors André Leon Talley and Marian McEvoy, who were close friends of Perry's, would join us on occasion and supply a running commentary, complete with histories and gossip. It was art, sex, drugs, cuisine — any and all conversations running at once. A grand variety of people from different walks of life. The beau monde.

In keeping with Perry's obsession with the British Isles, at one point he tried to establish the idea of afternoon tea served at the studio, and for a while every day at four, everything would stop and tea would be brought in, along with petit fours and crustless tea sandwiches from a place called William Poll, which are still my favorites. Any number of people would join for tea. Manolo Blahnik. Barry Kieselstein-Cord. All sorts of celebrated editors and photographers. It was a good idea, but it didn't last long. The schedule got the best of these teas, and after about six or eight weeks, it was over.

Tea service or no, the daily Perry Ellis salon marched forward, every influencer of the day in and out of those offices. Major fashion editors and buyers would stop in unexpectedly — people like Carrie Donovan, a treasure of a woman who ran *The New York Times Magazine* fashion pages. I immediately adored her, and she me. She called me "Yvessac" and said to Perry about me the day we met, "You really know how to pick 'em." Another constant presence was John Duka, who wrote a weekly column for *The New York Times* about fashion and style subjects called "Notes on Fashion," and who became quite a huge star on the scene in the early 1980s. (He is also rumored to have been Larry Kramer's model for the role of the journalist boyfriend in *The Normal Heart*.) John was witty and I was always impressed with his ability to write something interesting and culturally based — not just surface-scratching like other, more shallow fashion journalism. He was also very handsome and seemed to have all the confidence in the world, which inspired the opposite in me.

From the time I started at Perry Ellis it felt like I was under twenty-four-hour surveillance from Condé Nast, especially *Vogue.* If I hadn't already believed it, it was drummed into my head in those early days that *Vogue* was everything, and nothing else mattered. At Perry Ellis, if two magazines wanted the same dress, it always went to *Vogue.* It's a rule I embraced, and it stayed with me through all my years on my own. At the time *Vogue* was run by Grace Mirabella, a smart lady whose mystique was wrapped up and protected by two or three of her favorite editors, who represented the magazine. One was Polly Mellen, an exuberant woman who at the age of fortysomething looked exactly as she does forty years later — with her forever-white bob and fabulous legs. Polly had the uncanny knack of finding the new thing before everyone else and dropping it sooner. She was known for stomping her feet and clapping like a seal at fashion shows when she liked something, and sneering if she didn't. She exuded an energy that encouraged designers to do daring, sometimes outrageous, things. I admired her from afar for months, and when I graduated from Parsons she came to the senior fashion show dinner dressed in a crotch-length Stephen Sprouse fluorescent-green pailletted minidress with white tights and silver leather Mary-Janes. She approached me from across the ballroom at the Hilton hotel, and said: "Dearie, you're the young man I've seen at Perry Ellis. My, but you're going places, aren't you?"

There was Jade Hobson, who everyone thought would be Mirabella's replacement when she retired. Jade was Polly's polar opposite. She sat stone-faced through most previews and shows where Polly was bouncing off the walls. And finally at the end Jade would crack a little smile and whisper almost inaudibly, "Golly, that's chic." Jade was a knockout to look at and might have been mistaken for a fashion model herself. One day, right after I started at Perry Ellis, I was at the airport and I noticed a woman waiting for her car at the curb. She looked exactly like an Arthur Elgort photograph one might see in *Vogue.* There was Jade, complete with narrow knee-length skirt, flawless legs, high heels, clutching her fisher fur coat, big hair undulating in the wind, a Louis Vuitton suitcase at her feet. Jade really walked the walk.

Early on at Perry Ellis I was witness to some of the complicated and unkind politics of the fashion press. There was a fashion critic who hated Perry for dating someone whom that critic had set his sights on. He gave Perry bad reviews for the rest of time because of that. John Fairchild, the publisher and editor in chief of *WWD,* had a lot of fun making and breaking people. Lucky for me, he liked me a lot. He called me "Genius" whenever he saw me, and he praised me to the heavens when I went out on my own. The first day I met Mr. Fairchild I was on the street, styling one of the Perry Ellis dresses they were shooting for a preview. I retied a satin bow on the dropped-waist of the dress the model wore, which Mr. Fairchild noticed. He proclaimed, "Now that young man knows how to tie a bow! There's only one other person I've seen tie a bow like that: Mr. Yves Saint Laurent."

My mother and I dined out on that comment for months.

Designers start as early as a year in advance of their shows to have everything ready for the one big day. Fabrics are developed, as are accessories, venues are booked, dates are reserved in the fashion calendar. The purpose of fashion shows is to present the new collection to the press, and there are more and more of them every year. Editors shuttle from city to city and from show to show, and the competition for an elite A-list audience is fierce. Lately showmanship has taken a great position in fashion week, and the giant extravaganzas can often outshine the clothes. In the old days, New York fashion week occurred after the European shows, which began in Paris. This was a no-win scenario. If you showed clothes that didn't fall in line with what had been shown in Europe you were seen as démodé. If you did show clothes that reflected the European trends, you were considered a copyist. A strange phenomenon of the time: New York designers were *supposed* to be greatly influenced by the European collections, and if you went too much against the grain you were considered outré, contrary. The powers at *WWD* considered it the New York designers' duties to cash in on the trends that were begun in Europe, and their reviews reflected that stance. But things had begun to change when I worked at Perry Ellis, and he was at the forefront of those changes.

Perry believed that no matter where or when you showed, you should do something entirely original, which seemed like the object of the game to me, too. If I was bored with the status quo, Perry was revolted by it. It was his wont to change everything from season to season. For fall he showed tiny waists and ruffles, the following spring he showed long, spare, shapeless jackets and long pleated skirts. The about-faces were what his fans expected of him. Sometimes he accomplished this within the confines of one fashion show, making a case for one thing — a length, a color palette — and by the end of the show making a case for its opposite. Aesthetics swung in and out at breakneck speed in that studio, and at first Perry was praised for it. After a while he was chastised for that very thing. (A similar fate awaited me.)

Perry was one of the first people to challenge the idea of what a New York fashion show was supposed to be. In the day, European fashion shows were events, unlike the staid showroom shows in New York, where theatrics were put away and business took center stage. Perry wasn't necessarily interested in theatrics (though some of his best clothes were very dramatic in their own uberwholesome American way), but he was interested in glorifying the American fashion-show event. He had a huge showroom — a loft space with soaring ceilings — which lent itself to a grander effect than the average New York showroom show. He used loud, contemporary music, which was something that didn't really exist at New York shows till he started doing it. He was also the first in the world to send print models down the runway. To that point there were delineations between runway girls, who could walk beautifully but who weren't necessarily good in pictures, and print girls, who dominated the pages of fashion magazines. Even in Paris and Milan there was snobbery about this difference. When he hired Kim Alexis and Janice Dickinson for his fashion shows, the editors adored it because they could now see the clothes on the girls they were thinking about. Everyone followed suit after a few years of debates about how these print girls "couldn't walk," which was just a cover for the fact that everyone was copying Perry, who was the only one brilliant enough to figure it out.

I worked on many shows at Perry Ellis, and I remember them all. But the first was truly special — my initiation into the workings of a real fashion show. The design for that spring collection had taken place late in the summer and into the fall, just before I returned to school, and I felt myself to be a big part of it. The new collection was inspired by *Chariots of Fire,* which was set in the 1920s at Eton and had beautiful costumes by Milena Canonero. It had recently opened in theatres and was an obsession among the fashion crowd.

I snuck out of school as often as I could to see the really important fittings. I was obsessed with a tall, thin, blond model named Karen Bjornson, a favorite of Halston's, whose star power lingered well into the 1990s, and who I got to know. Jed knew I would be devastated if I missed her fitting, so that day he had me called out of class. What that didn't do for my image: being called out of class because Perry Ellis "needs you in a fitting." I owned Parsons for weeks after that. Then to arrive across the street and see Karen and the gang standing there waiting for me to start the fitting . . . I still don't know what I did to deserve that kind of consideration.

That November, aside from the nights I worked, I took three or four days off from Parsons to work on the show. It was the first collection I worked on from start to finish. The show began, the Vangelis music from the movie poured out into the showroom, the bright lights came on, and the show progressed without any obvious hitches. But backstage was an inspired mess — clothes flying, models running, and any number of assistants and hairdressers stalking the models to reposition a hat or retie a bow. From clothing station to runway, the models rushed back and forth in the nick of time. I was on the verge of tears throughout that first show, and at the end I found a vacant stairwell and wept. I get emotional around beautiful things, especially when I'm greatly stressed. And both beauty and stress were abundant that day. When I got home I found flowers and a note from Perry — he did the same thing for all of us who'd been involved with the collection. He had a way of making everyone feel they were indispensable.

When I got the job at Perry Ellis it was as if the universe were providing me with exactly the information I needed. I was able to pour everything I had into my work, and I had so much to pour! The more energy I had, the more there was to do. Then I'd go home and pick up a sewing project I'd left from the previous weekend or work on sketches of my own that weren't related to my job. People refer to it as workaholism, but it's the way I am. I'm more interested in the creation of things than I am with any other aspect of life. I feel best about myself, about my life, when it runs that way. After a day or two off I start getting depressed. And yes, perhaps I neglect aspects of my life in order to accommodate this work ethic, but it's who I've always been, and that seems to be getting truer. Those years at Perry Ellis weren't just about learning design, developing taste, and understanding the politics of fashion; those years were about discovering that it's okay to be this way. I was born to work. I live to work.

18

In the fabulous world of Perry Ellis, for all the newness and excitement, there were also a few personal setbacks. I was extremely conscious of the aesthetic and social hierarchy that existed in the design room, and I knew my place was low in the pecking order. For one thing, Jed and Patricia patrolled that gate night and day, making sure that I never advanced too much in Perry's good graces. I worked hard in that studio, but I didn't want the kind of career positions they had; it was always my intention to eventually strike out on my own. I looked up to Perry, and I always remained slightly scared of him. My work relationship with him was reverent, even if joke-filled, and the occasional allusion to friendly affection was all I could manage. Although there were days when I didn't interact with him, he was my all — a father figure even while my real father was alive.

The gay culture in that world nourished me in some ways and fed my self-loathing in others. In general, thin, handsome men and women abound in the fashion business, and the offices of Perry Ellis seemed to be their international headquarters. Jed and I were the jesters who entertained Perry and his gorgeous friends, and while they went on with their gorgeous lives, Jed and I, and the rest of the lowly design staff, were left behind to do the dirty work of organizing shows and seeing to the making of the collections. The more we catered to the whims of these beautiful people, the more alienated I felt from the whole fabulous scene, and the more proof I had that I was the fat, ugly kid from Brooklyn I saw in the mirror, unworthy of a second glance.

The harder we worked and the more devoted we were to fashion, the further we all seemed to get from our own sex lives — and the more we used fashion as a diversion from deeper, more meaningful things. It was a phenomenon at *Vogue,* too, and a few other seriously immersive fashion offices. One traded one's sex life for a life of fashion servitude. There was even a name for us — we were referred to as "Fashion Nuns." At *Vogue* they made a joke of it: *"The only dick you ever see at Condé Nast is*

Avedon."

But the world of fashion and my personal body image weren't the only things that stood between me and sexual awakening. The other was a threat that I had no control over, and that struck very close to home.

A young man who worked in the sales department at Perry Ellis, a gorgeous blond named Daniel, was suddenly stricken with a mysterious new disease called AIDS. One day he was there — beautiful, dashing, turning heads, dressed entirely in Perry Ellis — and a week later he was rushed to the hospital with heart failure and mysterious lesions. A month later he was dead. So many cases of this mysterious scourge cut close to the bone. One particularly heartbreaking case: I had become dear friends with a classmate of Kevin's at Juilliard, Christopher Renstrom, and his lover, Brian Greenbaum, a wonderful young movie producer. They were part of my surrogate family whom I saw three times a week, including a standing Sunday brunch at a little place on the Lower East Side called Everybody's, which was around the block from where they lived. Christopher and Brian were a kind of "married" couple years before gay marriage was even a glimmer in the collective LGBT eye. Out of the blue one day

Brian was taken ill and raced to the hospital. And from that day on he was never the same, wracked with all sorts of terrible ailments and ugly symptoms, from respiratory failure to lesions. I accompanied Christopher on the final occasions when Brian was rushed to the emergency room near their home. Brian died a few weeks later.

The following summer Laughlin Barker, Perry's boyfriend, came down with a case of hepatitis, and those of us who worked in close proximity were advised to be vaccinated. There was all sorts of good humor, even jokes in the design room in an effort to dispel our angst and paranoia, and after a month or so, Laughlin returned to work. Despite our attempts to make light of it, after the hepatitis there was an eerie pall cast over that happy place, and although no one talked about it, we feared the worst for Laughlin. Ultimately our fears were confirmed. He was in and out of hospitals for the following four years and finally died of lung failure.

So many of the fashion glitterati were to die over the course of the next ten years. John Duka, who had been such a fixture in Perry's design room; and Charles Suppon, who had only four years earlier awarded me his Gold Thimble, both died in the early eighties. And of course the scourge didn't confine itself to the fashion world. Both the New York City Ballet and American Ballet Theatre were hard hit, as was the Broadway theatre community. You couldn't go to a museum, a gallery, or a theatre in New York without coming in close proximity to at least one tragic history.

I took these losses personally on two levels. I grieved for the people I loved. And I was terrified for myself. Just as I was coming into my own sexuality, a terrible plague emerged — which seemed to place a target square in the center of my back, attacking all the people and things I cared about the most.

I left Perry's employ in 1982 to take another job that seemed to offer more autonomy. This was before I knew Laughlin was terminally ill. About a year later Perry called me and offered me a job designing an offshoot brand called Perry Ellis America, which I turned down because it was a jeans line, which at the time didn't appeal to me. Later it came out that Perry had AIDS, and I realized his outreach to me was part of an attempt to put things in order with his company before he died. His death hit me very hard but I was spared the funeral because I was on a business trip to

Hong Kong and couldn't get back in time. I wasn't ready to memorialize that period of my life and I didn't want those days to be remembered sadly. I remember him smiling and laughing.

But the epidemic didn't go away. It got worse and worse as the 1980s wore on. The disease became associated with death. My whole generation was affected, stricken with terrible fear. My friends and I were all sure we'd die young. And after all these years, I often think of myself as lucky to still be here.

There's a fine line between my natural aversion to boredom and my fear of commitment. It's a part of my personality I can't master. No matter how great things are at any given point, I start weighing the pros and cons of staying in the same place, and usually I come to the conclusion that it's time to get somewhere else. Partly this is due to my gift for seeing the bad aspects of a good situation — and just as often, vice versa. But it doesn't really have to do with right or wrong. I leave parties at the height of the fun, and sometimes I'm too impatient for the fun to start. While moving on too soon has been an occasional cause for regret, usually this instinct works out well.

By 1983, after three years of great happiness and fulfillment at Perry Ellis, I decided it was time to go. Frank Rizzo introduced me to Jeffrey Banks, a menswear designer who hired me to help launch his women's collection. When I told Perry, he deflected his annoyance with humor and said, "She's leaving me for a black woman!" As difficult a decision as it was to leave Perry Ellis, I was energized by the change. My college friend Peter, who'd been working for Christian Dior in Paris, had just moved back to New York City and was living with me, sleeping on a cot in my small studio while looking for his own place. We were having a lot of fun together, up to our eyeballs in parties, clubs, theatre of all kinds.

Had you told me ten years earlier at my bar mitzvah that I would be living my life in the epicenter of the design world, flying around the globe, fulfilling my creative bent, I might have believed you. But had you told me — the fat, pimply, bar mitzvah boy I was — that I would live out my identity as a homosexual and have a fulfilling sex life, I would have dismissed the idea as nonsense. But that is what came to pass. It was totally different than what I imagined it would be like. As a fat kid you grow up seeing a fat person in the mirror no matter how thin you get. When your father tells you that you have "other qualities," and that good looks are not your strong suit, you go through life thinking of yourself as unattractive physically, and when attractive people make passes at you, you assume it's a joke or a mistake.

When I was seeing Dr. Kahn those years in college before I came out, whining on incessantly about my sexual insecurities, he said something that affected me deeply. It wasn't necessarily what he said as much as the way he said it. In a very clinical way, almost as a medical assessment, he said, "You won't have any problem finding as many lovers as you want. You're tall and you don't smell bad and you have good hair and teeth." The matter-of-fact way he put it sounded less like an opinion and more like an evaluation of a laboratory rat being assessed for its eligibility as a test subject. It was reassuring in its unvarnished practicality. That was the moment when I began to think I might be okay. I was ready, even with a gamut of insecurities lined up against me, not to mention a deadly scourge, to enter the fray.

I can count on my fingers the number of boyfriends I had through those early years from roughly 1981 to about 1986. Meanwhile, many of my friends were going to the

351

baths or sex clubs and having sex with three or four people a night. The AIDS crisis was just getting started, but not everyone seemed willing or able to curb their libido. Safe sex eventually proved to be genuinely viable, but at the time it was still a theory. The only mistake-proof protection seemed to be abstinence, a state of being that came and went in my life depending on the frequency of depressing news. With so many friends and colleagues getting sick and dying, sometimes months passed — even a full year — that I remained celibate. The AIDS test itself was horrifying — leaving you in a state of panic for two full weeks till the results came in. AIDS made me careful about love and especially sex. I don't regret that, but it was confusing on an epic level — I was rendered terrified of men even as I pined for them.

In Jeffrey Banks's office there was a young man who worked as an administrative assistant, a small blond, I'll call him B. He was a stereotype of a certain kind of gay man in the early eighties. He had standard-issue good-looks and a standard-issue gym body, and in my estimation he wasn't particularly interesting or smart. When I first arrived in that office I looked down my nose at him, and he disdained me right back. To me, he had the unfair advantages of being thin, blond, and happy all the time. He was an early version of a *twink* — and it seemed everyone wanted him. There was an ease about him, a lack of complication. To him I was a snotty, weird-looking designer who dressed in this ridiculous way and went on about things that didn't matter.

One evening it seemed as though B was trying to befriend me, and he invited me to go with him to Uncle Charlie's, a large, fun, gay bar on Greenwich Avenue in the West Village. Unlike so many specialized bars of the time — you were either at a leather bar or a piano bar — Uncle Charlie's was surprisingly integrated. B introduced me to his friends, who were all young men like him — attractive, uncomplicated. And if I didn't already feel alien and out of place, I noticed one of B's friends rolling his eyes after we were introduced. B and his happy bunch disappeared into the crowd after a bit, and I was seated alone on a carpeted platform, finishing my drink and planning my escape, when I noticed a dark, handsome guy looking at me. He didn't look away until he caught my gaze, and I smiled out of nervous embarrassment. He came over and sat next to me and chatted me up for ten minutes. Then out of the blue he started kissing me. Even after the first kiss I thought he mistook me for someone else. Then it dawned on me, and I thought, *This is what being hit on feels like.* But being kissed like that in public was not only unexpected, it was dangerous and erotic. And I let it happen. I sat there getting kissed, and I liked it.

He was the son of an Israeli politician, slightly older than me, who had moved to New York recently and spoke English with an Israeli accent — a total turn-on hearing that accent spoken in a context other than a rabbinical one. He told me of his days serving in the Israeli army — another turn-on, having sex with a soldier. He was a psychotherapist who had recently begun his practice, the biggest turn-on of all. Also he was very funny and had a *realness* that I wasn't used to. The things he talked about were outside the realm of what my fashion friends did. He spoke of politics. Current events. When he spoke of art or even of fashion, it had different, weightier significance. He put everything, not merely the physical aspects, into a more political context. He listened well and gave advice. He had a darker sense of humor than I was used to. Late one night he feigned having a diabetic fit, which made me panic. He said he might die unless I found an insulin shot and only revealed it as a prank seconds before I confirmed the ambulance. We stayed together for about six months. It might have gone on longer, but meeting each other's friends was our undoing. His friends thought of me as superficial (an accurate assessment at the time). And my friends thought he was a bore.

But this first experience at Uncle Charlie's was a good one. And it boded well for the future of my dating life. I went through my twenties intent on making romantic connections more than sexual ones. In truth I think I was fooling myself that I could have handled a long-term relationship in those years. I was too busy with my work and better off on my own. Boyfriends were messy and slowed me down. But try as I might to have meaningless one-night stands, it was impossible for me. I was needy for romance, so I gave every guy a good chance. Or at least three good chances.

To my relief, the Fashion Nun Curse seemed to be lifting. I was on my way back from a business trip to Japan, on the leg from San Francisco to New York, and lo and behold, sitting next to me was an extremely attractive blond man. I could tell from his accent that he was French, but it was difficult to tell if he was gay. Before deplaning we made a date, which I took great care and pleasure preparing for. Every bit of my body was accounted for and groomed. I splurged at the little florist on the corner, who had the most irresistible pale-pink peonies with a particularly strong and beautiful scent. It was a perfect night in May. When I opened the door, we wasted no time getting to the point. Without even saying hello we lunged at each other, and we were naked and in bed within minutes. It felt like an hallucination — that anyone that attractive could want me for my body. He had silky blond hair, long sinewy limbs, round horn-rimmed glasses, and blue-and-white striped boxer shorts. He made me feel beautiful, which in turn sparked a kind of love that made it possible to suspend disbelief for long enough to feel beautiful. We dated for about six months — six months seemed to be my time limit. He was the closest thing to the man of my dreams that I had yet encountered. He seemed to have all the emotional depth of the Israeli shrink coupled with lightheartedness, a fun-loving side that was so attractive.

That first night we walked down the block to Cafe Luxembourg for supper. Life was good. He mentioned his last name and waited a long pregnant beat, as though I was supposed to know something. He was a French aristocrat, and he spoke of his noble background in a way that suggested it was a major aspect in his life. When I told my mother I was dating him, it seemed to warm her to the idea that I was gay. "I always knew one of my kids would end up with a Rothschild!" For a Jewish mother I guess that name was a kind of balm that made everything, even being gay, okay. When we broke up and I told her, there was a long silence on the other end of the phone. Then she blurted out: "Well. You blew it!"

While my personal life was full of excitement during my time at Jeffrey Banks, my professional life was markedly less so. At that time I was surprised to encounter a certain shallowness in my own personal character. Whereas Perry Ellis was smack in the center of the glaring fashion limelight, Jeffrey Banks was not, and I missed it terribly — the way a drug addict misses his regular fix. Jeffrey and I did everything we could to bring attention to the collections, which actually did get very favorable notice. There were a few covers of *Women's Wear Daily* and a number of fantastic editorials in *Vogue, Elle, Harper's Bazaar,* etc. But no matter what we did, we were still a fledgling brand, and Jeffrey was known for menswear while Perry Ellis, Calvin Klein, Ralph Lauren, and the other more established fashion houses continued to dominate the fashion pages. I didn't know I would miss the attention that much, but I did. I kept thinking it would pass as other things took precedence in my life. But that never happened. What I missed wasn't just pages of fashion reportage. It was shoots. Parties. Tables at Mr Chow. All the celebrities and socialites — the glitterati who seemed obsessed with us up there in Perry's inner sanctum. The Fashion Tribe.

And more than anything, I missed the fashion shows that came twice a year. At Jeffrey Banks we had beautiful, modest shows compared to the extravagant ones at Perry Ellis, which seemed prophetic and religious by comparison. All the star models lined up in their new hair and makeup looking like nothing anyone had seen to that point. The evocative, ear-shattering, edge-of-the-world music. The triple-strength lights that make everything look beautiful. The vast stretches of runway, which always felt like a walkway toward fashion history.

Whenever I think about that time in my life, I'm reminded of a scene with Anna Wintour, which presented the high contrasts between being in the fashion spotlight and out of it in six short words. It was 2008. I'd just had dinner with Mrs. Jayne Wrightsman and Anna Wintour at La Grenouille and then went to a Broadway revival of *Les Liaisons Dangereuses,* starring Laura Linney. It was a warm spring night, and as we lingered in front of the theatre before the show, I told Anna how hard it was existing outside of the heady fashion whirlwind. Without missing a beat she turned to me with a weary chuckle and said, "Well, darling, that's the big time."

19

Answering machines were new inventions in 1983, and I was obsessed with checking my messages — and not merely because I was dating someone named Mario who was no stranger to last-minute booty calls. One night after dinner at Cafe Luxembourg I convinced Peter to stop back at the apartment on our way out to a nightclub, and there was a message on my machine, but it wasn't Mario. It was my uncle Sam calling to tell me that my father had suffered another massive heart attack and had been rushed to the hospital.

I hastened there in a kind of trance to find all of my immediate family in the waiting room in various states of emotional devastation. My father was in intensive care, and I was only permitted to peer through a small window in the door to his room. For the next two days my sisters and I split round-the-clock shifts at the hospital, mostly looking after my mother, who wouldn't leave. Scared as we were, none of us really believed my father would die. We thought this time he might possibly have to have surgery, but we were used to the heart troubles, and we were sure he would recover.

When I wasn't at the hospital, I'd return home to find Peter there, which was a blessing. Having just lost his father a few months earlier, he knew all the right things to say. After the first day or two my dad began showing signs of recovery and all dire thoughts of losing him vanished. I even managed a coffee date with Mario, who left me one of the sweetest messages I'd received when he found out about my dad. Our hospital vigil eased and on the third night we felt okay about leaving him. Even my mother went home for a good night's sleep.

At about two o'clock the next morning the phone rang. I was still awake, since I was not one to fall asleep before three. It was my uncle Sam calling to tell me to hurry to Lenox Hill Hospital. Peter woke and offered to come with me, but I declined. It was a warm night, and I smoked a cigarette in the backseat of the taxi, the window open and the dirty, humid summer blowing on my face. At times of emotional trauma, when there are things too painful or frightening to confront, I end up finding the next most terrifying item to obsess over. That night, instead of confronting my fear of losing my father, I thought only of the freedom I had been enjoying since I began separating from my family, and I worried about how the next few days would affect the course of my free life. When I got to the hospital I hesitated outside, not wanting to go in. I knew the minute I crossed the threshold of that building I would have to abandon my great new life indefinitely — maybe forever. I stood there smoking, teetering at the jaws of obligation, which were ready to chew me up and swallow me. I feared that I would be called upon to leave my happiness behind and take up the old mantle of the dutiful son, a role I loathed but one I was specifically groomed for.

My father was in critical condition. He'd contracted pneumonia, and we were told his chances of survival were slim. In the ten minutes I was alone with him he was barely conscious, with tubes running in and out of different parts of his body and face. He looked exhausted, as if he'd aged fifteen years in the hospital. He kept trying to say something, looking up at me, smiling. Finally with a great deal of effort he said, "You're a good boy." I took his hand. Then he said, "Be a good boy." A few hours later my father was dead. When the doctor came out to tell us my mother screamed, "Louie!" — the nickname they'd called each other since their honeymoon. It was a terrible sound.

The following days were filled with great levels of sadness and anxiety. No matter what differences I had with my father, my endless tears were a testament to the love I felt for him. I was surprised by my response — I just couldn't stop crying. As soon as I stopped, I would start again. For days I'd fall asleep in tears and wake weeping. Any thought that came into my mind would make me sob. It was a low point. A descent not only into despair, but also a revisiting of my troubled past. Horrible thoughts raced through my mind of being trapped again in the ugly reality of that community in Brooklyn.

The funeral took place in the old shul founded by the Syrian Jews of my grandparents' generation. Located on a tight side street in Bay Ridge, in a series of small, dark rooms that had been joined together from a row of houses. Dour colors, mahogany wainscoting, airless, no windows in the main room. Old, dark red-velvet folding chairs lined up close to one another. The entire population of those past generations manifest in the gathered crowd — harder, even less assimilated, and fuller with judgment. On a bier, which in my memory looks more like two sawhorses, stood a plain and beautiful plywood coffin that resembled a Donald Judd construction — simple, sturdy, elegant in its efficiency, unvarnished, the light-colored wood glowing in all the darkness. It's the custom of the community to be buried in a simple way. All eyes were on me, waiting to see how devoutly I could pray for my father's soul. His sisters and brothers were watching me closely now — these people I was so scared of in the past, I felt an innate disdain for them, similar to the disdain I had felt for my father. I imagined my future as being nailed in that coffin, about to be buried forever. Singsong, minor key Arabic prayers ringing through the rooms. My mother, in torn black, clutching my arm. Obligation, like a weight and as hot and airless as the stifling room, presented the unspoken implication that *I was the man of the house now.*

After shul the cars caravanned to a Staten Island cemetery where all the Sephardim are buried. The nearest family members were all present — about sixty-five aunts, uncles, and cousins. We sweated profusely, the hot sun of August soaking our mourning black. Of all the days I'd spent as an outsider, I never felt more outside than on that day, among those people, everyone grieving in exactly the same way. For the next few weeks I was forced to move back to my mother's house. The religious aspects of the shiva process felt false and invasive, offering no room for my own grieving process. My new personal identity was on the line. I'd gotten used to living my life as an out gay man, and I finally believed that my feelings were more important than those Jewish teachings condemning me. That day not only was my father's life being eulogized, it felt like my life as I knew it might be over, too. My obligation was to keep up with the praying — the mumbling and swaying again — which felt like a big step backward.

Dreams of my mother emerging from the confines of the Syrian community were dashed to bits. She didn't become extremely religious like my sisters, but she would never become the Auntie Mame–ish character I had hoped she might. The division between her world and mine seemed to widen even as she tried to keep me tethered to her, to that world. As much as she wanted me to succeed, to have my own life, she couldn't let me go entirely. Her responsibility as the matriarch of the family weighed too heavily on her conscience.

For months after my father's death I was expected to go to temple three times a day and be part of a minyan: a quorum of ten men who have been bar mitzvahed, which is, according to the religion, the only chance the prayers might have of piercing through to heaven. Stepping into that scene felt fraudulent — if I participated in that, wouldn't it stand to reason that I believed in it? That I believed in god? That I upheld the beliefs of those men I prayed with? Having lived through yeshiva, any belief in god had been thoroughly knocked out of me. Every word of those prayers around my father's death felt like a lie, like a betrayal of the person I really was.

The mourner's Kaddish is a prayer the living say for the dead in order to insure their passage into heaven. When my father was alive he made me promise again and again that I would say Kaddish three times a day for him for the full required year, completely convinced it was his only chance of getting into heaven. For two or three months I pretended to say it — I wasn't really sure of the exact words, but it was easy to go with the flow phonetically, rhythmically, carried along by the other voices. I couldn't bring myself to learn the prayer, even though I read Hebrew and Aramaic, which I was taught at Yeshiva of Flatbush. It rang completely false. Up to that point I had been cavalier about my disbelief in god, but from that point forward I was clear and solid in my atheism.

The more I tried to fulfill the promise, the more of an affront it was to me. I thought if the roles were reversed, I would never hold anyone to something that wasn't meaningful to them. Even though I knew it was easier to just say it, get it done for a year, and then move on, I realized I needed to assert my own principles. It was something I couldn't discuss with anyone, I just followed my own heart. I was the one to make the judgment — which made it seem even riskier, making my conscience the arbiter of my father's fate. What if someday I woke up and found that I actually did believe in the power of Kaddish? Would I hate myself?

For what it's worth, I think of it as one of the best decisions I ever made.

No matter how much I loved my father and how much sadness it gives me to admit this, I was really only able to live my life — to thrive — after he died. There was no way

I could live as an openly gay man without the fear that he might find out and be crushed, or try to crush me. In the following couple of years after his death, most of my extended family found out I was gay, and although I was never close to them, I did fear how my openness might affect their relationship with my mother. Once I came out completely it became harder and harder to show my face in the old neighborhood. There was no chance I would consider staying in the closet, even for the purposes of a visit home. By 1982 for me the closet was in the past.

Still, there were certain conventions that I was obliged to fulfill, if only to make my mother happy. I was always present at Jewish holidays, though not at shul. (I stopped going to shul completely right after my father's one-year memorial service.) Two years later I stayed in Italy for a few weeks after a work assignment and missed Passover, which was seen as a total transgression. My uncle Sam actually called me in Milan to tell me I was "too old for this sort of rebellion!" (I was twenty-three.) I attended most family events — such as weddings, bar mitzvahs, and funerals — where I was entirely out of place. At one family wedding one of the cousins that I'd been close

to as a child, who had since become Orthodox, literally backed away from me when I
went to greet her, as though I were a
vampire about to bite her.

Yet without my father, my mother took
more and more comfort in the extended
family, and my exchanges with her began to
follow a certain routine. At dinner we talked
raptly about literature, fashion, politics, as
though it were one of our Saturday-morning
breakfasts of old. Then, like a kind of switch
had been thrown, she'd pull back and speak
of nothing else but her new grandchildren
— puzzled as to why I wasn't taking more
naturally to the role of uncle, or why I
seemed to be pulling away from my sisters,
who were becoming more devoutly Orthodox than we had ever been growing up. It
became harder and harder for me to justify
my presence at family gatherings. I had to
deflect my real identity; even though they
knew I was gay I couldn't talk about it
openly. I couldn't talk about my chosen lifestyle, my real self. And somehow I was
expected to swallow my individual identity,
respect the status quo, and love it still.

To be clear, I was at odds with every
thought that was being discussed at these
family functions. Not just sexual or religious
ideas — economic ones, political ones,

humanitarian ones. There's a certain blindness toward anything and everything that doesn't agree with their religious traditions, and a pass is given to terrible old ideas like racism and misogyny because they seem to serve the religion and the community. It's not aggressive or even perceptible a lot of the time, but it's a powerful undercurrent. Anything that mattered to me was made null and void by the built-in obligation of religion and family. It was a kind of orthodox, heterosexual tyranny that encompassed all parts of life and nullified any squeak of rebellion, any real innovation away from their reality. The message was: They were capable of loving me, accepting me, if certain aspects of my identity were left unacknowledged. It felt more and more like a grave compromise to my integrity. The chasm between us widened and nothing could be done to make it better.

Rather than complying, or worse, begging for tolerance, I chose distance. Nodding politely while watching the clock for the right time to start saying my goodbyes and finally taking my leave. There was no ecstasy like the subway ride back to the sanity of my life, or the taxi ride home after Yom Kippur or a family wedding. Each time I headed home after one of these events it took me longer and longer to shake off the lies. Eventually I would come again to the joyful recognition of how far I'd come away from my repressed beginnings.

In 1984, after I'd been there for about three years, the women's division at Jeffrey Banks was closed by the parent company. Successful as the launch was, they hadn't foreseen the huge investment that would be required to take it the full distance. I took the opportunity to resign, and I made no plans to take another job. I did a few odd things, including making costumes for a small movie about a lesbian vampire called *Because the Dawn,* starring a singer named Edwige, a gadabout on the downtown circuit. I thought long and hard about taking a part in an all-male version of *The Women* being performed by an experimental theatre group in the East Village called ABC No Rio. (I was offered the part of the Countess de Lave, a part I always thought I was born to play. *"L'amour, l'amour, toujour l'amour!"*) I tossed around ideas of getting back into show business full time, but, again, it seemed wrong to expect anyone in Hollywood or on Broadway to understand what to do with me; making a distinctive mark in fashion seemed more tangible. I talked myself in and out of the idea of starting a company and ultimately concluded it really was not the right time. You feel these things in your bones, and my bones weren't ready. All I knew was that I needed a little breather.

For four months I stayed in my little apartment and sewed a lot. I went out nights to old-movie revivals and new nightclubs. It was a beautiful autumn filled with cold, overcast afternoons in Central Park and I felt lucky to be out of the loop, doing as I pleased. More than anything else during that time off, I made sketches. Day after day, for those months, I sat with my paints at a big, round table that dominated my tiny room. It was a real pleasure for me to pick up my paintbrushes again. When I'd finished Parsons, my sketches devolved into much less elaborate things, made solely to communicate ideas to pattern makers and associates, whipped together in haste with colored pencils or whatever was lying around. Now I got to luxuriate in gouache. That group of sketches was a manifesto, a solidifying of ideas, a basis. There were sketches of ball gowns styled like overalls, and beaded, striped fisherman's T-shirts worn with duchesse satin evening coats made to look like L.L.Bean barn jackets.

Jumpsuits that tied onto the body like kerchiefs. Beaded tartan-plaid pantsuits and trench coats with crinolines. They were the most beautiful sketches I'd ever made to that point. (Recently I had a retrospective at the Jewish Museum and I used several of them in the show.) Those sketches were being done in preparation for something — what, I didn't know.

One day the phone rang and it was Calvin Klein's personal secretary calling to see if I would be interested in meeting him. I was reticent. Calvin was someone I admired, but I knew it would be difficult being around all those neutrals. Working for Calvin seemed like a big opportunity because he had recently parted company with his star associate, Zack Carr, who left to start his own line. But there was nothing Machiavellian about my choosing that job. I had no intention of replacing Zack, no illusions about working there, no desire to further myself at the House of Calvin Klein. As a matter of fact it was hard for me to pretend I even wanted to work in another design room. What drew me there was that glaring flaw in my character: the ugliest, most competitive part of my nature, which sometimes takes over. Objectively I know fashion is a rat race with, at best, dubious rewards, but any invitation to participate is irresistible to my shallower parts. I was drawn again to the glamour, the fun, the powerful klieg lights of fashion, which seemed to shine more relentlessly on Calvin than anywhere.

When I set off on the allotted day to meet him, a bag lady at the Seventy-second Street subway station looked at the acid-blue flannel paper-bag waist pants I was wearing and said, "You go around scaring people in that?" I raced home to change into something more subdued. But it was an omen about entering a place where compromise would have to prevail.

Calvin worked in a vast three-story loft on the corner of Thirty-ninth Street and Seventh Avenue. It was so big I often got lost. The showroom was decorated by Joe D'Urso and featured hollow carpeted platforms, track lighting, and pin-spotted white cymbidium orchids everywhere — every room looked alike and did nothing to anchor one's sense of place. All three floors had a hush about them; one floated through the busy hallways, eerily quiet, like the streets of Tokyo without the humor.

I was shown into Calvin's private office through the main entrance. There was also a sneaky door to it through the fitting room,

374

which enabled Calvin to escape the premises with no notice and still be perceived as present; or appear out of the blue, as a reminder of his omnipotence. That day I sat waiting in his office, studying the décor, a gamut of objects, from African masks to Stieglitz photographs of Georgia O'Keeffe, one of his main inspirations. He startled me, gliding in from the unseen entrance, like a good-looking specter. Tall, boyish, with a deep, breathy voice that enhances the overall seductive effect.

He reviewed my sketches, those dear things I had pored over for the last fifteen weeks. "These don't look a thing like my work," he said, and I felt a combination of disappointment and relief, convinced he had no intention of hiring me. Then he said, "But they could." I never understood what he meant by that. Did he like what he saw? Enough to integrate some of the ideas? Or was it his way of saying he was going to bend me to his aesthetic will? In the room that day he offered me a job. "We're leaving for Europe at the end of the week. If you start tomorrow you can meet everyone first." Much as I wanted a few more days off to process things, I couldn't resist the offer, and within three days I was on a plane to Italy.

■ ■ ■ ■

Almost immediately upon my accepting the job, Calvin was thrown from a horse and spent weeks out of commission. When he returned to work he brooded around the design room on crutches, like a well-dressed Brick from *Cat on a Hot Tin Roof.* Every girl and boy flirted with him, including me, in my own passive-aggressive, professional way. But Calvin was elusive. I was used to knowing the people I worked with, each design room forming a kind of family unit, dysfunctional or otherwise. Calvin was the negligent parent of about six or eight of us who vied constantly for his attention, like a bunch of starving children. *Actually starving.* I observed that the thinner you were, the easier it was to get his attention. Any ounce of extra weight was magnified in that design room tenfold, which was lethal when combined with my natural proclivity to feeling fat. I quickly lost twenty pounds. I ate nothing but almond butter and rice cakes, and I was always exhausted. I was the thinnest I'd been in my entire life. Definitely way underweight. But I looked great. I dressed like a punk Audrey Hepburn, in clothes I made myself: skinny side-zip ski pants with stirrups and tight short-sleeved turtlenecks. Christiaan, the famous hairdresser, told me never to wash my hair again and to use olive oil on it every day, so I had what might be called Jew-dreads. I wore kohl on the lower inside rims of my eyes, Erace on my lips, and white translucent rice powder, which gave me a glowy pallor. With my skeletal frame, it was chic in a ghoulish way, and I got Calvin's attention.

I learned a lot working there. Fittings were more formal than they were at Perry Ellis. Calvin would make surprise entrances from that private office door; at times I felt like applauding, the way an audience applauds a star on his entrance. We pinned our expectations on him to know the right thing, and he always did. He had a great eye for tailoring. Even though he couldn't sew, and I never saw him sketch, he knew exactly what he wanted — always something directly or indirectly related to a man's suit jacket. I'd watch him closely, even when he was working with lace or an evening dress he was tailoring, giving structure, editing away. He was a great editor. He knew exactly what to get rid of in order to tighten the tension around what remained. The Alfred Hitchcock of fashion.

We got to know each other a little, but he

remained sphinxlike. Boys had crushes on him. Girls had crushes on him, too. And he didn't do anything to discourage anyone. At that time he seemed to be the textbook definition of bisexual. A history of gossip about liaisons with men didn't preclude him from dating Kelly Rector, who ran the design room, and who I immediately liked. We trusted each other in those rooms full of tricky personalities. Kelly is gorgeous to look at, with a childlike awe for design that people sometimes mistake for haughtiness or condescension. The fact that she's so pretty and was in Calvin's good graces led people to resent her position, or to misread her thoughtfulness as disdain or lack of direction — similar to the way shy people can be misread as standoffish.

One day a few months after I started there, days after returning from Italy where we had completed our fabric buy for the season, Calvin announced another trip to Europe. It was a total mystery. There were vague plans to visit the fabulous embroidery firm Maison Lesage, in Paris, which was not a resource we had used before. Prior to meeting the rest of us in Paris, Calvin and Kelly went to Rome with the design manager Melissa Huffine and Melissa's then-boyfriend, Nuno Brandolini. Nuno is from a noble and very well-connected Italian family, so all I could come up with was that Calvin wanted to meet the Pope.

That Sunday, on my way to Paris, I stopped for a newspaper in the airport. On the cover of the *New York Post* was a paparazzi picture of Calvin and Kelly leaving a justice of the peace's office in Rome, having been married the day before, the wedding, presumably, arranged by Nuno. When I landed in Paris the next morning I couldn't help feeling like an interloper on what should have been their honeymoon. The appointment with Lesage at the Plaza Athénée went off as scheduled in the bridal suite. We continued on to other parts of Italy, an anomalous schedule of fabric shopping, sweater fittings, and what felt like wedding dinners. We continued on to London, and at the final dinner at Mr Chow's, Calvin ordered lichee nuts for dessert. When they arrived at the table and the waiter cracked one open, a torrent of ants poured out. I screamed and leapt away from the table. To that point, I think it was the only time I'd ever seen Calvin laugh.

About a year after that trip, Grace Coddington was hired to replace Kelly, who had decided to stop working. Rumors about Grace's departure from British *Vogue* were rampant, and when it was announced she was moving to Calvin Klein as design director the news crashed like a tidal wave. I idolized Grace from my days at Perry Ellis, where we had met briefly, and thought what fun it might be to work in close proximity. And we started off with a bang, always agreeing in design meetings, and dining or going to inspirational exhibits and shows together. When she moved into her new town house I sewed her some linen slipcovers, which she still refers to as the most beautiful she ever had. But a month or two later it occurred to me that the stiff, committeelike approach to design at the company saw no chance of thawing under Grace's rule. If anything, things became more and more bureaucratic there. My influence at Calvin Klein might have been felt for a season or two, but I was never truly integrated there. While the other designers were sketching mannish suits and coats, I was doing sketches inspired by 1950s Technicolor musicals. One day I passed Calvin in the hall. I was carrying my newest drawings, and he asked to see them. The top sketch was an ostrich-feather coat over a grey-flannel strapless top and trousers — my attempt at softening things up. He looked at me, perplexed, and said, "Okay!

Keep at it!"

In the fall of 1986, I began to realize that what was the beginning of something for Calvin and Grace was the end of the line for me. One day about six months after her arrival, Grace sat me down in the fitting room and broke the news that they decided I wasn't going to Europe on the trip to buy fabrics that fall. And that was the day I decided to quit, while I was still somewhat ahead.

20

I was on the phone with my mother late that summer and she said, "You know you have a small trust fund," which was news to me. She'd never mentioned an inheritance in the three years since my dad had died. That night I learned that my father left my sisters and me each fifty thousand dollars, and the money was there whenever I wanted it. It wasn't much, but it was something to consider.

Why Calvin hadn't fired me as yet was baffling to me. Great as he is, humor was never his strong suit, on or off the runway. More than once from that sneaky fitting-room door, he walked in on me doing Liz Taylor or Streisand impersonations for a rapt audience of designers, fitters, merchants — whoever was around. He'd freeze, smile ironically, and retreat to his office. I managed to hold my own there for a little over two years with mixed results, and finally among the layers of hierarchy, my bitterness started peeking through. One day, with the entire staff there, I disagreed with one of his decisions about a textile I loved, and in a fit of black humor I said, "Calvin. Are you getting creative on us all of a sudden?" A pall set over the proceedings as happens when a joke crash-lands. When I finally gave Calvin my notice, I think he was relieved.

I knew it was time to strike out on my own, and the trust fund was the good omen I needed. It wasn't so much the money itself — I would have struck out on my own even without the money. But I felt ready. The luckiest break I had was that I didn't realize how ill-prepared I was. I didn't know how impossible the road ahead was, nor how much money would be needed — I was armed with ignorance.

I yearned to make clothes that had been formulating in my mind from the days that I started sketching in my basement atelier. And since I'd started working professionally my vision had intensified, and I had a clear idea about what I wanted for the future. There was a balance I could strike; a reason to form a house. What the world was missing was American clothes with a real sense of humor. And color. Color would be a huge part of it. I wanted to create unexpected, jarring combinations of colors that couldn't be contained in a category like "pastels" or "brights," or, my least-favorite category descriptor, "jewel tones." I wanted a world where you'd choose colors from a huge array — so much color that a mistake would be a good thing; accidental pairings of bright pink, tomato red, pale saffron, and henna; or deep sky blue with purple undertones mixed with Yves Klein blue, yellow, and olive green.

My first task was to find a space to set up a tiny atelier. I had my heart set on being in SoHo even though a decade before my father had warned me against the abominations of the area. His first job in the garment business years and years earlier was in one of the sweatshops there, legendary for their horrid working conditions. Since that time those factories had disappeared and SoHo was a burned-out neighborhood. But by 1986, there was an enclave of artist studios and a few start-up galleries. It would be a while before the majority of new shops and restaurants would assemble, and for those few years you could feel the energy pushing forth through the cobblestone streets about to explode in the cast-iron factory buildings — a potent contrast with the squalor of its decrepit past. And: It was the only place I could afford.

A real-estate agent named Susan Penzner, who later became a good friend, brought me to a loft on Greene Street, small by comparison to any of the design rooms I'd worked in, but huge in my imagination. When I walked in, I felt that room in my bowels. I saw the studio in the same way I saw a puppet theatre in a garage before there was one. It felt like my place.

Sarah Haddad (who had since remarried and renamed herself Sarah Cheney) and I had remained friends, even though it was a number of years since we'd worked together after the IS New York label folded. Though I wanted to stay as far away from the community as possible, I knew Sarah was a strong-willed, capable person who really believed in me. I knew I could talk to her about my ideas and be taken seriously. The steep odds against our success never occurred to her; again, ignorance was a major asset. I knew it probably would have been better to have someone with a lot more experience as a partner, but from the first phone call I knew she was ready, and I knew that she was smart enough to pick up whatever she didn't know. I was feeling my way as I went along, and it was nice having someone enthusiastic and familiar in the fold.

It also seemed like I had my first commission: Melissa Huffine, who had worked as the design manager at Calvin Klein and who became a good friend, had been teetering nervously on the edge of becoming an Italian aristocrat. She'd finally become engaged to Nuno Brandolini after a long courtship, and they announced their engagement. She chose me to make her dress. It took months of arranging and fittings and every resource I had at the time. The dress was composed of an off-the-shoulder peasant blouse with full sleeves made of silk organdie covered by a meticulously cut corset of about thirty panels made in silk peau de soie over an enormous bustled ball-gown skirt and train. The color was dark cream, almost bone. In the late daylight, she looked like a John Singer Sargent painting. The bridal party added to the effect: little boys dressed in navy blue double-breasted suits and flower girls in dresses I made — cream silk pinafores trimmed in navy blue ribbon.

On the big day I was driven to Melissa and Nuno's house in Southampton where I oversaw the dressing, all the time containing my hysteria. Every socialite in New York was invited to that wedding. Oscar de la Renta, whom I didn't know at the time, was there. It made me so nervous to think that all those perfect people dressed in Chanel and Valentino would be scrutinizing my work at close proximity.

I've always had a tendency toward disaster fantasy. The first dresses I made for public spectacle filled me with a particular dread. Any time there was someone dressed in my clothes at an important event I imagined a seam ripping at a crucial moment or someone stepping on the train and ruining it. That day I was especially filled with such dread.

At the reception Oscar made a point of coming over and telling me how much he liked the dress. It seemed like everyone liked it. All the papers had items about the event and about my dress, referring to me as a new designer name. A day later the back cover of *WWD* was split between Melissa's wedding and the wedding of someone I had heard about, a very glamourous young editor at *Vogue* named Elizabeth Saltzman, who had already begun making a name for herself. Her wedding to Glenn Dubin took place at the Puck Building (hooray 1980s!) the same Sunday as Melissa's. Elizabeth's dress was a straight, white sheath with a train, made by Stephen Sprouse. Right after the ceremony Sprouse himself cut the train off with a pair of scissors, a modern, almost violent act. This was photographed for posterity and published in *WWD* alongside a picture of Melissa in my dress, which was the complete opposite — a study in taste and decorum. Pleased as I was about what my dress looked like and even the attention, I was nonetheless annoyed by the implied comparison. On their own each dress had merits and flaws, but next to the Sprouse, mine seemed staid. I was baffled as to what the dresses had to do with each other and why they were presented side by side. I knew the coverage was more to do with society weddings than wedding-gown designs but I felt inadvertently misrepresented and resentful of sharing the tiny editorial space. No matter how illogical my feelings — it wasn't about me — I couldn't help noticing how unfair it was to be juxtaposed thus. It was the beginning of a lot of that.

In those days all of the important designers — Geoffrey Beene, Bill Blass, Oscar de la Renta, Anne Klein — were located in one building: 550 Seventh Avenue. Donna Karan, who had recently set up her own offices, did so in that building, and it seemed to me like an exclusive club, outside of which you stood no chance of succeeding. By comparison, SoHo was a dead zone. The art scene was thriving there, but in those days fashion editors and buyers were offended if they had to walk one block out of their usual route, and most of the people I looked up to strongly advised me not to set up my studio anywhere but in the garment district. Kal Ruttenstein, who was the fashion director for Bloomingdale's, told me I was crazy and I didn't stand a chance anywhere but Seventh Avenue. Another young designer located only twenty blocks south of the fashion district who had gone out of business was painted to be a spendthrift by the press. One of the line items they focused on were his bills for private cars, which he was forced to send for people in order to get them to come see his collection. Something else Kal told me was never to send private cars for people, what he really thought was a piece of valuable advice.

But the thick fashion scene that prevailed on Seventh Avenue was antithetical to everything I wanted to do. I couldn't tell the difference between one designer and the next, especially in the stores after all the fuss and styling had been removed. I was like a conscientious outsider, and it was that distance that allowed me to think differently. SoHo was deserted in those days. Walking the streets any time of the week you might run across one or two people but not more. If you wanted a crowd you'd have to go a few blocks south to Canal Street or over to Broadway. If you were hungry there was a place called Food. It was a cafeteria on the corner of Prince and Wooster with a Socialist mien and bare-bone amenities. I don't even think there was air-conditioning. The light was dim but not on purpose; the place barely had light fixtures. The food was cheap and abundant and the clientele reflected the local population; often you couldn't tell the difference between an artist and a vagrant.

There was a beautiful anomalous restaurant called Chanterelle created and run by David and Karen Waltuck, whom I later became friends with. It was on the corner of Grand Street and Mercer. Whenever I wanted to impress the "uptown" crowd I would take them there. These were editors and friends who wouldn't go far afield of the old guard, elegant restaurants like La Caravelle or La Grenouille. Chanterelle was the place to prove that there was another kind of elegance in New York City. It was the most beautiful room, with austere cream-colored walls, a plain brass chandelier and dimmed lighting, and a single, massive flower arrangement located against the center wall of the room. There was a new design for the cover of the menu every few weeks, made by artists bartering for food — Cy Twombly, Jennifer Bartlett, Ross Bleckner to name a few. I took John Fairchild and C.Z. Guest there for lunch once, and reluctant as they were to admit it, they knew they were experiencing something as fresh and new as it was luxurious. It was akin to what I was trying to evoke in clothing: beautiful, original, technically flawless, and casual.

Really, the neighborhood was pioneered by the art community. Artists had studios there and galleries opened fabulous converted spaces that felt luxurious in their austerity and industrial-chic edge. Sonnabend, Castelli, Pace all had galleries that I visited regularly. (I had one of my smaller midyear fashion shows at the Pace Gallery on Wooster Street in early 1988, and Richard Serra called Arne Glimcher to complain about fashion photos being taken in front of his oil-stick painting, which was hanging in the gallery. It took a lot of cajoling from my friend Susan Dunne to stop me from calling him back and giving him a piece of my mind.)

With all the energy in the world I went to work setting up shop. My little space needed painting, so I painted it. I needed cutting tables, so I built them. Sewing machines were moved from my tiny apartment on West End Avenue (for a while I didn't know what to do with all that extra space at home). I hired a young woman recommended by Frank Rizzo, named Annica Andersson, who had just graduated from Parsons, to help me make clothes. It didn't take the fashion cognoscenti long to get off their asses. Within a year or two SoHo — and my studio in particular — was the place to be.

I started with a small collection for resort that came out of me like a jumble. There were bathing suits and cover-ups; lightweight coats in lemon-candy yellow or dark jade-green taffeta that could work for day or night; little evening dresses; an azalea-pink wool jersey halter dress to the knee with a huge taffeta ruffle at the neck; a big, white lampshade hat that I made with my friend, the great milliner Patricia Underwood. Every piece was a sort of fucked-up tribute to Audrey Hepburn. It was new, but it had a definite place in a woman's life, rather than being just a useless new idea. Right away there was a lot of attention. I wasn't worried about selling, I'd decided this would be a trial run and any actual sales would be gravy.

One day late that summer of 1986 the phone rang, and a voice said, "I have Dawn Mello on the phone." Dawn Mello, who ran Bergdorf Goodman, was one of the most visionary retailers in the history of fashion, and notice from her could make your name. She was cheerful and excited on the phone and said she'd heard good things about my work and that she'd like to send her buyers to take a look. I'd seen Ms. Mello at appointments at Perry Ellis and Calvin Klein, but we'd never formally met. We eventually became friends, but at that point in time she came across as aloof, intimidating. Toward the end of the phone conversation, which was going well, Kal Ruttenstein's words rung in my ears. I said "Uh. Mrs. Mello. Sorry. I would love for the buyers to come down, but I don't think I can send a car." There was a long pause on the other end and she said, sounding a little baffled, "Don't worry, dear. They'll take a taxi."

The buyers walked in, and I could sense their intention to order clothes, though I couldn't understand what had led them there. No matter how optimistic I felt, in the fashion business, as with all businesses, nothing is real till you have the order in your hand. We proceeded politely, nervously, carefully, to show the clothes one piece at a time. I booked two models to show the tiny collection, which was a necessity. The buyers were suspiciously friendly and awestruck themselves. It was my first sense that there was some sort of buzz out there about me, about what I was doing. I don't think it was because of the five or six years I spent in the industry in advance of launching my own label as much as people understanding how motivated I was to make a success. And maybe, too, how strong the clothes were. What strikes me in retrospect is how easily it could have turned against me, but for the moment I felt the presence of good fortune. By the time those buyers were ready to leave after that first appointment, the main concern was how quickly we could get clothes to the store.

I had been warned by everyone, including Kal, about the treacherous laws of supply and demand in the fashion business, how dangerous it was to take orders and not deliver, or, something I considered a high-class problem: getting too big too soon.

Those were pitfalls no one had any real solutions for. So many reasons to fail, of which I took no notice. Business in general is something I had no idea about, something I think no one starting out ever has any idea about. To be fair, it's not something one can figure out in advance; it has a lot to do with luck, especially for a Type A like me. I knew a lot about beautiful clothes, how to make them, how to instruct others to make them, and that was all. Business was a monster under my bed, a mass of problems, ready to elude me as easily as eat me alive. If I took time to figure it out, in my short life, I would have no energy or focus left to do what I was best at. The ideal situation is to have a trusted partner, in my case Sarah, who would handle all that. But deep down I knew that she didn't really have the experience we needed. And so I operated in a state of high denial mixed with a kind of religious determination and trust in a positive future.

Youth, darling.

21

My head was down, absorbed in my work. It was summer and the door was ajar, and I felt a stir; someone had wandered in. There were only two or three of us working at that time, and we looked up. It was a middle-aged woman with deceptively average-looking features: premature salt-and-pepper hair, watery blue eyes, and a puckered half-smile. She was dressed in Chinese pajamas and had a serene, otherworldly quality, and spoke in a deep, rushed whisper. She introduced herself as Julie Britt. She said she'd heard of me through Jade Hobson at *Vogue.* I was curious but too busy to inquire further so I quickly took her through the collection. She was almost completely silent as she looked, and that puckery smile never left her face entirely. She whispered, "Wonderful." Then she promised me she would be in touch and floated out.

A week later she called and asked to come

and meet me about a commission. By that time I had done a little research and found out she was a great stylist of major importance who worked with the best fashion magazines and photographers. When she arrived she went straight to the rack and pulled out three dresses and asked me if I could show up with them the following day for a shoot with Richard Avedon. Richard Avedon. Really. She said they'd like to have me on set to "dress the girls." As busy as I was at that time, keeping my eye on the ball, hard at work making clothes, I decided I couldn't miss this.

I took a taxi up the East River Drive on a hot summer afternoon. We were stuck in traffic and I sat there, sweating, filled with dread about my little business, commitments piling up, bills not making sense. My head was so full of stuff at that time, and I couldn't really believe I was on my way to meet this man I had designated a decade earlier as my personal saint. I thought the job might actually be something Avedon-related or some other kind of thirdhand association. Finally, the taxi pulled up to a small town house on East Seventy-fifth Street, and I paused outside wondering if it was the right address — a small place for such a huge legacy.

I walked into the little house with my garment bag and encountered a lady with oversized octagonal glasses, a dark ponytail, and a smile that revealed teeth which took up more than a usual share of a face. She was seated at a plain little desk, on the phone. She gestured for me to have a seat. After finishing on the phone she leapt up and introduced herself. Norma Stevens. Smiling like a Pac-Man she said, "Julie told me all about you, and we are all really excited."

The moment I set foot inside that town house the world got better. There was something you felt as you entered, that no matter what came out of that place, it would be the best. It was like passing through a portal from ordinary to excellence.

Norma led me through the building, first past a small kitchen with a communal seating area, then through heavy double doors to the inner sanctum. We passed a dressing room where I noticed a number of models — some famous ones like Kelly LeBrock and Janice Dickinson — and a big team of hair and makeup people working on them under the guidance of my new friend Julie Britt, who looked up and waved. Finally we reached the studio.

Richard Avedon was a small man with an

extra-large head covered in shaggy heather-grey hair. He wore aviator-style eyeglasses and was dressed in blue jeans and a blue button-down shirt. He was busy working out lights with his assistants. Norma waited for a break in the activity and whispered something in his ear. He came over, beaming. "Julie tells me you're a genius."

I tried to talk. I called him Mr. Avedon, and he stopped me midsentence. He said, "Call me Dick." It wasn't an option. He refused to be called anything else. Not Mr. Avedon, not Richard, only Dick. I think it had to do with his ideas about economy; Dick was the shortest form of address. Maybe, too, it made him feel slightly younger and hipper to be called by his first name, and more casual — "casual" being another of his imperatives.

I learned quickly that Dick liked to weigh each and every decision about a shoot and pass it before a kind of committee, which everyone who was invited to work in the studio that day belonged to. Each question that arose would be followed by a scholarly pause. Eventually someone would take their life in their hands and chance an opinion. Then someone would either agree or counter with another piece of advice, and the floor would be open for discussion. Eventually an answer would arise. It was different from being at Calvin in that the answer wasn't a foregone conclusion of beige. Also, here I felt I was on equal footing with the others. It was a good lesson that "design by committee" wasn't necessarily something to be scorned. As it turned out, I could collaborate happily with others more suited to my natural tastes.

The clothes I brought to the sitting that day remained in the garment bag. I couldn't figure out exactly what I was doing there. Eventually I would participate in five or six similar shoots, all part of an ongoing campaign for Revlon featuring "The most unforgettable women." They were designed as double-page spreads with four or five gorgeous women from all different generations: Christy Turlington, Iman, Tatjana Patitz, Cindy Crawford, Rachel Williams, Lauren Hutton. For each sitting Julie had arranged a theme. The first was flapperish; all the clothes were black with a lot of jet beading. There was one day when the girls were actually wearing dresses of mine, which couldn't be perceived because of the focus on this overpowering sculptural jewelry Julie had gotten from somewhere. One day there were these dramatic white gazar collars stiffened with wires that I helped to style around the girls' faces and shoulders while Julie and Dick oohed and aahed at my ability to manipulate these shapes. Another day I wrapped the girls in different animal-print scarves and throws that Julie brought in. That shoot jogged something in Dick's memory. He had one of his assistants dig out some contact sheets from his archives, pictures he took in the 1960s of Madame Grès wrapping Streisand's head in thick, white butcher linen. He had them Xeroxed for me, and I studied those gorgeous pictures for weeks.

Avedon and I became friends and dined together a few times in the house he lived in above the studio on East Seventy-fifth Street. A housekeeper would leave food in roasting dishes with notes attached: *Heat at 375 on convection setting.* The apartment had décor that captured a time in New York City from my childhood, the early 1970s. It had a dining table under a slanted skylight that ran parallel to a white, narrow, open-plan kitchen. The living room had a vaguely Japanese feel, fitted with cabinetry that felt like elegant fruit crates had been stacked. Around the various rooms were all sorts of fabulous photographs of his, tacked up or framed and propped against walls. I thought of it as the perfect setup: working all day in the studio and walking upstairs at night to bed.

He gave me fatherly advice about everything. And if I ever wondered why I had a complex about my weight, there's this story: When Dick and I knew each other I had recovered a little of the weight I'd lost at Calvin Klein, but I was still bone thin. At one point I brought up my weight and was about to tell him the story about growing up fat and losing seventy-five pounds in high school and the recent eating disorder I'd experienced. He stopped me and said, "You know, there are some men who just look better fat. Fidel Castro, when I first photographed him, he was thinner. The second time, years later, he had put on a lot of weight and was much more attractive. You're one of those people. You look better fat. Don't lose a pound."

I got to meet a lot of wonderful people working with Dick. I met Suga, who I think was the greatest hairdresser who ever lived. I also met Kevyn Aucoin, the fabulous makeup artist, who I would go on to work with exclusively. We became great friends. At some of those shoots I felt like I was contributing something. At others I felt useless. I was one more voice in the committee of people who agreed or disagreed with Dick. But each of the days was a fantasy, a heavenly break from the realities of my studio. And each day I learned something about beauty and refinement. The best lesson I learned was a kind of restatement of an idea I knew instinctively: that in order to create excellence I had to totally immerse myself in the task at hand and forget everything else.

One day Julie called and asked me about a piece from my first collection, a canary-yellow coat with an extreme drawstring ruffle-collar, and whether I could make it for her in black by the following week. It sounded like another fool's errand, but one couldn't say no to Julie. Or Dick. And I loved the rarified air of this new association. So I made the coat in black (Taroni) double-face satin, the most gorgeous fabric available on Earth. I taxied up with my garment bag for an extra-early call that day. When I got there Dick wasn't in his usual jeans but instead in a grey flannel suit and a tie. He seemed more anxious than usual. I said, "What's with the suit?" And he said, "For the great one, I wear a suit." Audrey Hepburn was coming that day for one of the "Unforgettable Women" ad shoots. Dick said the only way she would agree to do it was if he would do another portrait of her, later in the day, for a UNICEF press release.

Dick and Audrey Hepburn were kindred spirits. They were from roughly the same generation, both Taurus, both around the same height. He felt a kind of ownership of her and was invested in a way I had not seen before. Almost teary-eyed, he told me "Right off the boat they sent her to me. Even before they sent her to Hollywood." (It was unclear who "they" were. I assumed it was the Hollywood executives who had discovered her in Europe.) He photographed her extensively before she had seen her first screen test, and those pictures preceded her to Hollywood. Not to mention the countless times he took her picture after that. The movie *Funny Face* was inspired by Avedon. Fred Astaire portrays "Richard Avery," a thinly disguised version of Dick, who discovers a model, played by Audrey Hepburn, with whom he falls in love. Dick was very involved with the making of that movie as a special consultant, yet he was abandoned by the studio midway. Once he regaled me with tales about working on *Funny Face* and how much the studio hated him after they began shooting. They considered him over-involved, a nuisance, and he insisted that they once drugged him at lunch to keep him away from the editing room. According to him, he was their worst nightmare from start to finish. He found problems with everything from camera angles to finished color processes. He described it as something he regretted getting involved with, which was baffling to me, seeing as how it's such a great and lasting document of his world, complete with appearances by Dovima and Suzy Parker.

Audrey Hepburn walked in wearing a black raincoat to the knee, a kerchief over her hair, and dark glasses. Her arrival was greeted with no more fanfare than anyone else working in the studio that day. She went straight to Suga, whom she loved and trusted. Dick took me over and introduced us, then left us alone to make further preparations. She was smaller than she appeared to be in movies and had a big, photogenic head, huge, slanted eyes, the anomalous almost pudgy nose, all the features that had long mesmerized me — edged by the crepe that comes with being sixtyish. There was a wistfulness to her demeanor, a languor, an almost sadness that she did nothing to hide. When we were alone I froze, but she immediately made me feel at ease. She asked me for a cigarette, and we smoked together.

She had a jewelry roll with her; she un-rolled it and started pulling out all sorts of tasteful earrings and necklaces. She held them up to her face and sought my opinion. At first I was amused by these old-fashioned necklaces and earrings from a bygone time — tasteful Schlumberger, discreet Cartier things — but as she held them up, they began to irritate me. Dick returned to the room, and I mustered a very authoritative voice and said: "No jewelry. Anything will just be a distraction from that face."

There was a long silence in the room. The chopping off of my head was being contem-plated. Dick looked at Julie and finally cracked a smile and said "Absolutely!" and it seemed like the committee exploded into spontaneous applause.

Hepburn and Kevyn got along famously. She had a few directives and brought a few of her own makeup items, and he respect-fully worked his magic. Next it came time to dress her, and I hesitated. She intuited how nervous I was and said, "But that's your job, silly!" When she saw the coat on the hanger she sighed and said "Beautiful!" in a vocal expression of hers I'd noted before, which sounded almost like crying.

Sitting on the set that day watching her

and Dick work together was like witnessing a miracle. Dick said, "Okay now, Audrey. Look down. And each time you look up at me I want something fresh and new." She looked down. Then up with a half-smile. Then down. Then up with a mysterious gaze. And so on. Down. Up with a huge grin. Snap. Snap. My coat looked flawless. And her neck looked about a mile long. Her hand was in the shot, touching the big ruffle around the neck. I remember the discussions at Dick's studio afterwards, the art directors felt her hand looked too big. To be fair I think it was an ad for nail polish, so in the end they swapped it out for that of a hand model, and if you look at the picture now the hand seems way too small.

At the end of that long day, well after four in the afternoon, I left Dick's little brownstone. There were throngs — and I mean throngs — at least thirty photographers — waiting for Audrey Hepburn's exit. Nowadays agents call paparazzi to whip up attention for their star clients, and it's all trim and orderly by comparison. This was way before that. I watched her emerge from the building, this wisp of a woman, to face that big mess of photographers shooting her on the sidewalk, harassing her as she walked politely to her car. These men were not

Avedon, lithe in his grey flannel suit and his perfect lighting. These were fat, sweaty men in shorts. Huge men with massive cameras dangling around their necks, all there for those terrible pictures. It was feral. Predatory.

Since my childhood days of watching old movies on TV, I'd certainly never dreamt I'd meet the great one herself. As a young adult I thought I would encounter women of my generation who might live up to Audrey Hepburn. But there was never anyone who could come close to her. There have been so many stylish, beautiful women in my time. So many more beautiful than her, and many who have impacted fashion more, but never anyone with that kind of gravity. Am I deluding myself? Do we all feel this way about iconic people we grow up idolizing? Or might it just be true in this case, that no one else will ever come close.

22

For me, one of the greatest developments of 1986 was the discovery of an aboveboard traveling gay cocktail party that happened the first Friday night of every month in a surprise location. It was called "Boys' Night," and it was organized by a bunch of young men who worked for the Italian designer Massimo Vignelli. Boys' Night brought out all the aspiring young men in New York. There was a kind of heady freedom in the idea that one could go to a gay dance or a party without being hidden in some back room. One time Boys' Night took place at a hall in Columbia University, the next in the lobby of an ad agency. This idea of going to a grown-up cocktail party without a shady underside, where you could meet other interesting gay people and talk about politics and books, filled me with hope.

In those days exclusivity was part of being

gay. A double-edged perk. Though it may not seem so, there were fun aspects of being a subculture. After I got past the initial hysteria about my sexuality, the very outsideness of it became a kind of turn-on. Knowing you were different. For every disappointment in a loved one's assessment, there was joy in the discovery of an ally. The instant bonding with others you knew to be gay or supportive. It was like belonging to a secret, dangerous, and exclusive club, something I can't imagine anyone today would miss, but which was a fun bonus for me and my peers. The heady, glorious feeling of walking into a gay event or party, the knowledge that everyone was fair game, the beautiful solidarity, the instant feeling of community against all odds.

One Friday night I hosted a Boys' Night event at my loft on Greene Street. It felt like I was flying in the face of caution. Harmless as it seems now, and hard as it is to believe, any sort of gay event in the mid-eighties connoted more than a slight bit of edge. We were busy working on my first collection show, which would be some time that winter of 1986, so Annica stayed and worked while the cocktail party was in progress. I was correcting patterns while men were milling about and drinking. Interesting, good-looking, smart men.

That night I met a guy named Wayne who I ended up dating for a short time. He was from Memphis and waited tables at Mike's Bar and Grill in Hell's Kitchen, a place that served margaritas made with what must have been grain alcohol. Wayne had a strong, attractive look, dark spiky hair, black eyes, and a thick drawl. Also, he had a wicked sense of humor. He teased me a lot about being so organized and pulled together. He referred to my tiny apartment, which was overdecorated with mirrors, plaids, and animal prints, as a perfect "starter apartment . . . for Diana Vreeland." There was another boy from Tennessee, Wayne's best friend, whose name I forget, let's call him Don, also gay, heavyset, butch, who waited tables at Mike's and also worked the graveyard shift tending bar at an East Village dive where we used to hang out. Like Wayne, Don's sexuality seemed completely integrated, unapologetic, homosexuality in-your-face, no easy feat in 1986.

Late one night around that time, after Don pumped me with margaritas (I was always a cheap drunk — I drank very little owing to the sleep disorder), I was dancing and singing around my apartment. I had

Liza's *Live at Carnegie Hall* record blasting when I slipped on my zebra-skin rug and broke my ankle. The following morning I couldn't move it. Somehow I managed to get myself to NYU Langone, where my ankle was X-rayed and put in a cast. Just as my career began to soar, I was making every attempt at sabotaging myself. (Not to mention how embarrassed I was by the gayness of slipping on a zebra skin while lip-syncing to Liza's Carnegie Hall album.)

That day I got a call from *Vogue* saying Elizabeth Saltzman wanted to meet me in her office and look at some clothes. I wasn't sure how she knew about me, and I had no idea how I was going to get all those clothes uptown while on crutches, my ankle freshly casted. Wayne helped me load up two garment bags and shouldered me and my crutches into a taxi and up the elevator in the Condé Nast building at 350 Madison Avenue.

I was inspired by Elizabeth, as were so many designers at the time. She was the "it" girl. Beautiful, funny, and tinged with scandal. Her first marriage, which she undertook in her Sprouse gown the year before, had already ended. Now she was dating Ron Perelman, jetting and yachting to places most of us dream about. I couldn't

412

tell what she was planning — whether it was a story for the magazine or just covering her bases to know what was going on out in the market. That evening there wasn't a lot of conversation — she did a lot of screaming as she tried things on. When we did speak it was about sex and boys and movie stars. I spent about two hours in her office, and we bonded; that night I was her discovery. She was a gadabout, and I was a little bit of a bore, always too tired from work to really partake in all the beautiful-people stuff. We gave each other nicknames that people used to roll their eyes over: She was Eenie and I was I-nee. We hosted parties for each other a lot, and the following summer we shared a house in Watermill. There was only happiness around Elizabeth, and I smile when I think about her.

She immediately arranged a sitting with the photographer Matthew Rolston, and the following week I sat in someone else's loft in SoHo, my ankle broken, while Elizabeth styled my clothes and Matthew, wearing graduated pearls, like an old society matron, took pictures. Elizabeth's column appeared a few months later: several pictures of my clothes and a picture of me looking slightly shell-shocked. It was a small story in *Vogue* — a breakthrough I didn't know I was making — those outward signs only registering their importance for me in retrospect. I cared little about press then, but it really helped. By the time I announced my first fashion show I had everyone's attention. Ironically, I was too busy to notice.

Either I didn't have time or it didn't strike me as an occasion to celebrate. After Bergdorf Goodman placed that first order my mother said, "If you don't celebrate this, what the hell do you celebrate?" I didn't see the little order as an accomplishment; I saw it as a challenge. I did everything myself. I oversaw the cutting and sewing — I even packed and shipped the clothes myself. Annica became like my sister, and we worked more closely than I did with anyone else up to that point and ever after. It was a tiny order, but it was Bergdorf Goodman and everything had to be perfect. Even that first handful of pieces — maybe a dozen total — overwhelmed me. A strapless velvet cocktail dress with satin-piped gores; a little puff of taffeta and tulle that couldn't be called a jacket or even a shrug as much as *sleeves;* a few colorful jersey sack dresses, each in a small size range only because we couldn't afford to have the patterns graded past a size ten. The first shipment sold out fast.

Then came a tiny bunch of early spring clothes, including a white pique smocked "garden coat" that kept being reordered.

The first few shipments were driven up to Bergdorf's in Sarah's green Jaguar. She sat in the car while I dropped the boxes off at the loading dock and got the appropriate receipts. Within the first four days of the clothes getting to Bergdorf's selling floor they called to tell me Jane Pauley bought a raincoat. (It was an easy-fitting knee-length thing made of one of the best fabrics I ever had: a natural handkerchief linen coated in a microfine layer of bone-colored rubber. I finished it with blond horn buttons that weighed more than the entire coat.) Eventually Bergdorf Goodman would become my biggest retail outlet. My first collections were sold predominantly through trunk shows arranged under the auspices of someone named Betty Halbreich, who still runs the personal-shopping business at the store. She and I became great friends over the years. A few weeks after our second and slightly larger delivery to Bergdorf's, Betty called to say that Liza Minnelli had just been in and purchased a whole bunch of things, including one of the piqué garden coats. She also said that Liza was on her way down to see me and "She likes Coca-

Cola." I left Annica to straighten up while I raced to the corner and bought a six-pack and some flowers.

When Liza and her entourage flooded in that first time it felt like I'd entered an alternative reality. The first thing she said to me was, "I noticed that smock coat from the escalator!"

Within minutes she was stripped down to her bra-pantyhose one-piece, which did not go unnoticed by me, and my noticing did not go unnoticed by her. "You like it?" she asked. I swear I think the body-shaper movement originated with that one-piece of Liza's. She has fabulous, disproportionately long legs and a short waist (like me), and she was able to pull her pantyhose up to meet her bra and sew the two pieces together without the bra pulling down and losing its hold. It formed one smooth line from toe to bustline.

She tried on literally every single thing I had in the studio and ordered it all. It was something I wasn't used to, someone ordering things with such abandon. It felt excessive, and I began to discourage her from ordering more. It seemed based on a disorder more than her desire for good clothes, and my protective instincts kicked in.

It would be hard to overstate how thrilled

I was to have Liza Minnelli standing there in various states of undress in the middle of my atelier, changing in and out of *my* clothes. I'm pretty sure I told her how much I idolized her from my childhood and what a huge part *Cabaret* and *Liza with a "Z"* had played in my life. For fear of coming across as a stalker, I omitted the parts where I had studied her every movement and vocal mannerism in order to impersonate her. I was also really nervous. I mean — the levels of perfection she had been held to growing up with those parents — the grandeur of the golden age of Hollywood, not to mention her legendary friendship with Halston. Was there any way I could live up to that? Also, I was nervous about the passing time, all the commitments and responsibilities I put aside in order to play dress-up with this living legend.

Aside from the amazing one-piece undergarment, Liza had a lot of tricks she revealed to me over the course of those fittings. Some useful things, but mostly crazy old-fashioned ideas that didn't really pertain. She liked dress shields and had myriad ways of incorporating them discreetly. She extolled the virtues of these terrible dance shoes that "disappeared on the foot" because of the clear plastic upper. She wore them with everything, and trust me, they did not disappear. She showed me one thing I did utilize regularly — a configuration of elastic that ran between a woman's legs in order to keep big heavy skirts in place. I dubbed it a "Whoopee Strap."

Fittings lasted full days with Liza. She would come in the early afternoon and stay till dinner. Often she would take me out with any number of friends, such as Ellen Greene and Chita Rivera. Kevyn Aucoin was also good friends with Liza and we went out a lot together. But there were also many hangers-on, secretaries and the like, posing as stylists. I went out *a lot* with Liza. We often went to small downtown bars and clubs, including one called Eighty-Eights that had a wonderful, tiny cabaret upstairs, and which would become an important location in my future. Almost always, when Liza was in the house, it was all about her. Without fail, someone would convince her to stand up and do a number. After much cajoling and more declining she'd get up on whatever tiny stage and improvise a number with the starstruck accompanist. One night I went with her to the Rainbow Room to see her sister, Lorna Luft, who I had met at one of the marathon fittings. The show was meant to be a comeback for Lorna, but that night, with Liza in the house, the show was less about watching Lorna and much more about *watching Liza watching Lorna.*

I had a lot of fun with Liza, and I learned a lot. When I won my first CFDA award in 1988 she presented it to me. Standing backstage at the Metropolitan Museum of Art auditorium, where those events used to take place, I was frantic with nerves. She turned to me:

"What's your favorite food?"

"Um. Ice cream?"

"Okay. Ice cream. What flavor?"

"Mint chocolate chip."

"Imagine yourself two hours from now, no matter what happens, even if this night is a total bust, eating a big bowl of mint chocolate chip."

When I did that I was no longer nervous: fabulous lesson number one.

Making clothes for Liza wasn't exactly easy. For one thing, she was really fidgety in fittings. I used to say fitting Liza was like fitting a goldfish. She never stopped squirming and dancing and talking while I was trying to pin something on her. She'd break into a demonstration of her new dance routine. "Then I do a double turn and *Wham! Kick!* Then I whip off the skirt!

Bam!" (Yes, I'm proud to say I made Liza more than one breakaway skirt.) Difficult as those fittings were for actually fitting the clothes, they were enormously entertaining for me and my staff.

Liza was opinionated and had a real point of view, and I learned a lot in those fittings about how to listen and then gently steer people away from their own ideas in order to help them look better. Unfortunately, Liza was surrounded by people who didn't seem to have her best interests at heart. An interchangeable group went with her everywhere. I couldn't tell who they were, and I'm pretty sure she didn't know either. On one of the nights we were alone I escorted her home after the ballet and supper. Seven or eight crazy fans awaited her in the lobby and the doorman did nothing to shield her from them. I felt obliged to stay and see her to her door, and then I realized she was eating it up, signing autographs and posing for pictures. My instinct was to protect her, but I'm not sure she really wanted protecting.

In 1992 I made her costumes for a big show at Radio City Music Hall. She committed to that show like she was Joan Crawford making *Mildred Pierce*. When we weren't in meetings about the costumes, she was calling me with notes and ideas. I

420

made her three or four beautiful things for the show, including, for her opening number, one of the most innovative dance dresses I ever made. It was nothing more than a white chiffon tank top with a really short white chiffon knife-pleated skirt attached at the waist with an exposed grosgrain ribbon. The thing that made it so fresh and revelatory was that the whole thing was embroidered with crystals in a kind of polka-dot pattern, which gave the chiffon a heft and sparkle and, best of all, when the pleats opened, the skirt moved like liquid, and you could see entirely through it. Her body was in top shape at the time. If you ask me, she never looked better.

I got particularly close to her during this period. I had a crush on Billy Stritch, who worked on that show as her arranger and pianist. I confided in Liza, who looked at me askance and set me straight right away: "Darling. He's *my* boyfriend!" I really didn't see that coming.

The miracle of Liza onstage is one thing; the greatest example of making an entrance that I have ever seen. No one else walks on the stage and owns a room that way, whether it's a tiny cabaret or Radio City Music Hall. But really, the surprise magic of Liza occurred during intermission night after night in the Radio City green room, which had been decorated with hundreds of votive candles (another nod to Halston). It would fill up with "friends" and adoring fans who were lucky enough to be admitted backstage. She would show up at the exact crucial moment every night in a glamourous, red crepe de chine kimono and greet everyone in the room, making each person feel like they were special and at the grandest, most exclusive backstage party that ever was. What I couldn't figure out was how she had that energy. She would expend as much star power in the green room during intermission as she did onstage.

In 1990 Halston died, which was a big blow to Liza. He was her best friend and had dressed her better than anyone from the very beginning. He was as much a part of her image as any of the shows or songs that came her way. I knew he was ill and had shut down his atelier, and while I was glad for the chance to work with her, I also felt conflicted because I admired him so much. Liza arranged his funeral, which took place at Alice Tully Hall. She put together a touching slide show of his life set to a melancholy, jazzy piece of movie scoring from *Midnight Cowboy* called "Fun City." She asked me to speak, which I did. The fact was I didn't know Halston and so I have no real idea why she asked me; I can only guess I was meant to represent a new generation who had been influenced by him.

That funeral had a green room to beat all green rooms. Joe Eula. Marisa Berenson. Elsa Peretti. Every socialite from Kay Graham to Nan Kempner. But no one as larger-than-life as Liza, which I think was by design. When she spoke there wasn't a dry eye in the house. After that I realized no matter what I did to befriend her, no matter what I could possibly design for her, I was merely a stand-in, someone she reluctantly accepted in place of her beloved Halston.

Though I did try my best, it was impossible for me to fully commit to the idea of being great friends with Liza. It would have been easy to be pulled into her orbit, she was so generous and smart in so many ways. Had I not been so extremely busy, perhaps our friendship could have flourished. But I surmised early on how much attention she needed, and friendship proved impossible. I'd have to give up a big part of my life, and I had no time to spare.

About twelve years later Liza met David Gest, a music executive who stepped in and ran her life into disarray for a time. Soon after they married at the Marble Collegiate

Church on Fifth Avenue and Twenty-ninth Street, with a reception and "concert" afterwards at Cipriani Wall Street. At the ceremony I sat next to Lorraine Bracco, the two of us holding hands through the madness. The guest list included everyone from Mickey Rooney to Elton John and Anthony Hopkins. Liza's best man was Michael Jackson, and her matron of honor was none other than Elizabeth Taylor, who held up the ceremony for about an hour as we waited for her shoes, which she'd left at the hotel. I actually thought it was a ruse, a plan to halt the proceedings long enough for Liza to come to her senses. No one thought this wedding was a good idea. But on it went.

If the vows weren't crazy enough — David Gest swearing to love Liza; Liza swearing to take it "one day at a time" — the party was crazier than anyone could have dreamed. There were musical acts ranging from the Doobie Brothers to Andy Williams. I barely saw Liza that night to say hello, but I did watch her clothing changes — at least four that I can remember. There was one crazy dress after another, and I hoped no one mistook any of them for mine. Mad as it was, hideous as the outcome was, it was one of the more memorable nights of my life, and I still have a heart-shaped candy box embossed with Liza and David's initials, which was given out at the end of the night. I sometimes think of how perplexed my heirs will be when they go through my ephemera fifty years from now and find that box.

Later that year there was a reality show that VH1 had green-lighted about Liza's life with David. A huge dinner was assembled at her apartment, catered by Sylvia's Restaurant in Harlem, one of Liza's favorite places, with a *casual* "living room concert" slated for after dinner. Sandra Bernhard and I were dates. We arrived at dinner along with other celebrities, movie stars, writers, and artists — everyone from Ray Charles to Dominick Dunne and Liz Smith. After dinner Luther Vandross did a number. Then Ray Charles accompanied Sandra singing "Come Rain or Come Shine." Then Beyoncé Knowles did a number. (This was when she had a last name. She was just breaking away from Destiny's Child, and I confess I still had not heard of her. I noted in my journal what huge star quality "this newcomer" had. I also noted the very questionable dresses they all had on, including Liza, which was the work of Beyoncé's mother, Tina Knowles, who was making a dubious name for herself as a couturier.)

Finally Liza appeared and began singing, and just as she was belting out the middle chorus of "But the World Goes 'Round," some TV producer decided to shut the entire show down. Right in the middle of Liza's big number, this nondescript man walked up to her, thanked her curtly, and literally directed the cameras to stop taping. David lost his cool and berated the executive there on the spot. With little traces of foam in the corners of his mouth he screamed: "The lady is in the middle of a number! Do you know who you just shut down?" It was the one supportive thing David Gest ever did for Liza, at least that I could see.

Worse than anything was what he did to her apartment, where I had been many times and which I admired to no end. Halston had decorated it in the 1970s, and it was a vast minimal space of white marble, with Warhols of Judy, Vincente, and Liza side by side in the dining room. There was no furniture other than what was absolutely necessary. It was done in a simple, original, compelling way. Liza's bedroom was huge and entirely carpeted and wallpapered in red velvet. When David moved in, he reversed the minimal grandeur of the place with all kinds of fake boiserie and faux

426

antiques and stacked the walls with his gold records. More than any reality-show disaster, it made me so sad to think of that wonderful Halston interior, gone forever.

23

The Sunday before my first fashion show, my cousin Gail got married at the Pierre hotel. The wedding was a family event that I couldn't miss, and coming as it did only nights before my first collection, suffice it to say, it was a total pain in the ass.

In those days Bill Blass showed on Mondays at the Pierre, and he was in the next ballroom that Sunday making preparations for the following morning. My mother and I spotted him in the lobby, and my mother walked up and introduced herself.

"My name is Sarah Mizrahi," she said. Blass nodded. "And my son is Isaac Mizrahi. Have you heard of him?"

My heart sank.

"No," Blass said. He was so polite.

"You will very soon," she said, not a hint of irony in her voice.

Embarrassed as I was by my mother's smack talk, it felt prescient in some way.

Once I did become known, Mr. Blass was quick to remind me of that story any time we saw each other.

There were times in my career when I would doubt myself — not my talent, but my abilities to make something out of my business. Many times after I started my label I felt really close to going out of business, which seemed to happen so frequently to so many young designers. I whined regularly to my mother on the telephone. Finally, one day she halted me midsentence and let a beat of dead air fill the receiver before saying in her sharpest voice, just shy of a scream: "You are *not* David Cameron. You are *not* Stephen Sprouse. *You* are Isaac Mizrahi!"

I made up my mind after one of those conversations: One day that fall I came to work and said, "Let's put on a fashion show." A first fashion show is the beginning of everything. It was three times more laborious than any show I ever did after — not the actual physical labor — which was definitely challenging, but the intellectual effort. I was presenting the concept of who I was to the world. And who I wanted to become. It was my chance to introduce myself in a political and social way as much as in a design way. The venue, the models, the accessories, the music, were as important as the clothes. So, like Judy Garland and Mickey Rooney in a barn, Annica and I rolled up our sleeves and went to work. We did nothing else but make clothes that entire winter, except for the occasional sitting at Avedon or visit from Liza.

I worked for months on the color story for that collection. I ordered fabrics from all the mills, mostly Italian, I had worked with at Perry Ellis and Calvin Klein. I submitted swatches of everything from ribbons to candy wrappers, and pored over lab dips, which the houses sent me for approval before they dyed the fabrics. That whole Christmas break I edited and reedited those two pages of swatches till they were a pulsating, vibrant story of pure color. Once those pages were right, the whole thing was right. The colors were organized thus: On the warm end, the reds and oranges and pinks would work randomly together. On the cool end, all the blues and greens worked together. Yellow was the swing color that paired with everything. Mentions in the press after the collection were always about "neons" and "brights," but in fact there were no neons and as many dark and pastel colors as there were bright ones.

I asked Manolo Blahnik to make his own version of Hush Puppies. He burst out laughing, which was my first clue that I was on to something. (When he showed me the prototype a few weeks later, I knew it would create a sensation). All of the models I had worked with in my years as an assistant volunteered to do the show in exchange for clothing. I had some more established models like Dalma and Anna Bayle, two of the great runway stars at the time, and others who were just emerging, like Linda Evangelista and Christy Turlington. (This was way before the word "supermodel" was listed in the *OED*.)

The day of the show there were a few last-minute nail-biters. My favorite chiffon jumpsuit had to be remade because it had been mistakenly shortened to the calf. All the furs from the furrier were on a truck that seemed to be lost. There weren't enough shoes to go around, and there was a long list of "shoe swaps" (meaning models would have to pass off shoes to each other after they walked the runway), which is every designer's nightmare. A whole group of the girls coming from their last booking (the Giorgio di Sant'Angelo show) were very late to arrive and were still in the makeup and hair from the previous show, which took longer to remove than it did to apply the hair and makeup for my show. (This foreshadowed something that would happen every season for the rest of my life.)

The guest list and the seating were being overseen by Nina Santisi, with whom I had developed a close friendship since my Perry Ellis days. She was instrumental in co-ordinating the invitations and creating the seating chart while she was still working as an editor at *Glamour* magazine. She eventually worked with me full time and became an even closer friend. She knew of my every move and gave me some of the best advice I ever got. Nina always veers to the high road. There was a fashion critic who wrote something not so praiseful about my second collection, the only dissenting voice, and it was Nina who talked me off the ledge. From then on that editor was placed in the front row, the best seat in the house, and we never heard anything but praise from that party again.

On the big day, to my complete surprise, everyone we invited showed up to the slightly bigger loft I'd rented upstairs from my loft. I had erected a small *U*-shaped runway there, and the only thing separating the audience from the small, narrow models' changing spot in the hall was a thin, black curtain. Carrie Donovan, fashion editor for the *New York Times Magazine* came. So did Bernadine Morris, the chief fashion critic from *The New York Times*. Polly Mellen and Jade Hobson from *Vogue* attended. John Fairchild and Patrick McCarthy who ran *Women's Wear Daily* came, and with them Bridget Foley, who has since become an executive editor. My friends Manolo Blahnik and his business partner George Malkemus came with André Leon Talley to cheer me on. Wendy Goodman from *New York* magazine. Elsa Klensch, who reported on fashion for CNN. Dawn Mello from Bergdorf Goodman. Elizabeth Saltzman came with her mother, Ellin Saltzman, who ran Saks Fifth Avenue. Kal Ruttenstein from Bloomingdale's. Even Grace Mirabella came. Somehow they all thought it an important enough show to go all the way to SoHo to attend.

My mother came and sat in the front row. Until that moment she hadn't fully grasped what was going on in all those months of preparation. I think she was in a daze for the entire twenty-minute show.

As was I.

The truth is, I had no idea what was going on in the front of the house. I was so focused on the clothes and the girls, checking my lists, making last-minute edits, tying hush puppies and sashes. Finally the music started and the lights came up and the first girls were on the runway, almost as though in a dream — a beautiful, meaningful dream. The idea was to introduce color as the main theme for the season — also for the rest of my career. So I began the show with about twenty passages of grey, camel, brown, navy, and black. Neutrals. Day clothes luxuriating in sportiness. I designed three versions of a blanket with sleeves — one in alpaca reversible to satin, one in double-faced wool knit edged in suede, and one in mink. In the following passages I showed things like business attire or luncheon suits being handled like lumberjack clothes one would wear in a cabin in Vermont. Dressy as you might look, you're still very casual in a singularly American way.

Midway through the show the music got pumped up and the lights got brighter, and out came Linda Evangelista, in a big, bright-orange coat shaped like a tribal robe, worn with a marigold-striped, wide-legged wool jersey, empire jumpsuit, and lipstick-red suede Hush Puppies. The ensemble was called "Orange Orange," as in the Kool-Aid flavor. Next was a short, bright red, double-breasted swing coat on Christy Turlington, worn with bright-pink tights and rust suede hush puppies. That was called "Sally Tomato" for a character in *Breakfast at Tiffany's*. After that it was only a story about color. Acid colors mixed with pastels and earth tones. Vermont cabin on acid. Dresses and jumpsuits and tea-length ball gowns that looked like sweatshirts, and parkas in a jumble of color, all worn with the elegant hush puppies.

I was flying in an open airplane or going 150 miles an hour in a convertible — a feeling of great elation accompanied by terrible dread. Too late to change anything, loud music dictating the tone, models awaiting cues. The designs I'd been jealously guarding yanked from my hands and thrown into a magnificent disorder. By the end of that show I had a feeling of total exhaustion and a strange sense of bitterness. Before I made my appearance on the runway, Veronica Webb kissed me and whispered in my ear, "You're the new king of New York." I smiled at her, thinking she was saying something cute to ease the pain of my epic failure. It was a shock when I came out onto the runway and the crowd leapt to its feet in applause. I thought it was some sort of joke.

Sarah Haddad had a prescient dream the

night before that show. She described it as a stampede of people running up the stairs to our little Greene Street studio. After that collection it did indeed feel like a mad rush of editors and buyers coming at me up those stairs. The day after the collection a huge photo and a rave review appeared on the cover of *Women's Wear Daily*. Manolo and André Leon Talley took me to lunch at La Grenouille and toasted to my success as others in the restaurant looked on, pointing and gossiping. There was also a great review in the *New York Times,* the first line of which said something like "Remember the name Isaac Mizrahi." And most of the national fashion pages had glowing reviews of the show. Like magic, in the course of one day, everything changed. Back-to-back appointments with every major retailer. Photo shoots for days.

And they photographed me. I never thought about being a subject in that way. I hadn't thought about a public persona because I was so busy working on the collection. It never dawned on me to change anything about my appearance, to change the way I dressed, or to make something up for the sake of a bigger, better public image. I thought who I was, what I wore when caught off my guard, was much more interesting than anything I could have planned. Also I felt that my life, every thought I had, every gesture I made, was authentic. If someone were to find fault with that I could not hold myself responsible. There was no lying. No additions. No making things up.

Vogue did a big story about my fall collection, styled by Polly Mellen and photographed by Irving Penn, another of my personal fashion gods. I got the cover of *W* a few times, including the month following the show. It was a picture of Dalma wearing the "Orange Orange" ensemble, with me lying at her feet. When I saw the picture I thought how fortuitous it was that I happened to be wearing a canary-yellow blazer and how great it looked with the colors of the ensemble being photographed. I saw myself as a kind of fashion elf. I kept my head down unless I was asked, but then I was not shy to express myself and explain my work. Within a week Wendy Goodman (who has become a dear friend) did a six-page story about the collection in *New York* magazine and that same year, *New York* did a career-making story about me with a long exposé-style interview. I was perceived as an iconoclast, and from that moment on I was dubbed "the bad boy of fashion," something I was unable to shake, even well after my boyhood. I was "hip and cool" because my studio was downtown. But I'm not, nor have I ever been, hip and cool. At least not the way I see it. If I did collections inspired by homegirls or bag ladies it was not to be hip and cool. It was actually the opposite. It was to bring a kind of formal structure, a kind of glory to those subjects. The hip-and-cool thing was an expectation I had no intention of fulfilling.

The *New York* article, which was published sometime in 1988, made clear that I was gay. I spoke about it openly and was thrilled they had included the fact. Since I'd come out those years before I felt it was my duty to change whatever perception I could around the subject, if for no other reason than to make it easier for kids who were struggling as I had. But it was a very different time, and most established fashion designers weren't out. It was a time when people were being outed against their will, and some actually thought it was bad taste to admit such a thing in so public a way. Within a few weeks I ran into my friend Paul Wilmot, whom I'd worked with at Calvin Klein, where he was head of PR and marketing. He put his hands on my shoulders consolingly and said about being outed, "Darling, I'm so sorry for you. . . ."

I didn't realize there was anything terribly scandalous going on, although I was aware of a few weeks of radio silence from Brooklyn. Of the zero time I spent thinking in advance of what I might say in an interview, I had already vowed to myself that if anyone was interested in asking me, I would proudly tell the truth about being gay even if it meant my downfall — which some people really thought was a risk at that time. Truthfully I was too busy to hide anything, especially anything I felt was as irrelevant to my work as my sexual preference. It was a moment I could feel something was changing, and eventually the change came to pass. I knew the world could not remain as homophobic as it was, and I was right.

Four or five years later there was another cover of *New York,* a picture of k.d. lang with the headline "Lesbian Chic." By chance I saw Paul Wilmot that week at a cocktail party, and I said to him, "See, darling? I was a lesbian way before k.d. lang."

This should have been a heady time for me. If my life were a Hollywood musical, this would be the big splashy finale where I — played by Eleanor Powell — make it into the big time. Everything seemed to be going my way. It took the *New York Times* years

439

to acknowledge a young designer and review them like one of the establishment, but by the time my third collection walked the runway, I was being reviewed by the main critic, Bernadine Morris, alongside the likes of Calvin Klein and Bill Blass. And I was at the top of every fashion page of every major newspaper worldwide.

I was getting to know all the editors and writers as well as some of the more important fashion-business figures. I was oblivious, really, to the ideas of how to raise money, and though I worried about it constantly, I took no real actions to forge any financial partnership. The money Sarah and I put in was long gone, and we had interim financing from friends of Sarah's, one of whom was Jack Dushey, the original owner of Studio 54, and the other was Haim Dabah, owner of Gitano jeans, to whom I had sold sketches as a teenager.

Over the next few years my fashion shows became *the* shows to attend. There were masses of major fashion editorials every month. "Supermodel" was becoming an established word to describe the beautiful, powerful women who seemed to have "it": the perfect combination of star power and the ability to recede enough for the clothes to take center stage. Christy Turlington,

Linda Evangelista, and Naomi Campbell. Cindy Crawford and Claudia Schiffer were maybe even too super — too busy and handsomely paid — to be considered supermodels. I guess they were superdupermodels. It was a defining moment that was sometimes really scary because so much depended on supermodels' participation. Naomi, beautiful and clever as she is, never really had a sense of urgency and was late most of the time. André Leon Talley, who made his presence in my world heavily felt for about two years, and thereafter would occasionally grace us with a visit backstage, would precede Naomi, proclaiming, "Naomi will, in fact, be here today!" I stood by, thinking about how I had cast her in all my favorite looks and of the hours of fittings I'd completed. *Naomi is, in fact, coming! How lucky for me!* I would bite my nails off waiting for her car, or for Christy's flight to land. They flew all over the world on a daily basis. Twice a week to Paris or London or Milan, and sometimes even more exotic locations. Linda seemed to like my clothes a lot, especially my shoes, and was never shy about ordering things. When we asked her where to ship them she'd say: "Just send them to the Air France Concorde lounge, they'll find me."

These girls knew what they were looking at. They knew everything that was going on in every corner of the fashion world, which I intentionally ignored. From the day I started working professionally in the fashion business, I developed a strong aversion to fashion magazines. There was no way for me to look at them without feeling either defeated, or overlooked, or competitive, or self-congratulatory. I preferred to ignore magazines and instead I relied on what I saw on the streets, coupled with information provided by my staff and these super-girls with their incredible senses of style. The more they liked what they saw in the fittings, the more I knew I was onto something.

I used to joke that I could leave Veronica Webb in a room all by herself and she could conduct the fitting without me. Once I was pondering whether or not to include a stack of bracelets with an ensemble. "With the bracelets or without?" I asked.

Veronica turned to me. "Can you sell the bracelets? Are they available for sale?"

I said, "Yes."

"Then *with bracelets!*" she said.

Veronica has been a great friend since she was first discovered. At the time I was working at Calvin Klein. It always seemed like she was smarter, more complicated, more interesting than most other models. To me, she was the perfect woman. That face and that body, of course — every woman should be so blessed. But also, she read books. She wrote articles. She attended art openings and the theatre. She had the sweetest apartment on University Place and a dachshund named Hercules. She was as discreet as she was flamboyant. And she gave of her time so generously and believed in me — encouragement I needed. We have almost exactly the same taste — almost exactly the same style aspirations. We're both skeptical, we both like irony and silver linings. We both like color. I used to hear her voice in my head, advising me when I was sketching, and before I could ask myself, *What would Veronica do?,* the imaginary Veronica would whisper, "Make that one purple. Show that dress on Carla Bruni. Sketch that with a flat riding boot." She was my way into women, and I observed her very closely, bordering on stalking, like I was observing a facet of my own personality attached to a face and body I wish I had. She'd fly back and forth from Europe to New York wearing clothes she'd style together flawlessly, effortlessly. A short, pleated, empire-waist dress of mine with Doc Martens boots from Chanel and a vintage 1950s rhinestone cowboy jacket. She'd put things together better than literally any stylist. Linda also had a wicked sense of humor and could really put clothes together, but in Linda there was a haughtiness I couldn't pierce. Veronica had a human side. She was able to observe others while they were observing her, which some of the other girls just couldn't do.

I was traveling all over the world, too, and I had nothing but great prospects for the future. Ironically, after my first three collections, I started to feel engulfed and overtaken. When I look back on those early days in the fashion business, I think of them as some of the best days of my life — exhilarating, vital. But in actuality I was white-knuckling it. I was nervous to the point of hysterics at all times. The faster and harder the signs of success came, the more I worried, even lamented. I never felt deserving of such acclaim. And though I didn't question my ability to have ideas for clothes or stage fabulous fashion shows, I knew I wasn't good at business and money matters. I would lie awake nights wondering when everything would just cave in. My moods swung from extreme to extreme. I was king of New York one minute and captain of a rudderless, sinking ship the next. I kept wondering about my decision to give up show business. The truth became more evident as I got deeper into it: The garment business is every bit as, if not more, treacherous and tentative than show business. I'd heard from others that "you're only as good as your last collection," and that was ringing truer every day. What I thought was going to be a steady, secure climb was turning into a rather slippery slope.

24

Insecurity really hangs around. "Success" didn't magically render my past irrelevant. My mother succumbed to her afternoon "naps" in my childhood and I often give in to depression, too. I think of myself as an optimist — a trait, ironically, I also inherited from my mother. I eventually see the silver lining. But no matter how wonderful things are going a lot of dark thinking manages to take hold, and it's been that way for as long as I can remember. I strive for an unattainable perfection while awaiting catastrophe. I've done a very good job sublimating this awful pessimism I live with. I've consulted with shrinks and psychics my whole life, in order to sufficiently dispel the black cloud that follows me around. It's a kind of anxiety, which I think is pretty common among artists who can't see the virtues of their own work. The more I succeed the more I worry about failure. And it's not a bad thing. It might be said that — for better or worse — this bleakness is the greater half of the force that propels me forward.

The harder I worked at making beautiful clothes for beautiful people, the more I saw myself as a fat, ugly person. In a way I think that was a blessing. It's what made it possible to be objective about beauty — always serving it, standing on the outside of it looking in. I look at pictures of myself from that time and notice how thin I was. But I remember how fat I felt. And how fat I was able to make myself look. I wore unflattering clothes: crazy high-waisted pants that I made myself that would make anyone but Fred Astaire look fat, and a bandana as a headband. It was viewed as my quirky personal style, but friends, like Elizabeth Saltzman, asked me again and again why I dressed like "an old man." It was a question I couldn't answer. I refused to see myself as the subject of fashion — I could only see myself as the author of it. To a great extent I was freaked out about being noticed and this was my way of making a joke of myself before anyone else could. So I kept to myself and worked harder, tolerating no distractions. My blind ambition was such that I was able to deny any other part of my life that I couldn't understand.

In those early days I was adjusting to the intrusions on my privacy and my sense of fairness. Journalists who knew me personally and knew how much my mother was an inspiration to me were calling to interview her, which blurred the lines between my life and my business. It also fed my paranoia. Routine things any other businessman might have to submit to felt invasive and unjust. For instance: The first time I had to submit to a physical and a blood test from a bank that was basing a huge cash loan on the results, which was followed by two weeks of horror as I waited for the AIDS test to come back negative — all while under the scrutiny of a bank board, not to mention my entire company.

I was also grappling with the loss of control that occurs any time you're not making every single garment yourself. Buyers took me to task for early quality discrepancies, things I was even more aware of than they were but felt helpless to control. My mother would call and say, "I was at Bergdorf's today and there was a dress with the buttons falling off." That sort of thing was never helpful; it only made me feel more crazy.

At the same time I was being written about in gossip columns for the first time, which was unnerving. One day Nina approached me holding the *New York Post,* giggling over an item about me being sighted at a gym the day before, a place I had never been, wearing a leopard-print spandex bodysuit. That was my first-ever mention on "Page Six" and the beginning of my understanding of how careless the gossip press was and how impossible it was to control. It took many years till I was able to appreciate it as a kind of entertaining joke, and to this day I'm still sensitive about appearing in columns.

About a week before my third Spring collection I was invited to lunch by John Fairchild and even though I understood the implications of this lunch, I was up to my eyeballs in work and scared that if I took any time away from the collection I might not finish in time. Nina reiterated that this was more than an invitation; it was a kind of initiation into the fashion tribe, which I could not put off or pass on, so I accepted. Nan Kempner and Pat Buckley, two of the great socialites of the day, whom I had never met, were surprise guests for this, my first official John Fairchild lunch at the old Four Seasons restaurant. A month prior, at another dinner party, I was introduced to someone called Robert Couturier, another

449

star in the style firmament, and we became fast friends. (He's become a kind of brother over the years.) At one point, he walked into the restaurant that day and I excused myself politely in order to say hi, but when I returned to the table a few minutes later, Mrs. Kempner was fidgeting nervously with her cigarette, Mrs. Buckley's mien had turned to ice, and Fairchild was giving me the gimlet eye. I couldn't figure out what had happened.

The fashion show the following week was a smash hit, received glowingly by everyone except *Women's Wear Daily.* The tepid review ran on the cover with a headline that read: "Isaac Tries Too Hard." At first I took the review at face value: They didn't like the collection and that was that. Never one to linger over reviews, I let it go. (One of the biggest ironies about the movie *Unzipped,* a documentary about me made in 1996, is that it focuses the entire plot around my seeming obsession with reviews. In reality I only care about reviews as a means of selling things. I don't think I ever read a criticism of my clothing that actually affected me one way or the other. But bad reviews can kill your business, something I was learning the hard way.) Nina and I pieced together the events of the preceding weeks and we figured out that Fairchild and the ladies had been offended at lunch, the headline, the slap-on-the wrist review conveying a strong message: Fairchild and his pals are omnipotent, paying attention to anyone else when in the royal presence will result in some kind of penalty.

After a season or two, Fairchild came around and I made friends with Mrs. Buckley and Mrs. Kempner. But I couldn't believe anyone would do such a thing, play with a career, evaluate someone's work based on a personal whim like that.

If I had issues adjusting to the harshness of the limelight, my mother was in her full glory. She was the mother of the "bad boy of fashion." In the Sephardic community the red carpet was rolled out for her everywhere she went. She would say, "You wouldn't believe the way I'm treated. Like a queen!" It made me fume. The very same people who made my childhood so unbearable — and who had also made my mother's life so hard those early years, forced to watch my torment — were now showering her with public admiration. Now that I was a star they were only too eager to claim me as one of them. The phone rang off the hook with offers from Sephardic companies who thought they had an advantage in licensing deals when in reality it was the opposite. When I went out in public, if someone stopped me and asked if I was Syrian-Jewish, I'd answer with a scowl.

When my mother and I went out people would stop me and ask for autographs, which she ate up. She would say, "I always knew you'd be great. Someday you're going to be invited to the White House and Buckingham Palace." But her confidence did little to boost my own. The more she kvelled, the more my spirits plummeted. Her presence at my fashion shows only added to my worries. I was always terrified that she would unwittingly say something to the press that might explode in our faces.

Once, early on, she made a remark in a joint interview we did that she didn't realize would get reprinted. It was something about how she didn't expect me to have such a broad success, which was said innocently. But the remark was pulled out of context and turned on its head, and she was made to seem unsupportive. Finally I was justified in my warnings to her about talking to the press, and I let her come to the conclusion that it was in *her* best interests (not to mention mine) that she be kept far away from it.

I needn't have worried about my mother so much, because everyone seemed to love her. She was in and out of my studio regularly, and when she came to fittings she immediately charmed everyone in the room, including celebrities, supermodels, artists. My staff doted on her every whim. If she wanted a piece from the collection, there were three people who saw that the order was executed.

That spring I was on the rue Cambon passing the great original Chanel store when I saw in the window the most fabulous cuff, covered with fake pearls, and thought how much my mother would adore it. I went in thinking, *How expensive could this be? Twelve hundred? Fifteen hundred?* When the saleslady priced it at thirty-five hundred dollars I thanked her and sheepishly backed away. A few weeks later I saw Christy Turlington at the Met ball wearing the same cuff. Christy always goes out of her way to be sweet. After hearing the story she whipped the cuff off her wrist and demanded I give it to my mother, whom she'd met a few times at my studio, saying, "Karl gave it to me and I will never wear it again. I would love to think of your mother having it!"

My mother came to my fashion shows

religiously. She wouldn't miss one. She would plan her travel schedule around the dates, and she rewatches the shows on VHS tapes to this day. More than seeing herself as an advisor, she saw my interest in clothes as her genetic gift to me, like my full head of hair. She viewed my career ascent as an extension of her own life, above and beyond living vicariously through me. Around my fifth or sixth collection, she came backstage glowing and proclaimed, as though she were Diana Vreeland herself: "This time, dear boy, you left me in the dust!"

As long as I was working, I was able to keep my anxiety relatively under control. So I worked and worked with laser focus all day. Then suddenly the day would be over and everyone would leave and I would feel especially lonely and very scared of the emptiness. The more "success" I had, the more surreal it felt and the less I connected to anything outside of work. The more people I hired, the more terrifying it was having all that responsibility. And I didn't feel right talking about it because I was afraid saying anything would undermine people's confidence in me and suggest I was unable to deal with the pressures of success. I also worried about the level of sympathy my complaints would yield. I mean — talking about how difficult it is being a media darling and making clothes for rich, famous people could easily make me sound like a complete asshole. So I kept it to myself.

One night I was dining with Avedon in his great kitchen. I confided in him about this increasing emotional turmoil, and he practically demanded that I get back into therapy. He spoke proudly of the fact that he was in analysis four or five times a week. I thought, *If I could afford to be in analysis four times a week, I wouldn't need it.* But I knew he was right. It had been five or six years since I'd been in therapy, a record for me, and if there ever was a time I needed it, it was then.

My first shrink, Dr. Mossey, helped me get through yeshiva. And Dr. Kahn guided me through my late teenage years and helped me come out. So I took Dick's advice and started seeing a shrink again, and it helped. But what helped me more than anything were my constant consultations with various astrologers, tarot card readers, numerologists, mediums, and psychics. When you consider it's part of a fashion designer's job description to predict what everyone's going to want to wear, it's not so far-fetched that we sometimes get a kick out of listening to others' predictions. The first reading I ever had was when I was eighteen. The psychic's name was Guy Culver. I called him Madam Guy and we dated for a short time. The first thing he asked at the reading was, "Why did you leave show business?" I didn't really consider the weight of the question, because I'd convinced myself that I was doing the right thing. But the more I tried to justify it, the less Guy believed me. He said, "If by the time you're thirty you don't pursue a career in show business, it will pursue you."

The greatest advisor of my life was an astrologer named Maria Napoli. I started seeing her also when I was eighteen, a little after I had my first readings with Guy. She was *astrologer to the fashion stars*. She read for Donna Karan and her entire staff. She read for Norma Kamali. She read for Perry Ellis and everyone in that studio, which is what led me to her. I saw Maria religiously, at least three times a year, and only recently did she stop due to illness. I always felt happy when I left a reading with Maria. She could turn bad news into a win. Six months before my father died she mentioned that I'd experience one of the great nadirs of my life, but that it would ultimately be a breakthrough for me, and on the other side of the sadness would be great self-awareness. I guess in psychic terms, you'd call that a good bedside manner.

She lived at the same apartment building on West Seventy-eighth Street for the entire thirty-five years I consulted with her. Her living room had one shaded window facing a brick wall and was packed with stuff. Furniture. All kinds of pillows and throws. Bookshelves so laden with old books and so embedded in the space they felt like structural elements. Ratty old shoe boxes filled with stuff, and two or three Hermès Kelly bags mixed in with the chaos. Also mixed in were shopping bags from Manolo Blahnik, Bergdorf Goodman, little bags from various tea shops (Maria loves tea) filled with scarves, papers, cans of food, half-filled notebooks. I could barely fit through the door, which wouldn't open all the way because of the piles of books and papers. I'd step gingerly through the sea of stuff to the one seat in the room that wasn't piled with folders, scraps, pamphlets. It was opposite where she sat at a small, round table covered with a collection of crystals and half-burned candles that had never been dusted. Among the mess was a little Maltese named Fluffy, who had a high-pitched yelp and would bark for about ten minutes when you first entered, and whom she lovingly referred to as "Demon from hell." When Fluffy died she immediately replaced him with Fluffy II, who looked and sounded exactly like Fluffy, with slightly worse manners. Both dogs seemed to know the exact time in the session to suddenly yap — a terrifying jolt, usually in the most engrossing part of the reading.

After about fifteen minutes of Maria opining as to who made the best tuna salad in the city and where the best sample sales had been that week, finally the reading would begin. She had a Panasonic cassette tape player that she'd use to record the readings, and the first thing you'd do when you got there was hand her the cassette tape you brought. If the reading led to something particularly searing or gossipy she'd pause the tape and resume after the subject was fully discussed. Toward the end of the time I saw her, cassette tapes were more and more difficult to find, and yet I persevered. I have so many of these tapes from Maria — for that matter, I have recordings of all the readings I've had my entire life, all dutifully marked with dates and stored in chronological order in a huge box. The irony is that as fastidious as I was about capturing the readings, I never once listened to any of those tapes.

Of course, there are psychics who come highly recommended and who just stink. Early on in my career the photographer Bruce Weber sent me to a woman who told me I did "everything wrong" and that she "couldn't help me — no one could." I still hear those words ringing in my head today, any time I want to believe my life is a failure. There was a guy in LA who worked with past lives who said to me, "If anyone asks who taught you to play the piano, tell them Mozart." Another was a Kabbalistic astrologer, a *rebbetzen* living in Queens. She told me I was "going to meet a nice Jewish girl and have a son and a daughter and make your mother very happy. You were born to study the Kabbala, and you were born to support the Kabbala Center. That'll be two hundred and fifty dollars. Thank you."

Once, in my midthirties, a friend offered to read my tarot cards. We sat on the floor of the loft he was living in temporarily. It was sunny and hot in the apartment even though it was freezing cold and wintery outside. For the reading he used a strange deck that I didn't recognize — a Mexican tarot deck, his specialty. I threw the cards and he predicted a lot of very relevant things. At the end he pointed to a card that, like many of the Mexican cards, I had never seen before. According to him, it was the resolution, the fate card. It wasn't part of a suit like rods or cups. It didn't seem to have a moon or sun or any planetary attribute. It was a picture of a man on a stage, a minstrel dandy in a cutaway coat, straw boater, spats, holding a cane, wearing blackface makeup. He was singing and dancing. My friend turned to me and said: "You're in for big surprises. No matter what you think about your future, you're going back on the stage. This card. This is your destiny."

25

A great feature of my first tiny apartment was that the door to the bathroom had a full-length mirror, and by chance I discovered that I could pivot it so that it reflected the TV and I could sit in the tub and watch my beloved Sony Trinitron in mirror image. One of my favorite things was watching *Jeopardy!* while soaking in the tub, the TV on mute, reading the clues backwards, and answering in the form of a question.

I had returned from a trunk show in Chicago late one day and was snuggled in my tub, the evening news on TV, awaiting *Jeopardy!,* when suddenly Grace Mirabella's picture appeared on TV backwards. Twitter wasn't a gleam in the eye yet, news in those days didn't break in dribs and drabs, it broke all at once, like a big crystal punch bowl hitting the living room floor, which is what this felt like. Grace was the editor of *Vogue* for seventeen years and a supporter and a friend. I jumped out of the tub, and turned on the sound in time to hear that she'd been fired from *Vogue*. Rumors had been circulating that Mirabella was not long for the job, people had bets out that any number of people, including Jade Hobson and Rochelle Udell, would replace her, each with a hundred obvious reasons to succeed to the position. But the big surprise was that Anna Wintour was chosen as her replacement.

I had first met Anna about eight years earlier when she worked at *New York* magazine. My friend Peter won designer of the year at Parsons, and she came up to Perry Ellis to interview me about him. When she took the job at *Vogue* I was afraid she would see me as an invention of Grace Mirabella's and want nothing to do with me. But after a few months she came to my studio for a preview of the fall season, which I was about to show. I was nervous but she seemed to be nervous, too, which was a surprise. This was someone who was already being portrayed as an Ice Queen in the press.

She always came for previews very early in the mornings because she lives on the border of Greenwich Village and SoHo, two blocks away from my studio, and it was a logical start to her day. Dawn Brown, a young woman who worked for me in public relations, was charged with filling platters with gorgeous baked things from epicurean bakeries I would specify, and then laying them out for Anna and her accompanying editors. The platters would go untouched — none of them, especially Anna, was too big on breakfast.

That first morning Anna arrived at least fifteen minutes early and without a word of apology, as though it was something to be expected. She smiled a lot that morning. In those days she smiled and laughed and even took her legendary dark sunglasses off from time to time. She asked about my family, about movies I liked and books I was reading. After the third or fourth meeting she started asking me about my love life and was setting me up on dates. It seemed our chatter was never about fashion, it was friendly. Her opinion began to matter in my life as much as in my work, and she was the most important presence at my shows. I can remember being backstage my entire career, in the scrum of it, dressing girls, tweaking, retying, rebuckling but, more important, checking with Nina, who was checking with Anna's people about her ETA. When Anna sat, the show started.

She invited me to her house for dinners,

and at first I wasn't sure whether they were social or something else. I'd arrive and usually there was a pretty girl standing at the door in a small black dress with high heels and a clipboard. Over time there were more and more of these dinners, which defined themselves as a sort of salon — a changeable Algonquin roundtable of moderns from diverse fields. Designers were there to meet writers, politicians, artists. Anna made this effort to integrate fashion and make it feel less insular. Often after dinner she would initiate a conversation among the three or four tables in her dining room. Joan Didion. Oscar de la Renta. Jay McInerney. Nora Ephron. Sarah Jessica Parker. Valentino. Salman Rushdie. Charlie Rose. George Clooney. Mixed in with new society girls who were being ushered into *Vogue.* Lauren du-Pont and Aerin Lauder. I sat next to people as diverse as Judy Peabody, Robert Downey Jr., Dr. Mathilde Krim, and Marianne Faithfull. One night I sat next to Irving Penn, way before he took my picture. (Anna commissioned the photo for *Vogue,* and he sent me a print. For all the years I worked with Avedon, I couldn't even arrange to *buy* a print of the *New Yorker* portrait he did of me.) Mr. Penn (who, unlike Dick, did not answer to Irving or Irv, only Mr. Penn) and

I discovered we lived a block away from each other in the Village, and we walked home together after those dinners on several occasions. He started calling me Maestro, and I imagined it was because he either couldn't remember my name or he called everyone that.

One night the new First Lady, Hillary Clinton, was Anna's guest of honor. After dinner Mrs. Clinton took all kinds of serious questions about the intentions of the coming administration — topics from health care to the Middle East. She had just finished an earnest answer about the future of the school system, when I called out: "But what the hell are you going to wear?" Hillary laughed and the room relaxed. Anna loved that, I think.

Among this changeable feast of power and society Anna mixed in her favorite people, like socialites Anne McNally and landscape designer Miranda Brooks. Anna's husband at the time, Dr. David Shaffer, was always around, too, and eventually it became almost familial — these were people I expected to see once every two or three months at dinner. I saw Anna regularly for lunches, preview meetings, or at galas, where I was often seated next to her — including a number of times at the Met ball, which was becoming an increasingly important item on her agenda. Two weeks after 9/11 there was a gala that had been planned for New Yorkers for Children, another of her then causes, at Cipriani 42nd Street. There was a fear that no one would show up, afraid of the physical dangers, not to mention the implications of being seen in public after such a devastation. Anna used the event as a kind of social call to arms. She didn't tolerate cancellations from her editors, who were justifiably afraid to fly to the European collections, and she didn't tolerate cowardice from people who were cancelling on her dinner that night. Her office made special calls to guests; I was informed that I was coming and sitting next to her. And it was a great night. Everyone showed up. Streisand was there and the mayor made an appearance, and it was a huge first step in the city's social recovery.

Each month a new issue of the magazine would come, hand delivered from Anna with a note on her personal stationery stuck in the middle: "Isaac, I hope you like your pages." or "Congratulations, darling, I hope you love your cover" scribbled in her handwriting, which looks like an impatient child's. I saved every one of those notes somewhere. But more than anything I waited after each collection to get Anna's list of the clothes she wanted for herself. Buying pieces from the collection was her greatest compliment to me. She loved color. And anything with fur trim. She wore a brown suede embroidered cocktail dress with fringe more than once, and there was a black sequin parka that she wore regularly and was photographed in several times. Nothing made me feel as right about my life as Anna's personal approval.

I'd accompany her to events, like a dinner to raise money for suicide awareness, and another that helped victims of domestic abuse among so many other galas. She enlisted me to emcee the first *Vogue* Awards in 1995. As charitable and ambitious as she is, she's impatient with long, boring speeches, which was always a bonus. If you were her date or you sat at her table at one of the many galas, you were in and out in under ninety minutes.

She could be pushy with her generosity. Once, after an exhausting collection, all I really wanted to do was stay in bed, but she insisted I fly to Washington to attend a party she was giving for Princess Diana, whose attention every editor around the globe competed for. We often went to the theatre together, including to both parts of *Angels in America,* the best plays I ever saw. When she took up the VH1 fashion awards as one of her personal projects, she hired me to design the production. I worked with a set designer who didn't want to listen to a word I said. I was trying to create a minimal white set with a huge projection, and what they had planned was the opposite — everything but the kitchen sink. I had to quit the job twice, and Anna had to step in on my behalf to get the set I wanted.

She was really concerned for my happiness, always asking about men I was dating. Also making note of my weight, congratulating me when I was thin and teasing me when I wasn't. Her presence at my thirtieth birthday party was as important to me as Nina's, Peter's, or Kevin's. She sat across from me that night and smiled or rolled her eyes when someone made a stupid toast. I think she was as genuinely amused by me as I was by her. Also we were protective of each other. Like anyone in a position of power she has a lot of detractors, and I tried to deflect as much of that as possible. One afternoon early in 2005 I ran into Meryl Streep, who lived up the block from my place in the Village. By that time I'd made her some clothes and had gotten to know her daughter, Mamie Gummer. Streep said,

"I agreed to play Anna Wintour. Am I crazy?" She was referring to the upcoming movie version of *The Devil Wears Prada.* "First of all, I have to lose about fifty pounds. Second of all, what do I know about the fashion business?" Then she asked if I'd look at the script and give the producers and writers some notes. Before I agreed I took Anna to lunch to pass the idea by her. I hadn't read the book, but I knew it was a kind of satire, and I didn't know if Anna might think of it as a betrayal if I helped in any way. There were all kinds of rumors so I broached the subject gingerly, but she had the opposite reaction to what I expected. She seemed delighted and told me not to hesitate. I was inspired by how she was able to see herself as a subject and not let her personal feelings enter into it.

Much later on, in 2003, when I launched my Target collection and reopened my couturier, Anna supported those endeavors, too. I had lunch with her and explained the idea and, as always, she nodded in agreement. Even if she had doubts as to the viability of the idea she never did anything but encourage, giving me a big story in the magazine. Three full pages with a consecutive page of text and a tiny inset picture. I wrote her a note and sent flowers thanking her for the "three gorgeous pages," and I got a note back in her hasty scrawl saying, "Yes, darling, but the story was *four* pages."

In 2005 I arranged a lunch to introduce my boyfriend (now husband) Arnold to Anna. She and her companion, Shelby Bryan, met us at Da Silvano, a restaurant in the Village that was a hub for the glitterati until its recent closing. She scrutinized Arnold like a protective sister. She seemed genuinely happy for us and said, "Isaac, now you can have kids." It was the one and only time we all went out.

Our friendship hit a few snags along the way. I was jealous of others she paid attention to. And if she didn't like a collection, it hurt. Finally, about six years ago, I was backstage and asked with my usual angst about whether the important editors were in place. Anna wasn't there yet; I assumed that she was detained. But after about twenty minutes it was obvious she wasn't coming and we filled the seat. It was a blow. I took it as a sign that my years as a couturier were waning.

We don't see each other anymore, but for some thirty years she was an incredible champion of my work, always there in the front row, always encouraging and helping

me. She was *the* fashion editor of my life.
Also. My friend.

26

One day late in 1989 Nuno Brandolini called to say that Charles Heilbronn wanted to meet me. The name made no impression until Nuno told me Charles was the half brother of Alain Wertheimer, the owner of Chanel. He told me they admired my work very much and were eager to meet and talk about the future of my company. I was incredulous but also anxious, mainly because at that time it was crucial that I figure out long-term financing for my company.

In the early 1980s Alain Wertheimer accomplished the heroic task of taking Chanel, the company for which he staged a bloody fight with his father, and rescuing it from obscurity. He closed all five-and-dime and discount sales of Chanel perfumes and appointed Karl Lagerfeld to revive the fashion brand. This reinvention was the great success story of its time, and it inspired all those comeback brands, like Louis Vuitton,

Lanvin, and Balenciaga. I had nothing but admiration for Alain, and I went to the meeting feeling excited.

I met Nuno and Charles for lunch at Bouley, another downtown culinary landmark that had recently opened. Soon after that, a meeting at the Chanel headquarters was scheduled. I couldn't believe what was happening to me. It felt like the handsomest, smartest, richest man in the room was asking me to dance. The office was on a very high floor at 9 West Fifty-seventh Street and had a dazzling view of Central Park. When you walked through those doors you felt like you were floating above the city, and it added to the fairy-tale feeling of the scenario. Sarah and I met Charles, Alain, and someone named Michael Rena, a tall, handsome, middle-aged Englishman who was the managing director of Chanel. There was an intense glamour about that place and those people. It was a connection to Europe, to the old world of real luxury that's been overdeveloped in recent times. Now there's a Chanel on every corner of every major city in the world. In those days the brand was still mysterious and alluring. Alain Wertheimer was a small, pale-pink man with wisps of light-brown hair. His presence was strongly felt in the room, but was only heard in the form of monosyllables. "Hmm." *"Oui."* *"Non."*

I fell deeper and deeper in love with the idea that I would be the only designer ever to enter into a partnership agreement with the venerable old French house. History in the making. It encompassed everything dear to me — not least a kind of Francophilia that I, like most other young designers my age, harbored. Things were just better in France. There was an unadulterated respect for fashion in Paris. Fantasy and frivolity were encouraged, markdowns were scorned. In those days Chanel never even went on sale. There were rumors, harkening back to my days spent in the Loehmann's dressing room, that they would burn the clothes that didn't sell rather than break price. It was the most exclusive brand in fashion, and I hoped that the Wertheimer family, who had built a huge fashion empire with Coco Chanel herself, would help me build mine. Under the original agreement they would fund my company and I would maintain design control of my namesake label, keeping a higher holding to assure the upper hand.

I felt increasingly at home in that heavenly location above Central Park, and the more I went there for meetings the harder I found it to be objective. I wanted the partnership badly, and so did Sarah, who was running out of creative ways to fund the company, which was growing by leaps and bounds. But we weren't the only ones who wanted the deal. What I didn't realize was that my credentials were being checked. Alain had close relationships with Anna, Dawn Mello, and a few other editors and store executives who went out of their way to praise me. The day I was to sign the agreement there was some last-minute paperwork, and Michael Rena and I went to a coffee shop to wait. He told me that Alain's father was originally meant to sign a deal with Halston and never did, and he kicked himself over that for years. Alain saw this deal as a kind of correction of history. As it progressed I fantasized about how beautifully my brand would unfold and skyrocket. Sarah got along famously with these men, and they adored her, though they didn't realize she had less experience and business acumen than they imagined. Years later when we parted ways, it became clear that they thought that Sarah and I would make it happen, and we thought they would.

There were even rumors that I was being groomed to take over from Karl Lagerfeld when he was finished designing for the

Chanel brand. (I might still be waiting all these years later!) The only dissenting voice about our alliance was from Maria Napoli, who warned me against it on two or three separate occasions. For as many times as I've had readings, I never understood astrology, only the interpretation, and she kept pointing to two or three bad aspects. Try as I did to convince her it was the right thing, she stood her ground. But even after her warnings I couldn't bring myself to walk away, so after six agonizing months, a deal was struck. A few weeks after we signed the papers Alain told me the family had named one of their new racehorses after me.

For the first two or three years of the partnership with Chanel I exhaled, knowing all my bills would be paid and all my collaborators — fabric mills, factories — would stick around to see what might happen. I was able to do my best work, and it seemed like everyone loved it. For the time being I was able to keep my place in the spotlight, give the editors fabulous shows, and give the stores clothes that I thought would sell. The retail auguries were good; I was among the number-one productive brands at Bergdorf Goodman, where I was given a gorgeous stand-alone shop right off the escalator on the third floor, which I earned and maintained just by my sell-throughs. In those days markdown deals were the norm; that's where designers pay the stores back for the clothes that don't sell. So were rent agreements, wherein designers pay rent for space in the department stores. My growth at Bergdorf's wasn't based on any of those retail conventions. It was a good solid business and what worked at Bergdorf's eventually was supposed to translate to the bigger retailer picture across the country. The other stores — Neiman's, Saks, Bloomingdale's — were biding their time, placing small orders, using my clothes as "window dressing," which is what insiders call it, and hoping my business would grow just based on the enormous amount of editorial press I was getting. But there was no grand scheme. There was no plan in place to offset the costs of such an expensive business. Somehow the expectation was that eventually I would hit on the magic collection that would generate sales to make my business plan work. While other designer houses relied on markdown money, freestanding retail stores, and advertising to grow their businesses, I was struggling without those tools.

Not to speak of the ill-fated licensing

philosophy. For fashion businesses, taking a loss on their couture clothes is a given and licensing is the only means of making any money. That is, the amount of very expensive couture clothing a designer can sell isn't near enough to cover costs, much less make a profit. Hence the term "loss leader." This is why most labels license their names for handbags, shoes, perfume — it's one way to increase revenues to cover the cost of designer collections without a great deal of investment. It's the only chance anyone has of making any money. I came to understand that the Chanel company had developed all those ancillary businesses — like handbags, shoes, costume jewelry — not as licenses, but from scratch, in-house, almost one hundred years ago, when those sorts of operations were less expensive to build. They owned all the factories. Handbag factories. Shoe factories. Even the factory that made the juice for the fragrance. And it felt as though I was expected to build the same system. Insane as it sounds, we all thought, myself included, I'd follow suit and be the first American designer to use that ground-up tactic as a business model. We were banking on the fact that my company would reinvent the American designer business, and we abandoned any plans for licensing.

So. To review. I had no production facilities, no controlled retail distribution, no advertising, no resources to make markdown deals, and no licensing revenue. High expectations and none of the tools to get the job done. One psychic I consulted said, "They think you're Jesus Christ."

I convinced myself and everyone around me that I needed a bigger, better headquarters. For one thing, we were bursting at the seams. Also it was my thinking that if I weren't going to advertise, a bigger headquarters would affect editors who came to see me, and editorials would affect business. It was my moment to become larger than life, and I did not shirk that responsibility. I dug my heels into SoHo and the new cultural scene that was developing around me. My partners at Chanel were all for this sort of thing because it cost much less than advertising or a retail program. A glamourous new headquarters made sense to them.

Nina found a building that was for lease, a classic three-story cast iron across the street from where she lived with her husband, Ross Anderson, an architect who I hired to design the building. That building, 104 Wooster Street, came to define me. The way Mariano Fortuny felt about his palazzo or Florenz Ziegfeld, Jr. felt about his theatre. People came to see me there. It was more than an atelier, it was a salon. There was one dilapidated freight elevator that opened to the street and had cage doors that were operated for a while by a guy who was also the shipping manager. The second floor was the warehouse and shipping center. The third floor was the design, fabric, and merchandising offices. To look at, it was a mash-up of Japanese paper screen/airplane hangar/plywood. Sound slipping under industrial doors that hung a foot off the floor, and light slipping over walls that stopped three feet shy of the ceiling. It was a design commune where there were no secrets and I was the boss. Highlights from my collection of old hats were displayed on a unit of particle-board shelves that took up an entire wall outside my personal office. The fitting room hosted a crush of super-models, movie stars, editors, artists, writers, and friends from all fields. Julia Roberts and Rita Wilson. Dan Flavin and his bride-to-be, Tracy Harris. Candice Bergen and Kitty Hawks. Candace Bushnell and Darren Star. Sheila Metzner and Uma Thurman. Manolo Blahnik and André Leon Talley. Lori Simmons and Cindy Sherman. Voguers from the House of Mizrahi and ballet dancers from ABT.

On the top floor, lit up by the skylight, were the showroom and sales offices. Done in industrial aluminum and pale-pink-stained plywood, it had open spaces that felt very luxurious and a poured white-latex floor configured to imply a runway. It's where I staged many small showings of secondary seasons like summer or spa (a word I used to replace the word "resort," which I hated so much for its old garmento implications, nothing more than a ploy, another made-up season to get women shopping, and I forbade anyone from using it). There was a wonderful contrast from the decrepit conditions on the street to the fabulous light-filled luxury of my two top floors. The painter Alex Katz came by to see me a few times with his wife, Ada, who was a fan of my clothes. He said his favorite part of my renovation was that I kept the stairwell original and didn't touch it. He loved the "squalor" and how it set off the beauty and purity of the showroom.

Day-to-day stress notwithstanding, I was happy there. Everyone was. For the ten years we inhabited that place we were the happiest garment-business family in the entire world.

I convinced my associates at Chanel that it was time for me to develop a small advertising campaign. Not merely to establish my own design point of view, but more to show support for all the magazines and newspapers that had been so supportive of me. I thought of it as a token in the quid-pro-quo that the fashion business is all about. I hoped my tiny placement of ads would justify a little of the huge editorial presence I was given those early years. Also I hoped it would encourage business. While it was clearly not the blockbuster ad campaigns of other brands like Calvin Klein and Donna Karan, and was one page for every hundred pages of Ralph Lauren's ads, I saw it as an opportunity to make an abbreviated, yet potent, statement of who I was.

Nina had recently become friends with Tibor Kalman, and she arranged for us to meet. Tibor was an iconoclastic thinker, designer, and art director with a company that bore the enigmatic name of M&Co; I think the "M" stood for Maira, his wife, an illustrator and author who worked with Tibor in the design company. His office was a place where nothing bad could happen. It wasn't postmodern or retro, nor was it cool and hip. It was neutral. The staff dressed in white cotton shirts almost as if it was mandatory, and they sat in rows of desks, set up like a sunny schoolroom, on sturdy, mouse-grey office chairs. The products Tibor designed had already become famous, like the watch with noncorresponding numbers, the paperweight made to look like crumpled paper, and an umbrella lined in blue sky print. It was under his direction that my logo was redesigned to what it still is today, with its customized Bodoni capital *M* that is such a big part of my identity.

In our first meeting Tibor proposed finding the right photographer to take a "beautiful and chaste" nude of a woman to run as my first ad. But I had other ideas. I wanted Avedon to take a picture of my studio like the one he did of Dior's in the early 1950s, a kind of ode to dressmaking. But that was not to be. Dick had an exclusive fashion contract with Versace, as I gleaned from Norma Stevens. A few weeks later, at one of our kitchen dinners, as a consolation, Dick brought out a book of a young photographer named Nick Waplington, whom he'd mentored at a master class he taught in London the year before. I loved Nick's book and brought it to Tibor, who loved it, too.

It was arranged for Nick to follow me around and take pictures of my studio at work. Fittings. Design meetings. The ladies of the workroom. Fashion shows. Nick isn't a fashion photographer, he's more a ghost, great at capturing people off their guard. The pictures he made encapsulate the glamour of that time, the frenetic pace, the love that went into those clothes. More than anything, they captured the feeling of happiness in the studio. It was the ease and sense of security that took hold once I knew I had real financial backing. Also I was at the center of an ongoing dialogue among the fashion critics and editors, the likes of which I had not known before, nor since. I've done better work, been less stressed, even had bigger media exposure, but never the perfect balance that I had at that time. I wasn't weighed down by the past, and I wasn't worried about the future. Those pictures bring that happy, easy time right back. And more than anything, they bring back Tibor.

Tibor had a fleshy face, baby-fine receding brown hair, prominent Alfred E. Neuman-esque ears, and a boyish smile. I had a strong attraction to him, almost physical. He was the perfect man, and most of my thirties were spent woeful that I'd never find anyone like him to love. At the time Tibor wasn't bound by one job description, he was a great example to me in that way. He wrote things. He designed clocks. He curated museum shows. He edited a magazine. He did it all in an integrated way, yet he rejected the description of Renaissance Man.

I met Maira, Tibor's wife, when I was seated next to her at a birthday party shortly after I met him, and I loved her instantly in the same way. The work, the person; identities that were impossible to pull apart. There was a familial pull. Maira moved from Israel to New York as a child, and I loved speaking my jokey broken Hebrew to her, a vestige of my checkered yeshiva past. In a trice I was invited to dinner with the family at their apartment. I walked into the lobby of that gracious building in Greenwich Village and felt a kind of prophetic peace. Like something great was happening. Nina was at that dinner, and we all laughed at the same jokes, which ran the gamut from well-wrought one-liners to Tibor balancing a bowl of spaghetti on his head. Also the Kalman children were there; Lulu, who was about four and Alexander, who was just a toddler. I loved them on first meeting, the way one is meant to love a niece and nephew.

One day in the spring of 1991 Maira told me about an apartment right upstairs that was for sale. The door was open so we snuck in and toured it. I still have a picture of seven-year-old Lulu from that day, sitting on the mantel in the sunny shambles of a living room. After a lengthy renovation (which was also designed by Ross Anderson) I moved in and was made to feel even more like an uncle, a brother, a relative. The Kalmans were the center of my life. Countless last-minute dinners. Holidays. Openings. A book party Tibor held at the A&P in Chelsea is as memorable to me as any of my own fashion shows. If *My Man Godfrey* or *The Navigator* or *Jules et Jim* was playing at the Film Forum, we'd go together. And when Tibor and Maira outlawed TV in their place, Lulu and Alex would sneak upstairs to watch with me. We lived in a smart, cozy world, of which our building was the center. Work collaborations seemed to enrich the bonds in the way religion corroded them with my blood relations. I couldn't help comparing this new closeness with the increasing distance I felt from my relatives. I had to disguise parts of my life to be around my sisters and their children; I didn't hide anything around the Kalmans.

I got to know Maira's mother, Sara Berman; a sort of Israeli Gracie Allen. A beautiful woman in white. White hair, white clothes, any room she walked into was blown out with white light. She and I sat next to each other at the edges of overcrowded Seder tables year after year talking about art, her grandchildren, and *Jeopardy!*, which she loved as much as I did. She'd slyly weigh in about the occasional date I brought to dinner. On one of the last of Sara's numerous yearly trips to Israel she asked me if I wanted her to put a note for me in the Wailing Wall. After a long think I decided it couldn't hurt, so I gave her a slip of paper asking the fates to send me a husband. I attributed my meeting Arnold to her and that note.

More than anything, there were jokes and laughter. It was an upstairs-downstairs support system. Like Mapp and Lucia carrying baskets to the high street for gossip, there were strolls to Balducci's or Jefferson Market together; impromptu meetings in our respective kitchens; lunches at Japonica; dinners at Bar Pitti; and many meals at Florent, a restaurant that Tibor had a dominant hand in creating. Florent Morellet opened the place on Gansevoort Street in the burned-out Meatpacking District way before it became the gentrified shopping mecca it is now. It's hard to think of that spot without Florent there, even these many years since its closing. We were always there. It was the better part of an outing to the theatre; a center to meet for late-night recaps; a destination for long breakfasts the morning after; and the location for all kinds of birthdays and extended-family gatherings.

My friendship with Maira is a central part of my life. We collaborated a few times. She made prints for a spa collection in 1991, and then for my spring 1992 collection. At the de Young museum in San Francisco, I'd seen a show of Ballets Russes costumes that were hand painted by Matisse. Maira went to see them with my instructions "not to be influenced." (Read: *Please be strongly influenced.*) I wanted dots and stripes and checks, painted by hand as only Maira (or Matisse) could do. I had the black-and-white patterns Maira produced printed — on a huge variety of grounds, from handkerchief linen to silk crepe to lightweight wool, made by one of the great mills in Italy, called Canepa, with which I collaborated regularly. When Anna came for the preview of that collection she gasped and said she was "thinking of prints exactly like these"

488

even before she saw them. Those prints were what set off my friendship with Maira, and it was hard to tell what the admiration was based on, or where it began and ended. I once had a conversation with Tibor on the subject of Maira, who we agreed *always* knew the answer to *everything.* If one is unsure, one has merely to put it before her to know the answer. It doesn't matter if it's some sort of emotional trauma or an issue of type font. Maira knows the answer. It's hard not to love someone like that.

One day, sometime in the spring of 1993, she called to tell me the family was moving to Rome, something they'd been thinking about for a while. Tibor was collaborating on *COLORS* magazine with Oliviero Toscani, and Tibor and Maira decided to move there for a few years to fulfill their lifelong dream of living abroad. My sadness at the breaking apart of our little family was made bearable only by how happy and excited they were about the prospects of living in Rome. Nevertheless, the day they moved was a sad one for me. But an even sadder day came two years later when they moved back. Tibor was diagnosed with cancer. When he told me, I couldn't accept it. I hung on to optimism bordering on denial. Tibor would beat it. The illness was a temporary thing, a subject to be made light of, his wheelchair and his cane merely subjects of design scrutiny. He set me up with his young, handsome doctor, and when that didn't work out, on one of the last days I went to see him in Columbia University Medical Center, he said, "I always wished I could find a boy for you. If I get better it's the first thing I'm going to do." His illness was even material for jokes among us, a way of dealing with this horrific chapter that we all thought would end in triumph. But that was not to be. After a wrenching six- or seven-year battle, Tibor died.

I was a pallbearer at his funeral. All I could think as several of us carried him to his grave was that I was burying my brother. Or uncle. Or father. There was no greater modern-day influence on me. It was a mentorship, a friendship — there was no separating the two. It was about thinking, about design, about taste, but mostly about love. It was the entire picture for us in those days. Work. Love. Work is life. Also death.

Someone chartered a bus to the cemetery in Westchester, New York, where he's buried close to George Gershwin. In true Tiborian fashion, hilarious and beautiful printed matter was given out on the bus, including

handkerchiefs printed with arrows cor-
responding to the words "cry here."

27

The life I led in those years can only be described as *fabulous.* Quickly though, the fabulousness felt like a distraction from the point, which, for me, is art. The parties, the celebrity, the fêting, were exhausting but necessary evils that felt like payment for the position I maintained in the fashion world. It took up too much of my precious work time. Also it seemed there were others who did this public thing way better than me; I noticed designers who were only too thrilled to go to every gala, every obligatory lunch. Flowers and gifts to editors were their stock-in-trade and they took to it naturally, whereas (at least in those early years) I relied on Nina to tell me what to do. She'd leave issues of *Vogue* and *Elle* on my desk flagged to my pages, along with the editor's name to whom I would address a gushy note to accompany a massive flower arrangement. I showed up at dinners that

Nina insisted I go to. She'd give me the names of the retailers or the publishers and I would wish them my best. After a while I got good at it. And after a longer while I did it so well people began to believe me. Then I began to believe myself.

People were always asking me who my publicist was, as if we were aggressively going after publicity, but in reality we said no to articles and stories more than we said yes. I also sent regrets to more parties than I attended. Some of them I couldn't say no to. One such obligation was the CFDA, which I hated more than the numerous High Holy Days in Brooklyn, and it seemed like they had as many events. I saw it as another cliquish way to homogenize designers and strip them of their individuality. I went to the yearly Met balls, a kind of chore, only to make Anna happy, often sitting next to her. Once Liz Tilberis hosted a party for Princess Diana at Lincoln Center, and I was invited to sit at their table with Kate Moss as my date. When I arrived to pick up Kate she kept me waiting for an hour, and we arrived terribly late, giggling like two delinquent schoolgirls. But it was much more of an offense than I realized. Liz was furious, this huge hole in the royal table of honor for over an hour. Liz didn't speak to me for months, but somehow Kate — an English subject who should've known better than to keep a princess waiting — went unscathed.

I was fêted in Tokyo by *WWD,* chosen to represent America in the "Best of Four" alongside Vivienne Westwood, Christian Lacroix, and Franco Moschino, representing the pinnacles of our respective countries. It was a number of events that were *a-blitz* with media, culminating in a blockbuster fashion show. I was fêted at the American embassy in Paris when I launched my brand there, and André Leon Talley took me on a personal tour of Versailles, as if it were his own home. I will always associate the Deee-Lite song "Groove Is in the Heart" with that place, because that's what André had blasting in the Mercedes limousine as we drove up to the palace. Another time I was asked by Louis Vuitton to design a bag for the one-hundredth anniversary of the eponymous printed canvas, another huge media event that took place in Paris. I got RuPaul, a good friend, to perform as part of the show. The idea was that Ru would be bathing in a blown-up bathtub version of the handbag I designed and break out into lip-synched song. At the dress rehearsal that same day a light fell on Ru's head and he was rushed to the hospital but made it back in time for the show. That's what I call a trooper!

In Shanghai, Hong Kong, Singapore, Tokyo, and parts of Korea where I went when my brand launched there, I saw the insides of embassies and homes that were opulent and strange and luxurious — I could write a separate book about them. I was in Europe every other month — in Milan and Como working on fabrics, or in Bologna working on shoes. I had an Italian boyfriend, Antonio, whom I met all over Italy for trysts. London was a second home; my godson Alfred was brought up in Kensington and his parents and I were dear friends. I was in Los Angeles constantly, and for over a year I had a boyfriend there, Manfred, who looked like a young Warren Beatty and who I met twice a month at the Hotel Bel-Air for long weekends.

And it wasn't just the fashion world. Around that time I befriended a lot of great thinkers and influencers. I was set up on a date with Andrew Solomon, who became a dear friend. I got to know people like A. M. Homes and Matthew Marks. Through my obsession with dance I met a lot of great writers, including Susan Sontag. Herbert Muschamp, the fabulous architecture critic for the *New York Times,* was an influence on me. We went to parties and dinners together, and I was challenged by the excellence of his thinking. One day we drove to New Canaan, Connecticut, to visit Philip Johnson at the Glass House while he was still living there. Mr. Johnson and his friend David Whitney took us on a private tour of the house and the art gallery. At lunch that day Philip Johnson turned to me and said, "Mizrahi. What is that? Is it Jewish? Is it Arabic?" When I told him it was both he said, "Oh, lucky you. You get to root for whoever's winning!"

During this time I made clothes for every great star I had ever wished to dress. The likes of Diane Sawyer, Meryl Streep, Diane Keaton, you name it. People like Robert De Niro and Madonna came to my shows.

The first time I went to Oprah's pied-à-terre at a glamourous New York City hotel for a fitting, my mind was blown. There, a staff of stylists came in and out with bags and bags of shoes from Manolo and boxes of jewelry from Cartier and Van Cleef & Arpels, pondering this pump or sandal with that yellow-diamond necklace or pearl bracelet.

On the first break I'd had in about four years after I began my company I received a call from Marina Schiano, a very fabulous and influential style editor working at *Vanity Fair*. She insisted that I go up to the Berkshires to meet with Mick Jagger, who was having trouble figuring out what to wear onstage for the Rolling Stones "Steel Wheels" tour. Tired as I was, I was also intrigued by the idea of dressing him; also I was scared that if I didn't do as Marina said, she would never speak to me again. So I reluctantly cut my vacation short and made my way up there. I was kept waiting for a really long time before a young stylist ushered me into a room with racks and racks and racks of clothes that she had pulled for him to try on. All I had was a sketch pad. Finally he came in looking disheveled and sexy, yet so much older and smaller than I would have imagined. I was nervous, but he set me at ease right away, apologizing for the wait. We sat together and I sketched, presenting him with ideas. I suggested a cape, which he nixed. I suggested something inspired by a nineteenth-century British military uniform, and he said in his cockney accent: "I can't wear that. Miss Bowie already did military on her last tour." He nixed everything I suggested until Jerry Hall walked in the room, looking gorgeous, no makeup, barefoot, in cutoffs and a tank top. I think if it weren't for her we never would have settled on anything. Finally we decided on a blue leather jacket and some tight sparkly pants. I made the pieces and sent them, he paid for them, but it was never acknowledged or spoken of again. And I never knew whether or not he wore the pieces.

There were other times when minimal efforts paid off. The first time I ever met Sarah Jessica Parker was in 1997 on Conan O'Brien's show. She was the first guest and I was the second, but she stayed for my interview. She was wearing a dress from my latest collection, which she bought at full price from Bergdorf Goodman. It was a black-and-white calf-length gingham cocktail dress with a white tulle crinoline. This was before we knew each other, and she said she saw that dress and "had to have it." From that point on I loved her unconditionally.

But of course there are times when even the most wonderful clients break your heart. People who wore my clothes regularly, like Sarah Jessica, Julia Roberts, Missy Elliott, would return dresses unworn after I'd spent days draping and sewing and fitting them. Sigourney Weaver presented me with my second CFDA award wearing an Armani dress, claiming my dress didn't fit, but I knew it was because she didn't like the one I sent.

Once I fought with Janet Jackson's stylist over a bill. At some point, someone set a precedent and didn't tell me, and from that point on all designers were expected to provide free clothing. But I was used to being paid for my work. Whenever I'd worked with Janet in the past she'd paid, especially when the dress was custom made. So I mistakenly sent a bill to her stylist and a very uncomfortable row ensued that I hope never got back to Ms. Jackson. On the flip side, there was Nicole Kidman, who showed up at the Golden Globes one year looking gorgeous in a dress of mine, which her stylist had borrowed from my PR department. They'd forgotten to tell me, and it was a total, happy surprise.

I've dressed executives like Tina Brown and Wendy Finerman, and major political figures like Michelle Obama and Hillary Clinton. I made a few pieces for Elizabeth Taylor without any fuss. She was being shot by Bruce Weber for her White Diamonds ad campaign and I was sent some measurements that were top secret, faxed anonymously without any other words on the page. I looked at those measurements, and

I knew immediately they were from some time in the 1970s and definitely no longer applied. Annica and I found the most recent photographs of Ms. Taylor and came up with our own size specs. A few months later she sent me one of the ads, featuring my satin trench coat, autographed. She sent a separate note saying what a pleasure it was to have clothes that "actually fit."

I got a lot of great notes from wonderful superstars, such as Candice Bergen and Aretha Franklin. I made clothes for the Queen of Soul in a dreamlike trance of fandom. I got regular notes from Sharon Stone, congratulating me on my latest collection and offering me little tips and criticisms as though she were a member of the fashion press. I published a big ad campaign for my secondary line, with pictures shot by Dewey Nicks and featuring my old acquaintance Diane Lane. Stone sent me a note saying if I had "wanted the Sharon Stone look in my ads, I should have reached out to her instead of copying her with a look-alike." But the note of all notes came soon after I met Streisand and made a few things for her. A paparazzi picture appeared in *WWD* of her wearing one of my suits, a pinstripe wool, man-tailored job, double-breasted with peak lapels and wide-legged trousers.

The editor got it wrong and credited the suit to Donna Karan. It was just at the time when Streisand and Karan were bonding publicly, so it was an easy mistake. A few weeks later, to my delight and astonishment, I got a note from Streisand with a clipping of her in the suit, acknowledging the mistake: "We know better who made that suit." I told that story for months. When I told it I imitated Streisand's assumed pronunciation of the word *"bedduh."*

If collaboration and friendship are hard to separate, professional admiration is sometimes the key to love. In the same way that hating someone's work makes it hard to be friends with them, loving their work can solidify a friendship. In the push-pull of obligation, it can be convincing to see yourself in a society column hugging someone you've idolized. It makes the opportunity for a friendship seem like a good idea even if it's not. So many times I've admired someone's work, then was lucky enough to meet them, then discovered we had no capacity for intimacy. I was always aware of the difference between people I love to be with and others that were more photo op than friend.

I fell in love with two of my best friends

before ever meeting them.

In the early days of cable TV there was a talk show on Lifetime called *Attitudes* hosted by Linda Dano. It focused on style and featured all kinds of guests — movie stars, chefs, designers. In the first few years of my career I was booked onto that show each season and showed a small group from my latest collection. On one such appearance I was asked, of all the celebrities I hadn't dressed who I would most like to. I answered the question honestly: Sandra Bernhard. And a few days later I got a call from her.

She came to my studio, and the act of trying on clothes became an obvious metaphor for us: circling each other, trying each other out. She brought a friend with her whose personality fell away into the floorboards along with everyone else there that day. It was just Sandra and me, love at first sight: Veruschka's face, Katharine Hepburn's body, and the dangerous wit of Lenny Bruce. The challenge in dressing her was that it was hard to beat — or even match — how great she looked in her real life. I first saw her sometime around 1986, performing in a club in the East Village, in a man's suit and sneakers. She often turned up at my studio in a white T-shirt and men's trousers.

No way to outdo that, try as I did.

After that first fitting we had dinner or another social function together almost every night for weeks. She was getting ready to shoot the movie version of her one-woman show *Without You I'm Nothing,* and she was at my studio a lot, checking out clothes for it. I followed her around like a puppy — in her dressing room at gigs, and at the David Letterman show on a few occasions, watching her on the monitor offstage. Our friends got to know each other. Maira and Tibor adored her and she was dating Sally Hershberger, who I really liked. She came to Brooklyn for dinner at my mother's house a few times, and they hit it off. I stayed at her house in Los Angeles once or twice. I got to know her family — her mother, Jeanette, an artist, who was a constant source of inspiration and humor, and her incredibly handsome brothers. I used to fantasize that her brother Mark, the one closest to my age, would turn gay, leaving the field open for a romantic relationship. (Sadly, he never did.)

Sandra and I were gay at a time when we were still expected to be apologetic about it and we weren't. We disdained those who didn't share our pride and strength and probably came across as more hostile than we actually were. For the first few months of the friendship it felt like we were perched on a banquette at Indochine, on the edge of the world alone together, unapproachable, laughing. When Sandra was in New York City she stayed at the Royalton Hotel, which had just opened across the street from the Algonquin, and we had parties in her rooms with all kinds of glamourous supermodels and movie stars.

One night Sandra and I and a bunch of our close friends went out for dinner in Chelsea before a dressy affair uptown where Sandra was the guest of honor. She was wearing a chiffon pantsuit from my latest collection with a thong underneath. This was early on in thong-technology and, like shoes that feel comfortable in the shop and betray you on the street, Sandra was having big thong problems that night. After dinner, walking to the event, Sandra had been pushed to her limits, and right there on the street, while the others made a circle around her, I helped her take the pants off — no easy feat in superhigh heels, then the thong came off and, naked from the waist down, she flung it into traffic on Ninth Avenue. She survived the rest of the night *au naturel* in chiffon pants sans thong. It was one of the biggest laughs we ever had.

Then Madonna noticed Sandra. The nightly entourage got much bigger and harder to navigate. Madonna was of course the subject of reams and reams of gossip, but she never really had a political profile. Not before she met Sandy. This was in the early 1990s, and I will go on record to say Madonna learned a lot from Sandy about having a public voice. How to be edgy, sarcastic, even angry, while funny enough to balance it. She observed Sandra's personality, knew it was time for this kind of brilliant cynicism, knew how to bring it into the mainstream, make it her own.

Sandra and Madonna became close, and the politics of my friendship with Sandra shifted. What this new arrangement lacked in intimacy it made up for in glamour. Being out with Madonna was different. There were bodyguards now. Whether it was dinner at Barocco or a burlesque at Gaiety Theatre (one of the last gay strip clubs in Times Square), we were followed by a security detail. Once I met Madonna with Jean Paul Gaultier in Paris, and after dinner in Pigalle, she wanted to take a walk. There was no such thing as a casual stroll with Madonna, and we were flanked on all sides by her guards. Once in New York, after the only one-on-one dinner we ever had, she came to my apartment to see a book I mentioned, and when we said good night, there were fans waiting outside my door on the seventeenth floor of London Terrace.

My friendship with Sandra ebbed and flowed, but we remained close for a long time. The question of having a child together came up a few times, but I wasn't ready. It was early in the time of gays having kids and my mother wondered aloud how a child with two gay parents might fare in the world. Also, she was quick to point out that I was too busy, too caught up in my career to be a father. At the time that was true. When I look at some of my friends who had kids who really shouldn't have, I'm convinced I probably would have done well at the task. But when I think of my own confidence issues, the moment-by-moment emotional spirals I still experience, I think I made the right choice not passing those genes on. Sandra and I have maintained a friendship from afar since those days, but the few times I met her beautiful daughter, Cicely, I did regret missing the chance to have a child with someone I love as much as Sandra.

In 1989 I went to BAM to see a show, a gala performance of *L'Allegro, il Penseroso* ed *il Moderato,* which Mark Morris created in Belgium the year before. I had a huge reaction to that show that night — visceral, intellectual. I agreed with every idea and aspect of it musically, theatrically. It was a melding of ideas that didn't seem "postmodern" or clunky. It was a conglomeration of images — ancient Greek friezes, Bugs Bunny, Balanchine, a conga line, entrances and exits taken right out of a silent film — all resolved, seamless, and totally original, all the things I wanted to be evident in my own work. I laughed at the jokes, I wept in parts. The beautiful dancers never seemed to push an emotion, make faces, or smile without a very good, organic reason. They weren't dancers. They were people, performers who danced like angels. I literally fell in love with Mark watching that show, and I didn't even know what he looked like. When the curtain came down all of us in the audience leapt out of our seats, screaming. And afterwards I was a wreck. I had to walk around the block a few times so as not to encounter anyone or engage in small talk that would break the deep emotional spell that had been cast.

That night at the gala dinner Mark and I were introduced and — trite as it sounds — I could feel an intense chemical pull. Something opposite. Synchronized temperaments. The artist Jennifer Bartlett once referred to us as Odette/Odile — the white and black swans from *Swan Lake*. We even have similar builds, and to this day we wear the same size. He looked like a Victorian doll to me, with those shimmering blue eyes and shoulder-length ringlets — only missing a big, taffeta bow atop his head. I got home that evening floating from the experience of seeing the show, meeting him, in love with him and not sure when I would see him again.

About a month later Anna Wintour threw an intimate dinner for about fifteen at one of Ian Schrager's new hotels in Midtown. Manolo was there. So were Julian Schnabel and Anh Duong. And Mark was there, and I was seated directly across from him. In fact I got the distinct impression that Anna was trying to set us up. At one point she turned to him and said, "You know, *Maaahk*, Isaac makes beautiful dance costumes. You should get him to make some for you." To which Mark replied, "Oh, I only work with artists." In haste I said, "And I only work with thin dancers," a reference to the criticism emerging that he and his company of dancers were fat. (By ballet dancer standards, which had taken over at that time. I didn't agree, but it was the only rejoinder I could think of.) And so began our great friendship.

We made a date for dinner, and it was unclear whether the intentions were romantic. We went to my favorite place in TriBeCa, Barocco, and after the first ten minutes my whole opinion of him reversed. I thought he was imperious and condescending, which at that stage, made him more attractive. He spoke of music in a totally pedantic way, as though no one but he had any connection to the subject whatsoever. He spoke of Bach as though they had known each other and had conferred on the phone minutes earlier. He said unequivocal things about music, things that made the hair on my neck stand on end. I didn't disagree with his opinions, but I hated that he left absolutely no room for any other thought on the subject. That night, it was clear that we were not destined to be lovers, but not wanting to leave any stone unturned we made an attempt at a good-night kiss. After that any sexual feelings were put aside, and eventually Mark made it clear, as only he can, that there was no chance of us becoming a couple. "I have a policy," he said. "One genius per family." For years I wondered whether I should have tried again. I felt a terrible sense that I'd missed something, a terrible sadness that we weren't together in that way. But I also sensed that the relationship, which was flourishing, might be sullied — even ended — if sex were a part of it. I was — I am — in love with him, in a way one loves Jesus, a chaste love of the spirit.

A few months later, much to my astonishment, he called and asked me to make a costume for him. It was for a solo he was creating to Gershwin's *Three Preludes*. It would require a costume for him and a duplicate for Baryshnikov, whom I knew and had already worked with, who would be dancing the part in rep at the same time. I stood in my kitchen on the phone, pinching myself, thinking of the great opportunity to collaborate with this marvelous artist, but also being overcome by a weird, deep, almost protective love for him.

On top of his other qualities Mark is a damn fun guy. The revelry gene is so remote in me now I sometimes question its existence. I had my crazy youthful escapades, but by the time I met Mark I had so many social obligations to my business and my family, I had little patience for late nights or parties. But the happiness, the true irreverence of Mark and his company brought it out in me again. It harkened back to the fun I had in my past, and I felt young with him. Two of the best parties I ever gave were for Mark and his company. One in Edinburgh at the Balmoral Hotel and the other at Chez Panisse in Berkeley. Both of those cities I will forever remember as happy places.

One of my favorite collaborations with Mark was on a show he directed called *Platée,* a baroque opera that opened at the Edinburgh Festival and later at Covent Garden in London. Meetings began three years prior with Mark and the great set designer Adrianne Lobel, who conceived of the "swamp" where most of the opera takes place as a terrarium, with plastic plants, a huge bubble-jet photo background of a swamp, and an orange "plastic" water dish that dominated stage left and had a functioning fountain that spouted at key moments in the show.

Designing costumes for the stage presents a whole other set of criteria that is opposite to those of fashion. In fashion you try to create fresh new things in order to sell them, and if you don't, you can't stay in business. Costumes don't have to sell. They don't function like street clothes, they function physically on a whole other level; the difference in construction comes from the difference between how the body moves on the street and the hyperextended way it moves on the stage. For a designer working under the constraints of fashion, costume design can be a wonderful release. And in the case of this opera, the costumes needed to be dazzling, funny, colorful — basically, a designer's dream: swamp creatures, gods and goddesses. Working at the Covent Garden workrooms on Floral Street in London with all the craftspeople, wig masters, tailors, milliners, shoemakers — perfectionists all — added another layer of great satisfaction.

Our collaboration is a fixture in my life. I think of Mark's dance center as a home. I know the dancers and administrators in his company not merely as artists, but in some cases, as good friends. And my friendship with Mark thrives. He's a beacon of honesty and light in a chaotic world. No compromise for him, no politesse, nothing that takes him away from his vision. That honesty prevails in our friendship, too. And after all these years of knowing him and working together in an atmosphere I'd describe as an aesthetic romance, I like to think our best collaborations, the shank of our friendship, still lies in the future.

Knowing people like Mark, like Sandra,

observing the way these two artists work, fills me with inspiration. There's a truth their work speaks to, an integrity that making clothes, fulfilling as that is, can't compare with. Working with those people, watching them, makes it clear that the greatest joys of my life have been — and are yet to be — played out onstage.

28

There's something really intimate that goes on between a photographer and a subject. I always say there's nothing sexier than a man pointing his big camera at you and shooting. I've had at least three photographer boyfriends that I can think of off the top of my head, and I'm sure there are more if I really put my mind to remembering. Let's say I'm easy for a man with a camera.

One day in 1995 I walked into my showroom to be photographed for *GQ* by a handsome guy named Douglas Keeve. He looked like a tall, brooding version of Fred MacMurray, looming over me with his Leica. I wasn't sure what he saw in the viewfinder or why he liked me, but his attentions were obvious. I flirted, and it wasn't my imagination that he was flirting back. He brought something out in me. He made me feel attractive because he was delighted with me as a subject, and I was able to open up. We had a rapport. The pictures he took that day were less remarkable than the attraction, which was real.

So many of the men I'd met before Douglas were only eligible until you scratched the surface and found out they weren't smart, or they had some sort of irreconcilable sexual fetish that — try as I might — I couldn't get into, or they were emotionally unavailable in one way or another. Men who seemed right for me to date were either boring or nasty or smelled bad or were even, in one case, a white-collar criminal. Also I found that the men who wanted a relationship didn't want to have sex, and vice versa. Gay stereotype? Yes. But it was true among a lot of the men I encountered at that time. Love and sex seemed to be two completely separate issues. I remember when I went out with Mark, after the second or third date he turned to me and said, "I can't have sex with you because I know your last name and I like you."

But Douglas seemed ready to integrate. I met him for our first date on the corner of Seventh Avenue and Greenwich. We couldn't decide where to go, so we walked and walked all the way to TriBeCa, then back uptown, ending up at my apartment in Chelsea. We had a lot of fun on that date and for a while thereafter. But soon I could sense a darkness between us, a shadow cast over him, like a storm cloud, which was in turn cast over me. It was impossible to cheer him up. That, of course, made him even more attractive. I took on the responsibility for that sadness, and it became my mission to make him happy and when I couldn't I took it very personally. Whether or not he blamed me for it was a detail. I naturally assumed that I was the source of his unhappiness. After all, love was supposed to inspire you, and I obviously didn't do that for Douglas.

Still, I thought this was the way it was. I thought it's what all those couples meant when they said being together is "such hard work."

A perfect example of dreading the future, white-knuckling through the present, then looking back fondly was a birthday party Douglas and Elizabeth Saltzman organized for my thirtieth birthday. Maira took photographs from the night and made a small, beautiful book for me with the pictures. To look at those pictures you'd think it was the greatest night of my life, but living through it was another story entirely. I'm not the kind of person who is able to let go and have fun when I'm supposed to, and I especially hate being fêted. The dinner took place at Barocco and was full of big personalities who had no business being in the same room together. It's hard to integrate different factions of friends. Friends I made in high school should be kept separate from friends I made in adulthood, and my West Coast friends don't have to like my East Coast or European ones. And my mother is someone I'm always nervous to expose in any context.

The seating arrangement was a big puzzle: I thought it best to seat my mother close by me and Sarah Haddad, and Nina Santisi and her sisters Elissa and Laura made a nice adjacency. Ted and Janine from high school should be seated together. Annica Andersson and my cutters and sewing staff actually requested a separate table. Sprinkled among these: Anna Wintour and Grace Coddington. Sandra, Mark, Tibor, and Maira. It was a total of about seventy-five of my closest friends and associates. There have been bigger parties, more important occasions, but nothing like this, where every person I knew was brought together in the same room. I'd glance over and there was Douglas talking to Janine, who was filling him in about my life as a fat teenage actor.

On the other side of the room, my mother was talking to Anna, telling her god knows what about my childhood that I would so rather Anna not know. In yet another corner, there was Sandra, seconds away from making a scene about something. Toasts were made and there were mentions of puppet shows and female impersonations, things that felt too tender for public consumption in any context.

Making sure everyone feels noticed over the course of an evening is always hard work; that night it was like rolling a boulder up a hill. An ironic combination of feeling unworthy of attention and an obligation to pay a lot of attention to the big personalities in attendance. One moment I was self-deprecating and vulnerable, the next I was acting like a spoiled child, moping about how everything was wrong. And of course the biggest challenge was facing Douglas at the end of the night, intent on not hurting his feelings and pretending everything was wonderful and how happy I was. But try as I might, I just couldn't hold it in any longer, and when we got home I exploded. That was the beginning of our end. Some relationships are remembered for specific experiences around things like travel, or food, or a collaboration. My memory of Douglas is centered around breaking up, a process that dominated our time together more than the process of being together.

I should have realized how poorly suited we were. Our personalities added to the other's insecurities which, like dough with too much yeast, grew and grew, even after being punched down. My body dysmorphia was fed by the lean perfection of his physique, and his lack of professional confidence was heightened by my compulsive drive. To put it mildly, our neuroses fit hand in glove. He would descend into a mood and go for days without saying a word; meanwhile I talked a lot. Our fights, which were many, consisted of me unloading yammering, shouting, and him sitting there, silently, smoldering, to the point where I would beg him to say something, anything.

Even in light of all that, I was committed to being with Douglas, and I thought he was committed to me. I was willing to overlook everything so long as we were civil to each other and looked good together. I think that's a big component for young people in relationships — the appearance of things on the outside. Once I was involved with Douglas, I dreaded the idea of admitting I'd made a mistake. I couldn't bear the idea of people thinking I'd failed at love. He wasn't my first boyfriend, but it *was* the first time coming forth as a couple in my adult life, and I was already in my thirties — late, by some standards. Love wasn't the motivating factor at that point; being in a committed relationship was. In the meantime, Douglas and I remained a couple for about three years in our unhappiness.

I was asked to make a video that would run before a presentation of my second CFDA award. Even during the period of our unraveling, it seemed natural to ask Douglas to collaborate on it, since his interest had begun to shift from still photography to filmmaking. It was a short piece — nothing more than a bunch of gags — but it was met with big laughs, something that didn't happen in the fashion crowd too often. The audience loved it, and the mood between Douglas and me brightened temporarily as a result. It also cemented our profile as a modern gay couple whose lives were intertwined.

There are different accounts about the genesis of the idea for the movie *Unzipped,* but one glance at my studio in those days and you'd immediately think to set up a movie camera. You'd have to be living under a rock not to be struck by the potential. It was a very funny, glamourous place — a constant feast of models, movie stars, editors, friends. Nina, Douglas, and I decided we had nothing to lose and jumped in. Douglas started shooting. I was nervous about wrecking my relationship with him, but I submitted after several conversations with my shrink, who suggested that the smooth collaboration on the CFDA video the year before boded well for this bigger collaboration. I thought it might even help the cause of Douglas and me.

Over the course of the next year, *Unzipped* took a lot of my focus. It was annoying, embarrassing, arduous, and yet I knew how important it would be in the scope of things. One psychic even went so far as to say it would be the thing I would most be remembered for. I knew there had never been anything like it, and I knew it would be great. It became the focus of my life, yet working on it was difficult, especially in public. These days you're nothing without a reality crew following you around everywhere, especially in the fashion world. Since *Unzipped,* there are more published backstage photos of fashion shows than there are runway shots, and at least three fashion documentaries a year. In 1995, way before the advent of reality TV, big camera crews were completely frowned upon. They were seen as déclassé by the fashion cognoscenti, who were still dominated by old world thinkers like John Fairchild and the WASP socialites of the day, who remained unyielding in their snobbery. Filming in a public location was considered vulgar and I feared for my image. Especially in Paris, a place I felt so ambivalent about, where the cameras and crew instantly reduced me to the ugly American tourist I made fun of.

We didn't really know what making a documentary of this kind would require. So Douglas shot probably ten times as much footage as was needed for the seventy-minute movie we ended up with. Also we had no real end for the movie until the day after the fall fashion show. I don't think you could get funding now for anything that wasn't plotted from beginning to end.

There were so many surprises. Lots of days we didn't know what would happen — luckily a lot did. And even luckier, Douglas was there to capture it. It helps when your boyfriend is the chief shooter and it doesn't seem out of the ordinary for him to be wielding a camera in the most intimate moments. Moments in bed. In the bathtub. Moments that made the movie what it is. Other days we followed a well-planned shot list, and some of those things never made it in. Faye Dunaway came in to look at clothes for a very short-lived TV show she was cast in, and Douglas had a full crew that day. She was there for hours and tried on every suit and day-dress in the place, and it was all documented. When she liked the way something looked she'd speak of herself in the third person. She'd say: "Oh, this is very Faye!" right at the mirror. We crafted a segment for the movie that became more of a tribute to Dunaway than anything else, crosscut with footage from *Mommie Dearest* in the same way clips from other movies like *The Red Shoes* and *What Ever Happened to Baby Jane?* had appeared. In the end we cut the segment because we couldn't get a license to use the *Mommie Dearest* footage.

Douglas and Nina worked with a woman named Paula Heredia editing the film, and I checked in every few days to see rough cuts of segments. The hardest part of that was being a subject and maintaining any sort of objectivity. But I did it. I developed the ability to see myself as a fictional character, suppressing the urge to scream and call a halt to the proceedings. I saw this deprecating vision of myself as a positive thing — being the butt of a good joke.

As often happens on films, we went way over our deadline and spent more money than we'd agreed upon. I made an ill-fated trip to LA to meet with a young agent from C.A.A., which Hachette hired to represent the movie. This agent went on to become one of the most powerful people in Hollywood but, sadly, he did not understand my vision for *Unzipped*. In the middle of my pitch he stopped and asked with a blank stare, "You mean like a wet T-shirt video to give away with subscriptions to *Elle*?"

To keep things from falling apart, I promised the backers that if we couldn't get the film finished by the designated time I would take all financial responsibility for it. I think it was something like half a million dollars, which I absolutely did not have. I'd venture to say that the terror I felt at being ruined financially is what ultimately got that movie finished. We lost Paula to another project, so we had daily meetings and screenings, and it was Douglas himself, prodded by Nina and me, who finished the final edit.

Toward the end of the project we all fought bitterly. Nina, Douglas, and I were at the ends of our ropes. It became clear that my relationship with Douglas wouldn't survive the movie. At a crucial point toward the end, our funds were short again, a scary make-or-break moment. I remember coming close to a nervous breakdown in the car with Nina one afternoon — I shouted at her with such force that both she and I got frightened. Unbeknownst to Chanel, I approved an extra fifty thousand dollars, which I knew would be covered by the budget of my following collection. From the first mentions of the project I felt that my partners at Chanel really didn't understand *Unzipped* or the benefits of doing something like it, so I kept most news of it a secret from them. Everything was on the line for me: my career as depicted in the movie, my relationship, and my reputation as someone who could produce something good.

We handed in the finished movie just hours before the first screening. Hachette and Bergdorf Goodman partnered to host a publicized event at a movie theater on West Fifty-seventh Street, I can't remember what the theatre was called at the time. (It is now the Directors Guild Theatre.) The entire fashion cognoscenti attended. It was the first time in my life I thought about running away. And then the lights went down and the movie started. Laughter. More laughter. And even more. And that good silence when people are listening. At the end there were people cheering, standing. After all the fights and horrible feelings we harbored for each other, Nina, Douglas, and I sat in the back of that theatre holding hands in solidarity. We made something great, and it would bind us together for life.

The following months were like a dream of a nightmare. *Unzipped* went first to Sundance, thanks to Nina's labors, where it won the Audience Award for best documentary. And there, in those soggy mountains, with every executive present from both coasts, layered up against the melting snow, finally, *Unzipped* was sold. All the money recouped and repaid, I felt like a captive being let out of debtor's prison. Miramax bought the movie on the third day of the festival, after a short bidding war. I met Harvey Weinstein a few times during the course of that negotiation never realizing what a monster he was. I was too absorbed in what was going on in my life, my relationship with Douglas, and especially the sale of the movie. Of all the companies bidding on *Unzipped,* we sold it to Harvey because he assured us it would stay intact without having to be reedited, lengthened, or changed in any way. Years later I would see him out and about and he'd say to me "What a great movie we made together!" and I'd think to myself, _we_ made? *You mean I made and you bought?*

It was all very bittersweet for me that spring and summer. There was no joy being at Sundance, even with such a great success, which had been clutched from the jaws of defeat. I was staying in a separate room from Douglas, and I couldn't help feeling the irony of that fact. Too many awful things were said in the final days of editing, and we were clear with each other that it was over from that point. Then *Unzipped* went to the Cannes Film Festival. Estranged from Douglas, I promised Harvey Weinstein I would show up, and I did. He booked me a huge, gorgeous suite overlooking the Mediterranean that felt to me like the loneliest place in the world. I flew in with Linda Evangelista, Kyle MacLachlan, and Naomi Campbell, who were there to soak it all up. It was the most glamourous and amazing screening, with loads of big movie stars in attendance. And it was all about me. Yet there was no way to enjoy any of it. That is one occasion I will never look back on fondly, no matter how much time passes and perspectives widen.

After the screening at Cannes we got a standing ovation. Harvey, Sharon Stone, and I hosted a star-studded benefit dinner

527

for AMFAR at La Palme d'Or, one of the most exclusive restaurants in the entire world. I sat next to Elizabeth Hurley and Hugh Grant, and all I could think about the whole night was the irony, the question gnawing at me: What came first, love or *Unzipped*? Did Douglas use me to get this movie made? Did I use him? That night, those questions presented themselves in all their delusion, as a bitter trade-off: this massive success in exchange for a life with Douglas.

About two years ago, in tandem with a large-scale, midcareer survey show that took place at the Jewish Museum in New York, *Unzipped* was revived for a few showings, and I agreed to do a Q&A with Bruce Goldstein, my friend who runs Film Forum. I couldn't watch the whole movie, so I showed up just toward the end and watched the last few minutes standing in the back. The end of the movie has me walking home to my apartment, Douglas filming me, having been to the kiosk on the corner to get my reviews. I regarded myself as I was twenty years earlier. I was simple and young and I could move in any direction I wanted. I had nothing. I wanted nothing. I was safe because the future was before me. Now, in the middle of everything, it's so much harder. I think more and I act less. I'm not as sure about what I want as I am about what I don't want.

Then, in the last moment of the movie, we're walking back to my apartment and Douglas, off camera, asks, "Was it worth it?" I answer without thinking: "It's always worth it. Even when it sucks it's worth it." I watched in the dark and cried.

29

In those days documentaries about designers didn't exist. There was a real snoozer about Giorgio Armani that came across as a vanity project, or a cross-promotional opportunity, more than anything. *Unzipped* was a breakout hit. It had a theatrical release, which no one thought would amount to anything but which actually did a nice business for Miramax. It has since had a great deal of exposure on video and TV and has presumably made a great deal of money (nary a penny of which did I ever see). As much of a success as it was, it didn't really serve me well at the time. I was good at drawing attention to my brand, creating a culture for the clothes, a reason for people to relate to them and buy them, but there was no basic support for my clothing business. Still no production or distribution channels. And any licensing begun at that time was way too late. It felt like the Tower of Babel was ready to topple.

When I signed the agreement with Chanel I knew they were the number-one luxury brand in the world, and I assumed they had some sort of a plan to grow my business. I think they thought *I* had a plan. It turned out neither of us did. I was a designer, not a merchant. I might have collaborated with business visionaries, marketing people, advertising agents, but that was never in the offing. After the sixth or seventh year in business with Chanel, it became clearer and clearer that my business was coasting on my ability to hold the attentions of the fashion press. I parted company with Sarah, which was a blessing and a curse. While she was in over her head, she supported me and was loyal to our cause. Others were brought in who made attempts to guide the business, but by that point it was too late. Because the economics of the deal changed so radically, a new contract was drawn up. Even as my business was misguided, it was growing, and I had not foreseen that building such a business, with no retail or licensing revenues to help, was such a money-losing proposition. When I entered into the deal I still had controlling shares. Over the course of the following seven years I would lose more and more control because of the growing losses.

Eventually I lost control completely.

It wasn't Chanel's intention to stack the decks against me. The big discrepancy in vision was between the way business in the world at large was conducted, versus the way Chanel did business in the ideal world they had built for themselves, starting all the way back in the early 1920s. So I continued making these elaborate, attention-getting fashion shows and having what turned out to be fruitless meetings with Chanel executives who were trying to be helpful. Eventually they did little else besides monitor the diminishing returns as reflected on spreadsheets. They were full of useless advice, and were not at liberty to lift a finger to help. As far as building a sustainable business was concerned, it was a real waste of those years.

Six months before my thirty-seventh birthday, completely out of the blue, I got a call from Bernard Arnault from LVMH, Chanel's archrival. Needless to say, a brief, rather awkward conversation ensued. Follow-up meetings with his people outlined a job to remake Louis Vuitton. Like so many others who continued to design their own collections while designing other revival collections, I was courted for the job at Louis Vuitton, which wouldn't preclude designing my own collection. One problem would be the irreconcilable differences in place between LVMH and Chanel. They were competitors to the point where some might consider them mortal enemies. But I brought the offer to the attention of Charles Heilbronn and Alain Wertheimer, who seemed amused. They humored me, and for a moment I thought they might be interested in reconciling the feud. Plans were made for me to go to Paris with Charles to meet with Mr. Arnault, but at the last minute the meeting was canceled, and it was never rescheduled. I suppose it was just too big a fissure for the two mammoth companies. I was thrilled by the thought of all that prestige and all those clothes and fashion shows. Also by the thought of conquering Paris, which in itself was a double-edged sword; the place the entire world perceives as the center of fashion, and a place I'd grown to dislike. But to be perfectly honest, I didn't really want the job. I was bored with the status quo of my life, interested in adding diverse projects — expanding into show business — not adding more of the same. My inborn need to leave the party just as it's peaking began to set in.

At that time, fashion as I knew it was taking a turn that I didn't understand. My *fabulous* shows were adored less and less. It was becoming more and more about expressionless, underfed young girls who can't smile as they barrel down the runway. Not only was the physique thinning, the intellect of fashion was also going anorexic. It felt to me like the editors held private meetings on their way back to New York on the Concorde after the European collections, and made secret decisions about the way clothes had to look — and especially about the way they couldn't look. Even before my clothes hit the runway, they were wrong. The world was closed to my ideas. I could feel the collective editorship in the audience staring at their notebooks and pouting through my shows, which they only attended because they felt obliged. The joy was drained out of the subject. "Heroin Chic" was in, and I was out. At some point in 1997 someone convinced me to hire a stylist to work with me on the shows, and it was a great struggle allowing any other opinions, but I had to try anything. Finally, at one of my last shows, the stylist put a sign on the wall for the models that said NO SMILING PLEASE. Now I'm not one who likes big fake smiles, but that sign felt ominious. It might have said instead: *The End.*

■ ■ ■ ■

Late in 1998 I was called to the Chanel headquarters. I didn't expect what was to follow. It was a freakishly cold September day, and the usually idyllic view of the park from the offices was obscured by a thick fog. I was shown into the main conference room, where Charles Heilbronn and Michael Rena were waiting for me. There was very little small talk. Alain Wertheimer was conspicuously absent. Michael Rena opened a folder and produced a shallow stack of papers with numbers on them. Without exception, I understood not a word or digit on them. "At this point we have to do something about these numbers. We're not prepared for you to lose more than three million dollars a year. You'll have to make cuts. If you keep your losses below three million a year, you can go on for the rest of time."

At that moment everything in the room froze, voices muted, nothing moved. I had the feeling of being stuck in time. What I had agreed to ten years earlier, the hope that this partnership might push me over the top, had been misconstrued on my end and theirs. All I could think, sitting there in that stifling conference room, was that the better part of my life those years, every great idea, every great effort, all the love that was poured into those collections was reduced to a sad stack of spreadsheets.

When I got home I saw Tibor. My destiny lay in running into him at that moment. We sat in the lobby, which is very odd considering we could have gone to either of our apartments. I described the scene I had just come from and posed the dilemma. I told him how confused I was, how much I wanted to stop functioning for a minute and contemplate. I confessed everything to Tibor that night, including my deepest fears about letting go. About having looked up to people like Geoffrey Beene, George Balanchine, Stephen Sondheim, even my best friend Mark Morris, people who are masters of their crafts, and the delusions I had about becoming a master myself. I realized at that moment that designing clothes forever was not in the cards for me. So many great artists reach a pinnacle in their achievements and spend the rest of their days building on those ideas, masterfully making work that refers back to that original genius. Especially in fashion, *that is what you do.* But it wasn't just new fabric, new clothes I sought, it was a whole different world. Sitting there in that lobby talking to Tibor was better than any therapy session. Listening to myself talk, I started letting the idea of mastery slip away in favor of artistic peace of mind.

At the end of the monologue Tibor asked me a simple question: "What do you really want to do? We got in the elevator and by the end of the short ride my mind was made up. "I'm closing," I said. And Tibor smiled and shrugged. "I knew you would," he said. "It's so much more interesting."

That night I sat in the bathtub feeling free. I knew what I wanted would not come in the form of running that company for the next twenty years and when I told Charles Heilbrunn of my decision he respected it. Frankly I think everyone at Chanel was a bit relieved. I knew the next chapter of my life would be about something more important. I was about to embark on developing my talent as a thinker, a writer, a performer. Guy Culver, Maria Napoli — the words of all the psychics were coming back to me now. "If by the time you're thirty you're not pursuing a career in show business, it will pursue you." If five years late, this was destiny fulfilling at least half that promise. The really difficult half. The half that got me to start thinking differently.

My practical nature kicked in, and I felt almost embarrassed that people might actually think I cared about the exact minute when shoulder pads or a skirt length became obsolete; the relevance of opaque hosiery; when bright-red lips were preferable to nude-colored ones. I wanted to write an editorial and send it to the *New York Times* apologizing for being such a fraud, pretending to care about such foolishness, while at the same time setting the record straight about all the love imbued in my clothes. I wanted the world to understand how I detested the idea of fashion — that exclusionary business of making women feel their identities were obsolete in order to sell them new stuff. What I loved, what I was driven by all those years, was nothing less than my love for new thoughts, beautiful textiles, women. Now I set out to prove that this love would conquer all.

When I announced my doors were closing, instead of my fantasy editorial, an article ran on the front page of the *Times,* accompanied by a picture of me. The only redeeming thing about it was that I looked thin (more redeeming than you'd imagine). The headline was one of the most memorable of my life, etched in my brain forever, like a premature obituary. It said: *Designer*

Most Likely to Succeed, Doesn't. I perceived that not for what it meant literally, but as a sign of hope, a real end to things and a beginning for others. I didn't understand it would be seen as a failure, even after that headline, which appeared, I repeat, on the front page!

Women's Wear Daily devoted pages and pages to the story with accompanying pictures, as though my clothes were some sort of war heroes. That morning in early November 1998, I assembled my entire company and broke the news. I cried and thanked them. That night Mark and I were Anna's guests at a party for Matthew Bourne's *Swan Lake* on Broadway. I considered canceling but thought it best to just face the world. The funny thing was that through all the potential shame and sadness, I felt amazingly free and resolved. It was only later, at a reading with Maria Napoli where she pointed out that I was going through a "public humiliation," that I actually grasped what was happening. That night at the show with Anna and Mark I was actually surprised that the world didn't perceive it as the end of a jail sentence the way I did. Those days afterwards I felt the way I did in high school, like I could finally breathe.

I permitted one interview with the *New York Observer,* through which I concealed my relief and excitement and feigned a kind of regret, if only to maintain friendships with people to whom I thought I owed that remorse. It would hardly seem sporting to say how happy I was to be moving on after all those people supported me in making it to the top. To the rest of the world, this was a disaster. The phone rang off the hook. It was the time of the answering machine, before caller ID, so for months I would wait to hear a voice before picking up the phone. One friend kept leaving me messages. The first was something along the lines of:

"Darling. So sad to hear about you closing your doors. Call me back." *Beep.*

His second message, a week later, was:

"Darling. I hope you're okay. Why haven't you called me back!?" *Beep.*

The third, a month later:

"Darling. Why the hell are you not calling me back? I just want to hear your voice and tell you how *sorry* I am!" *BEEEEP.*

I've always been really good at knowing the difference between my own paranoia and people's intentions. And I got very good at perceiving the subtle differences between genuine concern and schadenfreude. There were, of course, people who honestly cared about me. There were others who were more interested in gloating about what they viewed as my demise.

Then a stroke of fate. At exactly the right time a young lady emerged in my life, like Joan of Arc, a saint in shining armor. Marisa Gardini had worked for Raoul Felder as a divorce lawyer, then moved to Vienna with her husband, Craig Kinosian, also a lawyer. When they moved back she decided she wanted to get into fashion and entertainment law. Her sister Gina Gardini was working with Miramax during the launch of *Unzipped* and recommended Marisa for a job with Nina. Marisa ascended the ranks from intern in the PR department; a few short years later she was running human resources. When we closed she stayed on to help with the exit packages.

During that transition she'd appear regularly at my apartment for my signature on contracts and documents. We struck up a rapport. After the official closing there was so much to do, and we agreed that we'd continue working together. At first I thought of her as an associate, an incredibly bright person who seemed to have a lot of the right qualifications — mostly that she was enthusiastic about working with me. We lunched at Japonica and made plans. There was a deal with DreamWorks to develop my graphic novel, *The Adventures of Sandee the Supermodel.* There was a deal with HBO to develop a series based on my life. There was a deal with Oxygen to do a talk show. There was even one very successful shoe license that had been signed too late in the game and had not been terminated. She helped with these projects, and she was smart and straightforward. Respectful but honest. Her lack of experience didn't faze me, and eventually I thought of it as a bonus. Again naiveté was power. She didn't know what couldn't be done, so anything was possible.

Within about three months she approached me with her husband, saying they could win my trademark back from Chanel based on a few assumptions she made after looking at the original agreement. Before she brought up the subject I had turned my back completely on the idea, but she convinced me that I should win back the right to use my own name. We embarked on a long, arduous, nerve-wracking battle, and after three years she and her husband succeeded in winning the suit. That was when Marisa and I formalized our partnership, which lasted the next sixteen years.

I reveled in freedom after closing my doors. It was a new world with time to do things, to go to the gym, and buy groceries, and go to the movies. And mostly the freedom to pursue my first love: show business. On top of all the entertainment projects I was working on, I had a few stray things, including writing for *InStyle* magazine and designing costumes for Twyla Tharp at New York City Ballet. Even with all the meetings and management of my projects I had a lot of extra time, and I began writing things. Essays. Stories. I did a lot of journaling. I created a routine around it. I'd stay up all night writing then wake really late (a whole complicated way of dealing with insomnia), go to the gym, eat lunch, spend the afternoon on calls, and start writing again after dinner. There were days when I couldn't write a word and others when I couldn't stop. It became an anchor that gave my life a shape.

I wrote a number of small, funny essays that were more like rants or screeds. What they really felt like were monologues, scripts on random subjects such as "travel" or "men" or "mother." By that point I had assembled pages and pages of them. And it seemed like a good time to start putting together a one-man show. I gave these essays to my friend, a producer named Dori Berinstein, who had worked on *Unzipped.* She liked them a lot, and she loved the idea of my attempting a live show. One thing I was clear about was that music had to play a big part in it. Maybe harkening back to my days as a female impersonator and a performing-arts student, singing felt like the perfect form of theatrical expression, and I was determined to sing.

I met Stephen Sondheim at a dinner party at my friend Jonathan Sheffer's one night, shortly after the release of *Unzipped.* Steve was a big fan of the movie and we became friends. To have grown up idolizing him to such a degree, and then to have him tell me what a fan he was of *my* work, and then to engage in this friendship for those few years felt like I was living a kind of fated miracle. Steve was about sixty then and was emerging into another realm of great public appreciation. He was finally being fêted as the king of musical theatre. He was a perfect friend. He was full of great stories and advice. A god with the personality of an imp. A bearded cherub with crazy observational skills who excelled at dinner conversation and who seemed to get a kick out of me, too. He sent typed notes in the mail (all of which I kept), some accompanying copies of obscure tapes of his early work, which I treasured — like a tape of a musical he wrote for TV called *Evening Primrose* starring Anthony Perkins. Another note accompanying a copy of the original production of *Pacific Overtures,* which couldn't be seen anywhere but the New York Public Library for the Performing Arts, addressed to "Darling poor old ugly rejected you," and saying I might be "truly thrilled" by the costumes.

There were fabulous dinner parties at his house with people like Julie Andrews, Mia Farrow, Judi Dench, William Goldman, and Mary Rodgers. I invited him over to play bridge with my friends, who were in awe of him. He introduced me to Arthur Laurents and I took them to Chanterelle for dinner, where Laurents berated me for most of the night because I made the mistake of expressing occasional impatience in the theatre. I invited Steve over to meet Mark Morris, another forced meeting that somehow went awry. Mark was never the best at making first impressions, and the two seemed to clash on every subject. Steve and Robert Osborne, our mutual friend, regaled me with stories about old Hollywood one night at dinner, and after Steve saw a revival of *The Women* that I costumed on Broadway he left me a message saying something to the effect that he was rarely "moved" by costumes, but in this case he really was. I walked on air for weeks after that. Steve had an adoring acolyte in me, and in him I had a friend, a giant who affected me more with two words than a torrent of words from anyone else.

I'm not exactly sure what went wrong in our friendship, but at some point I was excommunicated. I think it was something I did or said inadvertently that caused Steve some kind of pain or embarrassment. I confirmed the radio silence when I saw his assistant (also named Steve) in the Village and confronted him. "Did Steve dump me?" I asked semijokingly, and his face clouded up. "Hmm" was all he said, and he walked on.

But before I was excommunicated, Sondheim had introduced me to a young musician named Peter Jones. Peter and I worked on some musical arrangements together. We got along well and had similar ideas and tastes in musical theatre. After a few weeks of rehearsal I felt I was ready to dip a toe into the water, and so I booked three nights at Eighty-Eights, the small cabaret in the West Village where I'd gone a few times with Liza. I had debilitating stage fright before that gig. Stage fright plagues me to this day. It feels like facing my own death. But the pleasure I took in preparing for those shows was deep. I wrote in my journal, *"I am living every day in a more intense way than before. Doing more. Letting go more. Feeling more, both poles, ecstasy and dread."*

I started the show walking through the audience singing a Cy Coleman song called "You Fascinate Me So" with wonderful tricky lyrics by Carolyn Leigh. I thought I'd mess it up, but I nailed it every time. After that opening, the rest always felt like a cinch. A good lesson for future shows: If you make the right entrance, you've won. Even if fear overtakes you later in the set, it's not half as bad as appearing nervous at first. If the audience senses you're nervous they'll eat you alive. You have to appear to be having fun, and the best way to do that is to *actually* have fun. In order for me to do that, I knew that a lot of the show would have to be extemporaneous. No matter how much I prepare, I think of myself as best in the moment, when I can incorporate things that pop up, and connect with the audience on the spot. The trickiest part of pulling that show together, which has proven the trickiest part of putting any show together, was deciding what to prepare and what to leave to chance.

One night Liza came to see my show at Eighty-Eights. Her presence should have made me feel even more nervous, but it actually made me feel more confident. I think it's because she knew how hard I was working on it, how earnestly I had thrown myself into it — and because she did it herself, she understood how hard it could be. I gave a great show that night in that little club, because I really let things happen rather than feeling beholden to patter that I had written in advance. And I accomplished the impossible that night, which was to wrest the audience's attention away from her and focus it on myself. Afterwards, backstage, Liza said, "Kid, that was more terrific than I expected." Then she gave me a hilarious and baffling note about my rendition of "Think Pink!," which I did early in the set. It's a Roger Edens tune that Liza's godmother, Kay Thompson, originated in the movie *Funny Face.* Liza said, "Kid, when you sing the word pink, think *rose.*" That's all she said. No more explanation. And yet I completely got her meaning and that sentence went into my permanent collection of favorite Liza-isms.

Les MIZrahi, which was at first a joke title and later became the actual title of my one-man show, had a few false starts. I workshopped it first with Moisés Kaufman, and then later, for a longer time, with Joe Mantello. But it wasn't till my friend Wendall Harrington brought it to the attention of Douglas Carter Beane and Mike Rosenberg, who were running a small theatre company called Drama Dept., that it really took shape. We struck a deal for a workshop production, and within a few weeks I was at the Greenwich House Theater (now called the Barrow Street Theatre), working on my show.

I got the idea to ask Richard Move to direct me after working with him as an emcee for one of his great shows at a downtown club called Mother. Working with Richard on his show made it clear to me that show business wasn't only a matter of stardust and stage effects. It was broken down into steps, ones involving hard work and development. All my recent experience, working with those other directors, working at Eighty-Eights, working on Richard's show, proved to me that if I faced my fears, I might be capable of creating something significant. Richard reassured me of my

549

powers, of the powers of rehearsal, and a lot of my neuroses fell away the harder I worked. I engaged in one of the most fortunate relationships of my life with someone named Ben Waltzer, who I met through Mark's friend Ethan Iverson. Ben became my musical director and accompanist, and it was only after I met Ben that I felt right about my ability to produce music on a stage. Appearing with him also cut my debilitating stage fright in half. It was at that time that I was able to see myself, finally, as a subject. I was thin and agile from all the physical challenges, and I created costumes for *myself,* which was a real novelty. I wore tails from Savile Row in one segment, a Sulka polka-dotted smoking robe in another, and a suit that was covered from top to bottom in crystals — including the shoes (women's shoes I bought at Comme des Garçons) — for the finale. I changed costumes behind a light-box screen onstage, like a stripper, with my silhouette for all to see.

The opening number was a Sondheim song called "Me and My Town" from a show called *Anyone Can Whistle.* I wrote a new set of lyrics, which turns into a big call and response number with the band. I wanted Steve's blessing so I sent him these new lyrics, and he seemed not to hate them — which from Steve, who is notoriously critical, felt like praise. Of all the terrifying things I've done onstage, the most fearsome came right after that number. A sewing machine would be wheeled out onto the stage, and I would proceed to cut out and sew a coat, one of my favorite designs from my first collection, all the while performing a monologue about being at Loehmann's with my mother. I was like one of those Chinese acrobats spinning plates while riding a bicycle. I argued and argued with Richard about it, trying to convince him that it was impossible, but he finally won. And it was a real standout in the show as well as a lesson to me about what I was capable of learning. I proved to myself that with the right amount of preparation I could be called upon to do anything onstage that the most seasoned performer could. Also that improvement is cumulative. One gets better and better. One's voice opens up after time, and it's easier and easier to rip one's heart out and leave it onstage. The only trick is you have to keep at it. Keep doing it all the time.

Getting those audiences to love me night after night felt like slaying dragons. The physical exertion of working on that show was therapeutic. I was eating anything I wanted and down to a size 30 waist. I was finally onstage and not behind it or seated in front of it. It made other disappointments and frustrations seem unimportant. For all the stage fright in advance and the sleeplessness afterwards, the rewards of that time, working in that little theatre every night, with my darling band, playing to those smart audiences, made me understand how simple and good life could be.

During the run of my one-man show I felt lighter and younger — actually attractive. Finally I felt like my body was as sexy as anyone else's. I began experimenting with sex and meeting lots of men. It was thrilling to feel a little out of control and have a belated slutty phase. I spent many a sleepless night on the Sex Line, which was a telephone precursor to Grindr. After you called in, you would be directed to a series of brief chats with all the other men on the line, and you could beep from one caller to the next if you'd had enough. And they could beep off, too. Mostly the conversations were very short.

"Hi. What are you looking for?"

"A bear top" — *BEEP!* On to the next caller . . .

"Hi. I'm on the Upper East Side — *BEEP!*

"Hi. I'm six-foot-two, twenty-six, blond, mostly smooth" — *BEEP!*

And so on.

They'd say what they were looking for and what they looked like in short, broad strokes until two people sounded right to each other, and they would take the conversation further and further until they decided to meet up — or at least exchange phone numbers to engage in phone sex that didn't cost seven dollars a minute. I met a lot of fascinating people this way. Also a lot of frauds. And even this happened: One night at about 2:00 A.M. I was beeping from caller to caller when I stopped to chat with a random gentleman. We were on the line for a good long time, and it seemed we were well matched. Finally we got down to the idea of meeting up, and when I asked where he was he told me the East Twenties. Suddenly it got clearer why the voice on the other end sounded familiar. Then it came rushing at me.

"Mark? Is that you?"

And with great alarm, almost hysteria, the voice on the other end answered, "WHO IS THIS!?"

It turned out my best friend Mark Morris and I were closer to each other's sexual fantasy that night than we might have guessed. We spoke on the phone for an hour after that, mostly screaming with laughter. I was working on costumes for his company at that time, and the next day when I went to his studio for fittings, I learned Mark had told the story in class to his dancers — we joked and laughed about that for years.

Really, the best part of having this crazy sex life wasn't so much the sexual gratification as it was having something hilarious to talk about afterwards. So many times I would meet people for fetishy sex just for the experience. Who knows? If I tried something I might like it. I remember my mind's eye floating up to the ceiling, like a camera, looking at myself in those situations, thinking how easy people with fetishes have it. They simply re-create that particular circumstance and they're aroused. I also remember most of those times when I wished the guy would stop what he was doing and leave so I could call Mark and describe what had just happened in lurid detail.

The Sex Line wasn't my only source for sex. Walking the streets became more than a way of getting from one place to the other or window shopping. Now it became the most interesting place to meet men. There was also the gay beach in East Hampton, which after sundown becomes a cruising spot, mostly for vertical sex. At the gay beach one would occasionally run into men one knew. "Heterosexual" men. Or men known to be in long-standing relationships. Or famous men. There was always the fear of being arrested. One would hear that the police had raided the beach and taken people into the precinct. I thank my lucky stars that nothing like that ever happened to me. Through all those nights I seem to have been lucky in a lot of ways. And for all the danger surrounding the scene — the risk of violence, disease, humiliation — it was a great deal of fun, and I would say worth every minute. The cumulative effect of having been with a number of men who found me attractive was that I finally started to believe I was *actually* attractive.

Here and there I would meet someone and date him for a while, but nothing ever stuck. There were men I dated with whom I was compatible in some ways, but not others. There was a wonderful guy, a gorgeous blond, who, after we dated for a bit he told me I had inspired him to go into rehab for heroin addiction. I was set up with a gorgeous fellow named John, who I dated for a long while before we ever had sex, which turned out to be a big disaster. I dated another fellow named Daniel, who I think I had the best sex of my life with, and whom I loved in a lot of ways, but with whom romance was a nonstarter. I tried to make a thing with one guy named James, who liked to have sex in alleys and public bathrooms, but the relationship could never find its footing because it turned out he had a wife. Another was a painter who also worked as a hustler. I tried to convince him that he was a good enough painter to support himself, and his answer was "I like turning tricks," which I understood to the point of being jealous.

Going through the motions of dating so much taught me a lot about men and convinced me that love and romance were impossible. I really thought that at the time.

A few weeks after the opening of *Les MIZrahi,* sometime in October of that year, I was sitting in my apartment late one afternoon after having bought a new toaster. The toaster didn't mean anything really, but it became a symbol of my self-sufficiency. I wasn't rich, but I was able to look after myself. I was ecstatic to have made it through my recent history, such a public fall. I had faced stage fright. Conquered the press. And once again, the moment-to-moment of living through it was stressful, to the point of near-misery. But when I looked back, that was the happiest time in my life. This thing that made me so happy, performing onstage, was no longer a mystery. Walking to the theatre in Greenwich Village every evening. Warming up my voice and body. Standing before a crowd every night and working hard. And feeling like I had conquered the world after each and every show.

Toward the end of the extended run I was aware of the impending void waiting to descend. What could ever replace that show? I had invested every part of my emotional inner life into the creation of it. More than any fashion show I ever made, this was my personality, my ideas, my words, my body on the line. By that point I had many other things on the horizon — a talk show, a pilot I was writing, a movie I was consulting on — but that show was the closest thing to my heart for those two years since I had begun writing the essays. Or really since my earliest dreams of working onstage, in a spotlight.

Around Thanksgiving it occurred to me that the only thing that might fill the oncoming void was a dog. Another lifelong dream. I imagined a dog would bring constant companionship and loyalty, and a deep, very private love. Also it would be a physical commitment, walking, training, and taking care of this puppy. And so toward the end of my run in *Les MIZrahi* I began to look in earnest.

After months and months, I met Harry at a Christmas cocktail party charity event for a local dog shelter. My friend Kitty Hawks had accompanied me to many of the city's shelters, even once to the pound (where I vowed never to go again because it's just too sad). That night Kitty brought Harry from his holding crate to meet me and said, "This is your dog." I immediately knew she was right. A mix of Border collie and golden retriever, he was the most elegant shade of auburn, the color of a red fox. Smart. Also a bit aloof, another good sign. I thought if he didn't care so much, we stood a better chance of living happily together. I filled out the paperwork that night and couldn't think of anything else till the following day, when I was set to pick him up. I saw Maira later that night, and I drew a cartoon of him from memory on a slip of paper, which captured his exact countenance. The next day Harry and I walked from the shelter on East Forty-sixth Street to my apartment in the Village. Harry came into the apartment and any trace of aloofness fell away immediately. He ran from room to room and jumped on the bed and on the furniture in a manic fit, as if to say, "Happy to be here!"

I brought Harry with me to those final few performances of *Les MIZrahi*. He stayed in my dressing room and was there when I came offstage. Nothing could assuage my dread of moving on from that show, but Harry had a way of changing the subject. He looked at me, and I felt less lonely. A kind of bliss set in between us that lasted the entire sixteen years we lived together. He made my shack in Bridgehampton habitable. Before him, I was much too scared to spend the night there alone. Eventually it became an idyllic retreat for me, and so many happy days and nights there followed — one memory in particular, walking in the moonlight with Harry off-leash, snow up to my knees and up around his snout. Harry was everything to me. After all those years of pining for a man, I was surprised when I got something I considered better. I got a companion who asked no questions and only gave love. It was that secure feeling Harry brought me that led me to understand the true idea of partnership and enabled me to be less desperate and more open.

After one of the final performances of *Les MIZrahi,* Isabella Rossellini came backstage and met Harry in my dressing room and said, "Ah. Harry. He is the couture of dogs. Mutts are the only ones of their kind. Not another one like Harry on Earth."

30

Dori Berinstein, a good friend and one of the first producers to get involved with *Unzipped,* was working with Geraldine Laybourne and Oprah and some other TV executives who had the very avantgarde idea to launch an interactive TV network, right on the cusp of the internet explosion. To their credit, they were a little ahead of the curve. They started the Oxygen network in 1998, and in that incarnation it was poised to be not only the first TV network to acknowledge the World Wide Web in so direct a way, but also the first network targeted specifically to women. Dori and I met for a drink sometime in the fall of 2000 and discussed the idea of creating a talk show together. None of the people involved were true talk-show producers, so we pursued totally original ideas. I wanted to do things with people other than just sit and talk. Being a multitasker myself, I thought talking while doing something would make it more likely for things to get said, revealed. People are off their guard when occupied, and hence more relaxed about revealing things. The pilot episode was centered around fittings on a dress for Sarah Jessica Parker to wear to the opening night of her husband Matthew Broderick's show *The Producers.*

I wanted there to be a musical element to the show, so Ben Waltzer was hired to be on set. He could accompany anyone who might want to spontaneously burst into song. And there were so many who really did want to. Jacques Pépin, after deboning a chicken, sang "Les Feuilles Mortes" and Belinda Carlisle and the Go-Go's, who assembled in the studio for an interview, ended the segment ad-libbing "Vacation" with Ben following along on piano. Debbie Harry and I got through a version of "Heart of Glass" and Lauren Ambrose performed "God Bless the Child" on the spot; and Sandra Bernhard made up a song with Ben about our friendship, her baby, Cicely, sitting on her lap.

Our first studio was located in a storefront on one of the quieter side streets in Chelsea. I had the idea to set the whole thing in front of a white cyclorama, a wall that curves and becomes the floor — no corners. When photographed it looks like a white void, everything appears to be floating in space. I set a piano and some elegant furniture in front of this cyc, and it looked modern and beautiful. The art directors on the network begged me to rethink the idea, but I wouldn't budge. They explained how much easier it would be if the set was painted a shade of pale grey that would read on TV as white, an idea I wouldn't even entertain. The first few airings of the show were so blown out because of the whiteness of the set, we heard from different carriers that people weren't registering pictures, just blank screens with sounds. Finally the technicians figured out how to transmit the show by some means or other and in the end we succeeded with that white set, and I venture to say started a whole bunch of other "white set" talk shows.

Most of the guests were friends of mine who I reached out to personally. One of the main reasons we had such great bookings originally was because we gave ourselves flexibility to shoot whenever talent was free. So we kept odd hours but had some amazing guests doing some amazing things. Natalie Portman and I washed my dog, Harry, who was a regular on the show. We followed an *Esquire* shooting on the set of *Zoolander.* I made costumes for Baryshnikov. I played Ping-Pong with Janeane Garofalo and pool with Lili Taylor. I did a sewing demonstration with Helen Mirren. I sang with Andrea Martin and we laughed so hard — to the point where the interview went out of control. I supervised a haircut for Rosie O'Donnell and we cried together about Columbine. By the second season of *The Isaac Mizrahi Show, New York* magazine proclaimed it was "the show to do," and soon publicists were calling us to get talent booked on.

At least one-quarter of my seemingly boundless energy at that time was focused on ignoring the call of fashion. All those years an addiction had grown, and now the task was set before me to break the habit without the benefit of a twelve-step program. Even with the TV show taking off and all the new entertainment endeavors, every time a fashion magazine crossed my path, I felt haunted. People would thoughtlessly ask if I was "all ready for Fashion Week," and I'd suffer a great pang of dread and a downward spiral into a black hole. I knew it was irrational, but the void that fashion left felt bigger and bigger.

■ ■ ■ ■

The year I turned thirty-nine I made a deal to come up with a series about my life for HBO, and I chose Marshall Brickman to collaborate on the script, someone I looked up to and was thrilled to get to know. It was a good script that never made it to series. In the process of working together Marshall and I became friendly for a time, and I started to value his opinion more and more, especially after he let slip a remark that haunted me for a long time and eventually acted as a kind of jog to my conscience. We were talking about the character of *me* that we were developing for the show; a heightened, more ridiculous version of me but me nonetheless. After living through *Unzipped* I was getting good at being objective, good at sending myself up without hating myself or feeling sold out. Marshall said something like "Well. *Isaac* is a little past his prime. I mean. Forty and still not with anyone. It's *abnormal.*" He actually used the word "abnormal," which jarred me at first, because even though he was talking about the character of Isaac, that fact was true about the person Isaac, too. I thought, *Shit. There's some unspoken rule about people who cross over into their forties alone and are too set in their ways to ever find true love. I have one more year till I'm officially abnormal.* I called him on it, and he backpedaled and apologized, but I never got over it. Isaac the character *and* Isaac the person: doomed.

Later that year, on an unusually beautiful spring day, June 21, 2001, I met my mother at her lawyer's office to discuss selling her house, which was a big deal for her and also for my sisters and me, since this was the house we'd grown up in. It felt like I was turning a definitive corner. I dressed in a suit to impress the lawyers, and the meeting went way over, into the afternoon, which I hadn't expected. I was very late to walk Harry, who had only been with me about eight months. I swooped in, gave him a treat for not messing in the apartment, and flew out the door again, Harry on his leash, me still dressed in the suit and tie. As soon as I got to Twelfth Street and Fifth Avenue I noticed an incredibly attractive man way across the street, walking in the opposite direction down Fifth Avenue. We made eye contact, but we passed each other without either of us crossing the street and taking the initiative. As I've mentioned, it was a time in my life when the most innocent of walks around the block might lead to some sort of impromptu sex. This mode of operations was justified by Maria Napoli, who told me not to be afraid of these encounters, that they might lead somewhere interesting. But this gorgeous man and I crossed paths, made eye contact, and that was that. *Oh well,* I thought. *Another Jewish affair.* And I continued on.

As I was getting close to Sixth Avenue and Thirteenth Street, the handsome stranger came running up behind me. I intuited his advance and turned, watching him approach, his gorgeous looks coming into focus: Six-foot-one, curly dark brown hair, and eyes like black dots on a smiley face. High, Native American-looking cheekbones, chipmunkish cheeks, and a cleft chin that makes him a kind of Puerto Rican Cary Grant. He looked at me with such interest, taking such care to notice, it actually made me feel like *I* was the attractive one, a reversal of logic. He was dressed in a long-sleeved crewneck T-shirt, baggy, wide-legged khaki pants, and flip-flops. He came right out and said, "You're that designer, right?" — which didn't come across as coy manipulation; it was a way of dispensing with pretense. We walked the rest of the way home, and when we got to my door I said, "Well. Um. We should keep in touch or something. I'd love to get your phone number but I don't have a pen." This was before we had cell phones on us at all times. I said, "Why don't you come upstairs for a second?" A rather standard-issue pickup line for such an auspicious occasion. Upstairs — well. I'm sure you can imagine the end of the episode better than I can tell it.

Arnold and I had two or three formal dates after that first encounter, then all pretense fell away and we started seeing each other regularly, getting very close, very quickly. There was something entirely different about this courtship. Aside from the great physical attraction, we were very honest with each other at all times. All earnestness. No posing. He brought it out in me, and I in him. I guess that's a description of the word "chemistry." After the first month we had a fight, but it didn't break us up; it brought us even closer. Then toward the end of that summer we were driving back from Bridgehampton on the Long Island Expressway with Harry in the backseat when traffic stopped dead. We were literally there for five or six hours at a complete standstill. Normally something like that would make me panicky, claustrophobic, but being with him that day felt fun, like a survivalist adventure.

When we first met, Harry was protective

of me and would growl when Arnold approached, sometimes even nip when he got too close to the bed. More than once he made Arnold bleed. But Arnold laughed about it, which made me laugh. It also made me like Arnold so much more. Very few people can make me laugh, but Arnold really can. Laughing that is close to seizure. We laugh at things that no one else would ever find funny or even get. The things we laugh at defy description, at least in writing. It's like another language we speak. Not to say that we don't have our bad moments, but for two such prospectively dark, moody people, we cast light on each other in the private world we occupy together.

When we met Arnold had just moved back from LA and was looking for an apartment. We both thought it would work to live together temporarily. But the minute Arnold moved in, we knew it was a mistake. I felt my little haven was being invaded, and he could feel the unwelcome. It was a one-bedroom apartment — hard to share on any terms. The bathroom alone; I was horrified at the thought of someone moving their toiletries into my shower and medicine cabinet. And I've always been bossy in the kitchen. I like running it in what I think is the most efficient way, and anyone messing with that puts themselves in terrible jeopardy. Also: Sharing a bed is hard enough for people who don't have sleep issues. For me it's impossible. Nothing is worse than lying awake while someone next to you is fast asleep, breathing deeply, snoring, while you lie there seething. It's the loneliest feeling in the world, enough to make you hate anyone. The problem was I'd lived alone since I moved out of my mother's house nearly twenty years earlier, where I had my own bedroom from the age of eight. I was "abnormal." Set in my ways.

On the morning of September 11, 2001, I was getting ready to leave for a meet-and-greet on an all-star production of *The Women* at the Roundabout Theatre, which I had signed on to as costume designer. It was a busy time for me. My TV show was about to premiere that week, and I was scheduled to leave for LA the next day to do a round of talk shows and appearances to promote it. I was rushing around the apartment getting ready that morning while Arnold took Harry out for his morning walk. Before long, Arnold returned, somewhat hysterical for someone usually so calm and collected. Before I understood what was going on, I thought something had happened to Harry. I turned on the TV, and then Arnold, Harry, and I stood on the terrace looking straight at the World Trade Center, watching firsthand as the horror unfolded before our eyes.

Working on *The Women* was a kind of security that I needed. Making clothes for those starlets in those extenuating circumstances; Cynthia Nixon, Kristen Johnston, Jennifer Tilly, Jennifer Coolidge, Rue McClanahan, and others; dressing them in clothes that recalled another time — fur shrugs, fascinators, seamed stockings — listening as the world expressed its shock, gathering backstage around a radio to listen for news . . . it was a dead ringer for 1930s wartime. It made anything we were doing onstage feel surreal. We tried to keep our spirits up; what I remember more than any part of the show were the late-night drinks with the girls afterwards, and the feeling of closeness that only comes backstage. Arnold and I clung to each other, too. We stayed together a few months too long just for the comfort of not being alone during that horrible period.

In January of 2002 a semblance of normalcy returned to New York City, and Arnold moved out. I was happy to have my world back, my bathroom, my kitchen intact. A breakup was inevitable. We tried to

571

rethink our relationship, but it didn't work. By the spring of that year I was dating other people, and so was he.

After almost a full year passed, I started to miss Arnold a lot. I thought about him day and night. I called him, and before I could explain the reason for my call, he said he was about to call me, that we needed to meet. It felt like something out of a Hollywood musical, where two characters in love come to the same realization at the same time and finish in a flourish of tap dancing. We met at the studio I was using as a tiny headquarters for my new couture business. It was nighttime and we were alone. It was dark in the room, and I leaned down to kiss him. He pulled away. "No. Wait," he said. "I met someone." My heart began to sink. He'd asked to meet in order to get back a small framed photograph of himself as a child he'd given me, which I kept on a shelf in my bedroom. Now he wanted it, I imagined, to give to his new boyfriend. Then he told me he got a job in Santa Fe and they were moving there together. I gave him the photo and he left, presumably forever.

All my psychics predicted I'd have a breakthrough in show business. I waited and waited. Aside from my talk show, nothing materialized. Three times I appeared in Woody Allen movies; I practically made an industry of playing myself in different TV shows; I was set to direct a movie I spent a year developing, and that fell through; Marshall and I handed in our script to HBO and they passed. Mike Myers studied me for about a year with the idea of playing me in an adaptation of *The Adventures of Sandee the Supermodel,* which had been published five years earlier. The script came in from the writer, an underwhelming adaptation, and that was the end of that. Even after my one-man show, which got great reviews, the phone stayed put on its hook. One by one the projects were disappearing, yet I was more and more committed to making a full transition to show business.

In 1996 I met Jim Brooks at a dinner party at Lisa Eisner's house in Bel-Air. He was working on a movie called *As Good As It Gets,* and he had the idea that I should read for the part of the neighbor. At that time a gay character in a movie that wasn't a psychopathic killer was still a novelty, and I really thought I had a chance of getting it. I read in New York at Jim's apartment on the Upper West Side with Owen Wilson, who was being considered for the part of the hustler. I was flown to Hollywood to read with Helen Hunt and Jack Nicholson. At the reading with Nicholson we were left alone for ten minutes. "See these shoes?" Nicholson said, pointing to his Versace loafers made in a discreet leopard-print suede, "I wore these for you." I was mute with flattery. He went on. "Listen. So you know. I really want this part. But my agent said to play it cool because they haven't negotiated the money yet. So if I seem like I'm a little bored, don't worry."

Jim called me again and again to read for that part, and I thought I had it in the bag. Then I found out that every gay man Jim Brooks knew was reading for it. I saw my friend, painter Ross Bleckner, at a party, and he mentioned that he'd been in, too. I think Jim was doing everything he could to understand gay men in order to direct an actor (he ultimately cast Greg Kinnear) with some kind of knowledge and authority.

Five years later Nancy Meyers was working on *Something's Gotta Give,* another movie with Jack Nicholson, and expressed interest in having me read for a small part, as Jack's personal assistant. The one day she could meet me was a day I was set to fly back from Japan, so I rerouted to LA via the only available flight, with a change of planes in Denver. I made all my connections and landed with no time to spare. I changed in the backseat of the car into a suit I thought would be good for the character if he was Nicholson's personal assistant. It was a grey-flannel bespoke suit I'd just gotten made on Savile Row, and I flew with it in a garment bag, through all the connecting flights, holding it like a newborn baby, trying desperately not to wrinkle it. I got to the audition and read my scene. After a long pause Nancy Meyers said; "Wow. That was really good. *Really really good.* You're good. Really." Another pause. "Did you ever consider doing this? Like, for a living?" The question hung in the air. I didn't know what to make of it, and I still don't. I thought, *Well. I just flew halfway around the world to read for this part and I nailed it. What else can I do to convince you that I am actually doing this?* I should mention I did not get the part; it went to Jon Favreau, and a lot of it got cut from the actual movie. As I was leaving the audition Ms. Meyers said, "Oh. One thing. Where do you get a suit like that?"

I began to think my psychics and the universe were at odds. It was trying to tell me something: not to quit my day job.

■ ■ ■ ■

I bought the studio apartment down the hall from where I lived on Twelfth Street in 1996 to use as a private study, and by 1999 it was a place for Marisa and I to meet while we were working on my TV show and all the other projects I had lined up, including a commission to redesign a hotel in Midtown. One day early in 2002, I returned from a taping to find a message on the office voice mail from a licensing agent reaching out to us about a possible one-off project for Target. I came close to deleting that message. I let it languish and forgot about it for weeks. Finally, in passing, I mentioned it to Marisa.

From the moment I heard the message I knew that if I could create an ongoing partnership with Target, the potential was huge. It had always been a dream of mine to make really great accessible clothes, and if it were possible to do so, it would be at Target, the only one of those big-box stores that possessed any style or humor. Nowadays everyone has a masstige collection, but in those days the only example of such a thing was Halston's go at JCPenney twenty years earlier, which ended badly for all involved. But at the moment when I was contemplating all this, I witnessed something, a touchstone, that justified my vision. I was having lunch at one of the fanciest restaurants in New York, looking out at the street, when a conspicuous Ford SUV drove up, and out poured the fabulous Miller sisters, who were then the epitome of international high society. They proceeded into this fancy restaurant without batting an eye. If the Miller sisters were being chauffeured in an SUV, when at the time, the only mode of acceptable transport was a Mercedes limousine, they might also have the cheek to shop at Target if the clothes were exactly right. I took it as a sign that my vision was correct. The phrase I kept repeating to myself that night was: "All for fashion and fashion for all." The next morning I came to my senses and dropped the idea, feeling the old dread that usually accompanied inspiration, defeated by the gargantuan undertaking even before the first call was returned. It was Marisa who convinced me to engage in that conversation, and since I had no real yearning to go back into the clothing business, I figured I had nothing to lose.

I'm pretty sure what I envisioned was not what the licensing agent had in mind, nor, for that matter, what Target really wanted. It took a good deal of convincing to get everyone on the same page. I agreed to fly to Minneapolis for lunch. As Marisa and I were making our way through LaGuardia Airport that morning I had a terrible panic attack and had to lie down on the floor in the middle of the terminal. We almost missed the flight. This big feeling of retrograde was closing in on me. I had convinced myself that my big break was coming in show business, like some young Hollywood waiter, and this deal with Target felt like a distinct turn away from that. I had an emergency consultation with Maria Napoli, who told me the Target deal was fated, a chance for me to make an even bigger name for myself, and that it would lead to other great opportunities in show business. So on I progressed. I created a small collection of clothes, booked some models, and staged a small fashion show for the Target executives on a second trip to Minneapolis.

It was another case of not knowing what one can't accomplish that made me able to embark on the venture. There was nothing like it yet, no precedent, and the people running the show at Target seemed poised, ready to make it happen. My main contact there was someone named Michael Francis,

a tall good-looking guy with a great personality and a way of wearing a suit and tie —
I love a guy in a suit and tie. But it was more
than the fact that we got along so well. I
knew he understood my vision and would
stop at nothing to help me make it happen.
Any idea I had, any thought, was not out of
the question.

In 2002 Minneapolis felt like an uncon-
quered American city that was about to have
a big moment. The city was a fresh, freezing-
cold place, with limitless views of skies from
conference-room windows, always clear or
white with snow. I spent a lot of happy times
in that city those years. The headquarters
itself was a friendly building, full of contemporary art that Michael was in charge of
collecting. I adored seeing that art because
it was a good cross-section of Americana
that I would otherwise have missed entirely.
A massive, molded-glass pillar by Howard
Ben Tré; a Sheila Hicks tapestry entitled
May I Have This Dance?; a soaring Dale
Chihuly Murano glass sculpture; a two-
story Gwynn Murrill eagle that dominated
the entrance. There were Rauschenbergs,
too, and Mirós and Bertoias. Arriving that
first day, passing by a huge Amy Brazil
Target dog paved in a zillion rhinestones,
made me think, *Hmm. This might work.*

People there didn't seem as jaded as New Yorkers. They also weren't as dramatic. They kept their emotions guarded. Most of the senior merchants would sit in concept meetings with utterly straight faces. No smiling. No show of emotion. And just when I thought I was bombing, someone would pipe up, veritably no expression, practically without volume: "That's amazing. Congratulations." This lack of emotional range was jokingly attributed to the lineage of colder climates. The Scandinavians, the Vikings, they would point out — were not the most demonstrative people.

I signed the deal seconds after Marisa and her husband, Craig, got the rights to my name assigned back from Chanel, which made it all the more dramatic. And when it was done, I made a vow that I wouldn't revert to old habits. If I was going to make clothes again it would have to be in an entirely new way and on my terms. In the year or so I spent away from the business I developed ideas about what luxury was and what it was on its way to becoming. I had less and less interest in what the world perceived as designer brands that cater to a very select few. With some exceptions, most of the stylish people I knew were not couture customers and I wanted my work, on

580

all levels, to reflect this modern phenomenon. As important as craft is to me, there is nothing as important — nothing as luxurious — as good thinking: the right ideas executed the right way for the right purpose. Couture might be important, but it felt irrelevant unless it was connected to a bigger picture, a more inclusive idea that didn't need to justify itself with snobbish people or massive price tags.

So at the same time that I launched the Target brand, I trepidatiously reestablished a couture studio. These clothes were only available privately and through Bergdorf Goodman, but they were conceived and executed as one with the Target collection and meant to be worn together. The couture customers who were turned off by my association with Target were people I wouldn't have wanted as customers anyway. One socialite actually said, point-blank, "I can't buy your clothes anymore," but others were delighted, and I had people buying couture suits and coats from Bergdorf's with sweaters, shoes, and T-shirts from Target. The Target clothes held their philosophical own stitch for stitch against the couture pieces. Making those fashion shows was more fun than anything I had done in years, pairing twenty-dollar pants with seven-thousand-dollar sweaters, and thirty-five-dollar trench coats with fifteen-thousand-dollar cocktail dresses. And again I found myself in the limelight, with people like Taylor Swift, Martha Stewart, Charlize Theron, and Gwyneth Paltrow wearing my clothes, themselves only too excited to say they shopped at Target.

When the collection launched in the spring of 2003 it was the most successful launch Target ever had with an apparel brand. We had one of the first (if not the first) pop-up shops. It was located at Rockefeller Center, and the lines snaked around the block for the entire time the store was open. Not only were we selling on this epic level, we were selling things they never thought possible, like jackets, skirts, and my favorite category, dresses. (There's something soul-satisfying about a good, inexpensive dress.) It was a theory I felt in my bones. I stuck to it and I was right. Within a year and a half I noticed everyone — Karl Lagerfeld, Vera Wang, Jil Sander to name a few — doing collections for H&M, Kohl's, Uniqlo, even Sears and JCPenney.

And yet. Parts of me felt like I was back at square one. I yearned for a life in show business, but I was still hawking *shmatas*. A performer, a writer, trapped in the body of a fashion designer.

31

After two years of being separated from Arnold I realized I'd made a great mistake and I started to panic. I set out to find him, which wasn't easy. This was in 2003; social media wasn't even a thing, really, and he wasn't listed in the Santa Fe phone book. I'd gotten two of my computer-savvy friends — one of whom was Barry Sonnenfeld, the great film director, who at the time wrote a monthly column in *GQ* about the internet — to help look. Nothing came up for Arnold Germer. After a few months I started interviewing private detectives. (Oh yes. I am that obsessive.) Then, by chance, I was on the phone commiserating with my friend Richard Desroche when he interrupted me. "How do you spell Germer?" he asked. I rolled my eyes. I mean. If Barry couldn't find anything, how could Richard, who barely knew how to return email? Seconds later he said, "Here it is. Germer. G-e-r-me-r? It's an address in Santa Fe, New Mexico. And there's a phone number." This was so early in the technology, but that's an example of why I hate the internet. Ultimately it *did* work in my favor, but to this day it seems totally random to me. In any case, after months of searching, I now had Arnold's phone number and like high-school stalkers, Richard and I agreed that he would call on some pretext. Before I could stop him to prepare what he'd say, Richard was dialing on another line and, seconds later, he was talking to Arnold.

That summer and fall Arnold and I spent hours and hours on the phone. I learned that the romance that brought him to Santa Fe had turned into a friendship instead, which meant I had a chance. Then in early October of 2004 he came to New York to visit his family and we had lunch. There's a moment after you reconnect with an old boyfriend when you remember why you broke up in the first place. It all comes flooding back. They don't look as good. They immediately say something to remind you what it was you hated about them. That day the opposite phenomenon occurred. The minute I saw him I remarked to myself that he was better looking than I remembered. And sweeter. And smarter. And funnier. And, more important, our chemistry seemed not to have waned.

He made a plan to come to New York for Thanksgiving, this time to be with me. He stayed at the Inn at Irving Place, where I met him that Wednesday night with Harry. The three of us spent those nights at the hotel, and it was a romantic holiday weekend to end all. Certain memories go down in the books as being perfect, and this was one. Thanksgiving has always been a very special holiday for me. For one thing, it marks the definitive end to the dreaded summer. But the real reason is that as soon as I moved out of my mother's house I made it *my* holiday, associating it with my life apart from blood-familial obligations, spending it with my chosen family. The weather that particular weekend was cold, overcast, fall-like, a little drizzly, and smelled of wet trees and chimney smoke. Being together was like a living dream of love, walking back and forth from my apartment in the Village to the hotel, a short distance through Union Square, Arnold's hand in one of mine, Harry's leash in the other. Four days more perfect than I could have imagined; maybe the best four days of my life.

For the rest of that year we spoke daily. He didn't travel to New York for Christmas, for some unknown reason, which I didn't think to worry about. I was appearing at Joe's Pub in a new cabaret act I had worked up, and I was in preproduction for a Web project I had written and was directing. I was also working on a big renovation of my house in Bridgehampton, a house, I told myself, that eventually we would occupy together. There was something cozy about being home for the holidays, alone with Harry, pining for Arnold, dreaming of the future. In my journal I wrote ". . . willing to wait for however long it takes for him to be one hundred percent sure about moving here. All I need is for him to tell me I'm his and he's mine. We could live apart indefinitely as long as we're sure of that."

As it turned out, there was more to his absence that Christmas than he let on. There were a few issues that seemed insurmountable, which I wasn't aware of: He was committed to his job working for a nonprofit organization that meant a great deal to him. Also living in Santa Fe had been a welcome change for him, having lived in New York City most of his early life. Right after the New Year, I got an email from him explaining all that and putting an end to all our plans. Contact between us broke off indefinitely.

■ ■ ■ ■

For the first few months we were apart I went physically ill anytime I thought about Arnold. There were nights I remember lying awake, writhing in bed, pure Martha Graham, feeling the agony of loss. It was months before I could even think of dating anyone else, and I felt that dreadful thing one feels when a situation has turned for the worse and there's nothing you can do to make it any better. A clock you can't turn back from a bad outcome.

But good luck prevailed and the situation turned. We began speaking again. At first it was once every few weeks, and eventually we reverted to our habit of speaking a few times a day. Progress was slow. So slow I thought it might never happen. After I had been confiding in Maira about our progress for eight or ten months, she asked, "How long is this going to take?"

A full year after his first trip to New York, Arnold finally moved back in late October of 2005. I suppose the pull of New York, the pull of our love, was greater than his fascination with the Southwest. Also perhaps the job, which for the first few years had been exciting, became less so.

I helped him find a one-bedroom in a newly renovated building in the financial district, an early skyscraper that was designed by the same architect who designed the Dakota and the Plaza Hotel. It was on a very high floor and had the most glamourous views of the river and of downtown Manhattan, but it also looked directly into the pit of Ground Zero, something that put me off. I spent very little time in that apartment. At Christmas that year I helped him haul a tree up there. I was excited about decorating a tree but discovered after the first twenty minutes what incredibly hard, exhausting work it is and abandoned it, leaving him to finish it on his own.

We lived apart in the city most weekdays, but on weekends we lived together in the newly renovated house in Bridgehampton, inhabiting it in a kind of ecstasy, with Harry and Arnold's new dog Dean, a beagle/Jack Russell mix. Since then we've spent most of our free time at that house together, and it often feels like a love nest out of an animated Disney movie, complete with bunnies and bluebirds. Since he returned to New York in 2005, we watched the subject of gay marriage evolve. Arnold and I entered into a dialogue about it and, as the country embraced the idea, we promised each other that the minute it was legal in New York, we would get married. In 2011, when it was announced, Arnold and I were watching the news. He turned to me and said, "Congratulations, Cutie, you're engaged."

Up to that point, whenever I'd bring the subject up to my mother she would say, "What do you want to get married for? If things are working so well between you, why upset the applecart?" She had a point. One thing I learned from experience was that if your life works, you have to be very careful about changes, because the tiniest little things can really wreak havoc. And this was no tiny thing; it was matrimony. But my mother's advice not to get married only made me more intent on doing it. I saw her reticence around the subject as an admission of the kind of burden marriage represented to women of her generation. She was raised to serve a man, and now that she was single for these years, nothing was going to sell her on the idea of marriage again. "Why would I want to get married to someone this late in the game?" she'd say. "I've had enough taking care of people for one lifetime." She spent the first thirty years living in her mother's house, then being subservient to my dad — not only to his physical needs, but also to his ideas and political beliefs. Finally she was free. And determined to spare me that drudgery.

Arnold Germer and I got married at City Hall on November 30, 2011. There was no family present. We wore jeans and went directly to Bridgehampton afterwards. We drove around Sag Harbor that evening and came upon a small place we'd never been to, an old-fashioned Italian restaurant called Il Capuccino with red-and-white-checked tablecloths and Chianti bottles wrapped in wicker hanging from the ceiling, like a scene from *Lady and the Tramp.* Our courtship is full of these serendipitous romantic occurrences. It was a month before Christmas, and the next day we went to a tree nursery down the block from our house. This time I was fully committed to the rigors of decorating a tree. After all, this was *our* tree. Being Jewish, I never felt completely right about having one of my own, but now that I was married to a shiksa god it was my right. We got a beautiful Scotch pine and some plain white lights and decorated it with brown-paper bows I made.

A few days later I was on the phone with my mother, who seemed happy for us. One of the first things that came up was how I'd tell my sisters. I didn't know how they would react and neither did my mother. It was obvious they knew, because there were items in the press. But there was something about confronting them with it that made me so uneasy, like I'd be admitting to some sort of sin. When I told them, they were gracious and reiterated again how much they loved Arnold. But still the subject of our marriage is slightly taboo. If things have evolved over the years — nowadays when I get invitations, they're addressed to me *and my husband* — it doesn't erase the past, knowing I'd been such a source of unease, even embarrassment, to them, and knowing it's still not something to be spoken about in the company of their kids.

To my mother, it's a tragedy that her children should be rent apart for any reason, and yet she supports her daughters' beliefs with no pushback. And I understand that position. Although there's no way to resolve it, she will never stop trying to get me to conform in whatever way I might have to in order to encourage a sibling closeness. She's never asked me to compromise my lifestyle, but she's baffled as to why I don't want to be among them as much. It would seem she'd be willing to sacrifice anything, my personal integrity included, for the sake of not disturbing that world, to uphold the illusion that we're still a close family. She'd like it if I could revert back to my teenage years, when I silently conformed to those family ways. In those days they didn't need to know the whole truth, and as long as I was present *on their terms,* they accepted me. She still pushes for a little of that old *don't ask, don't tell* policy. When I'm with her, most of her conversational effort is spent making a case for those traditions, much the way a salesman makes a case for snake oil.

Being with Arnold harkens directly back to those early days in my childhood, even before I knew there was a word for what I was, when I'd fantasize about being in my bed with my dark-haired husband and our ragdoll children. Ironically, because of my sleep disorder, Arnold and I do not share a bedroom and very rarely sleep in the same bed together. But the security I feel being married to this most wonderful man adds so much to the balance of my life. Being married helps my outlook in a lot of ways. Even for someone whose personal world-view is so dark, I'm able to tap into the vast source of optimism which our union repre-sents, and ultimately I see a silver lining.

In the summer of 2012 Arnold and I

moved into the apartment that we envisioned from our earliest days of being together. We were able to convert the little Greenwich Village one bedroom into a large three-bedroom place after we purchased the apartment next door and combined it with the original one plus the studio I'd acquired at the other end. We'd dreamed about doing that from day one and finally some time in 2010 we got the call that the place in-between was becoming available. We'd looked at other places but Twelfth Street was our dream; perfect location, perfect situation, perfect views, a wraparound terrace that faces south and west. The remake was designed in tandem with David Bers, a wonderful architect who, on our first walk-through of the three properties, called it our "manifest destiny." This time, moving in together went a lot smoother and Arnold, Harry, Dean, and I felt a kind of security, a sense of family, I didn't think was possible.

And yet still I wake up in a state of panic, fear, and sadness every day. It's tied into my difficulty sleeping. There's something terrible about falling asleep, knowing you're going to wake up, another day older, another night gone forever. Sometimes I wonder if this wee-hour bleakness began when I was a young child, tied to some memory of being alone in that hospital. No matter what time I wake up, whether it's 2:00 A.M. or 5:00 A.M., all I see is a violent world that I can't rationalize. My mood improves after random increments of time — anywhere from five to thirty minutes, sometimes longer. I've spoken about it with my various shrinks so many times, assuming everyone feels this dread upon waking, but I was told it's not as common as I think.

Insomnia has been a part of my life for as long as I can remember; it's one of the last mysteries in my life. I'm superstitious — afraid that if I talk about it too much after all these years, after getting it to a point where I almost don't notice it, I might upset the balance. People are often baffled by my disdain of travel; my need to extract myself from dinners or events that happen after a certain hour at night; anything I know will affect sleep adversely. But the ultimate truth is that sleep, or the lack of it, runs my life. In my youth I had terrible anger about being awake while everyone else seemed to be blissfully knocked out. But after all these years, and after having consulted with doctors and sleep clinics, I've grown accustomed to it and accept it as a big part of my identity. There's something noble about sitting up. Something strangely peaceful about being tired all the time. By now I even prefer it. When I gave up smoking sixteen years ago, it was hard for me to stay awake, and it seemed like nicotine had been the problem all along. But after about six months my metabolism adjusted, and I stopped sleeping again. To be honest, I was relieved. Sleeping all those hours every night I got so much less done. No reading. No catching up on reality TV. I felt like less of a person. When my friends ask how I get so much done, I have two answers for them: I don't have kids, and I don't sleep.

As I mentioned, Arnold and I have separate bedrooms, so that my insomnia won't disturb either one of us. (I think keeping separate bedrooms, where possible, is actually a great idea for any marriage.) Now when we're in the same house I feel ensconced in a kind of joy and safety that I've never felt before, and sleep comes easier. When I got Harry eighteen years ago I noticed a slight adjustment for the better in my sleep habits. Every night for about twelve years, as long as Harry could, he would jump up on the bed and stay by my side till he intuited that I was asleep, at which point he'd retire to the couch opposite my bed. Being in Long Island, in closer proximity to the negative ions of the sea, helps. When Arnold adopted Dean, our family — our lives together — felt complete. Unlike Harry, Dean loves to sleep on the bed with me, and on the nights when Dean is by my side, his deep sleeping, rather than being annoying as it might if he were another human being, leads me by example.

Harry brought real joy into my life. Both directly and inadvertently; after all, it was walking with him that led me to Arnold. But the joy of knowing Harry also brought the knowledge that I'd outlive him. Without reason, I'd look over at him and give in to that sadness. And when he died on May 12, 2016, it was the hardest day of my life. In that moment, organically, I shifted from skeptic to pessimist. And it's getting worse as I get older. But I think it's a kind of breakthrough. A blessing. Harry's death confirmed the sad natural order of things, which I had now lived through firsthand. Now that I'm certain how fucked-up the world is, the human condition is, I feel less personally responsible for any outcome. I don't make it happen, so I no longer strive for any kind of perfection. More than that, I think perfection is beside the point. I let go of perfection and gave in to chaos. Now all that's left is to try my best, try to relax, complain over a nice dinner with someone who will listen and complain, too.

In the middle of the summer of 2016 Arnold discovered a picture on Petfinder. A sweet-looking puppy who had the name Kita, a black Border collie mix who, though darker in color, looks and behaves exactly like Santa's Little Helper from *The Simpsons.* She was being made available through a rescue agency in Brooklyn called Stray from the Heart that specializes in rescuing the street dogs of Puerto Rico, or "sato" dogs, who suffer terrible abuses there in a place called "Dead Dog Beach." Every week, hundreds of dogs end up there, and they starve and die. The picture of Kita was compelling enough for Arnold to call the adoption agency and arrange a foster situation. Within two weeks she was flown over, and we met her plane at JFK and brought her home. We changed a few letters in her name and now she's called Kitty, after Kitty Hawks, my friend who originally put me together with Harry. (Also Mrs. Kitty Carlisle Hart, whom she resembles.) She has long legs, and the personality of a bird, and more than a few traces of Harry in her. At first, Kitty was skittish and cold. But within a few short months she completely overcame her reserve. Now she interacts with Dean as part sister, part tongue-in-cheek young trophy wife, and she's a mainstay of our family.

From the time they met, Arnold and my mother liked each other. He likes the idea of having a shrewd, erudite (read: Jewish) mother-in-law, and she likes him because he's young and handsome and not lazy. Also I think she adores having a Puerto Rican son-in-law, if only for the brief respite it provides from the Syrian-Jewish nonassimilative environment that surrounds her. My marriage to Arnold might be exactly the justification she needs after a lifetime of trying to negotiate the racism she grew up with — including my father's. "Don't listen to him," she used to say, changing the subject. She still lives among a kind of antique racism in the old neighborhood. I imagine that for all she puts up with to coexist peacefully there, she secretly takes pleasure in the fact that integration — my own personal assimilation as proof — seems to have won out in the educated culture at large.

Arnold found the way to my mother's heart, completely by accident. Once, about nine years ago, she complained about the long waiting list at her local library for Philip Roth's novel *Nemesis*. This is a woman who used her library card as a badge of honor her entire life and would never dream of buying a book. It's just not done; one doesn't *buy* books. For one thing it's expensive, for another it's a form of vulgarity that only "nonprofessional" readers indulge in. Also, books pile up. What happens to them when you're finished? But at some point in recent years it became harder and harder for her to get to the library. And when Arnold heard about the Roth novel, he took the initiative, ordered it online, and sent it to her. When she reconciled herself to the occult overtones of books just appearing from the ether, I think she saw this as the greatest form of love one human being can bestow on another. When her guilt subsided about owning the book, having it all to herself, she was filled with joy. Another justification for this great luxury of book-owning was her discovery of a book repository in the basement of the building she lives in. You put the book there on the table in the basement, and someone else gets to read it. Now Arnold and my mother have a deep, abiding love for each other. Arnold checks in with her each week and finds out what books she wants, and he orders them online, and — like magic — they arrive within two days at her doorstep. I hear them on the phone once a week:

"Do you want the large type? Paperback or hardcover?"

We speak every day, my mother and I. Now she's elderly, which is a big adjustment for me. She walks with a cane, sometimes even a walker, and forgets the thread of a conversation. Every time I speak to her I have to tell myself it isn't the last time. There's great love between us, and there's a nagging feeling of guilt that I haven't dropped everything in my life to be with her. A guilt she does nothing to assuage.

I went to dinner at her house last week.

"It's so great to see you," I said.

"I wish it could happen more often," was her response. Then she added, "Wow. I really am the typical Jewish mother." She chuckled, expecting me to challenge the remark, which I didn't.

My love for her is unlimited, but my patience is not. Those comments that raise my hackles seem to come at me like darts instead of her intended paper airplanes. For the most part when we speak or visit she dominates the conversation with talk of her grandchildren and great-grandchildren, which is what one would expect of a ninety-year-old lady who is lucky enough to have so many of them. Nonetheless, I can't really relate to these stories because I barely have a relationship with these kids — it was always awkward trying to get to know them. Once when I was with my sister and her six-year-old son he asked, "Are you going to marry a girl? What's taking you so long?" There was no appropriate answer to that question under the circumstances, and the room was thrown immediately into distress. I have no idea what my sister's reaction would have been if I had taken it upon myself at that time to say something about men loving other men and marrying them. I know for sure my brother-in-law would not have appreciated it. It would definitely have caused a chasm in the already delicate structure of our relationships.

It's like there are two sides to my mother. One side is the little old lady who is cared for by her adoring daughters, with adoring grandchildren and great-grandchildren, all comfortably ensconced in a community with narrow ideas and provincial attitudes. The other side is the keenly intelligent city dweller, who is extremely well-read and who relates to my life and would gladly support me completely if not for the allegiance she's sworn to the former.

The other night at dinner she said, "Isaac.

I'm a woman of the world!" Then she added, "I'm also such a hypocrite," which is something I hate to hear her say. I hate for her to take all the blame.

Arnold and I sit in Il Cantinori, our favorite restaurant, waiting nervously for my mother to meet us for dinner. She's so fragile these days, and normally I can suppress thoughts of her vulnerability, being immobile, relying on her live-in aide to get her from place to place. But sitting there waiting has me imagining all kinds of bad scenarios. We do this regularly. She sees this as killing two birds with one stone, seeing her son and getting out for a night in her beloved New York City, which would not happen otherwise. And I love seeing her outside the context of her life in Brooklyn.

Finally her black Lexus pulls up and stops at the curb in front, and I run out to meet the car. My mother's tall, imposing driver, Robert, hops out of the front seat. He greets me, we shake hands. Then he opens the door and helps my mother out of the car. I feel guilty because he's assuming the responsibilities of a son — driving her, adjusting her legs as she maneuvers in and out of the car, doing her grocery shopping, changing lightbulbs.

I walk beside her as she makes her way up the one big step into the restaurant and very slowly to the table, leaning on her cane the entire way. The maître d', Frank, who knows the drill, calls for two cushions, which get whisked into place before she sits. She's wearing a pink bouclé jacket and diamond-studded coral earrings shaped like turtles, vintage Kenneth Jay Lane. Also an old scarf of mine, a huge peony print on chiffon, an abstract blur of peachy color. I notice the shoes she has on. They're Manolo Blahniks that he did for a collection of mine in the 1990s: black satin flat sling-backs with square rhinestone buckles. Mental note: Dressy flats are so relevant again and about to happen in a big way.

Even before her body hits the seat she starts off the conversation: "I watched you on QVC last night. Very nice." She's referring to one of my many weekly appearances on the air at QVC, a thriving, wonderful business, the most important of the few licenses I've maintained in the apparel business. "I bought a pair of shoes. I love those moccasins 'cause they're gorgeous. And they're so comfortable. Also I love that Shawnie Sue. She looks great in everything." She refers to Shawn Killinger, an on-air host with whom I've developed a huge viewership, a great rapport, and a dear friendship. My mother finishes the thought with a sentence I hear at least once a week: "I love watching you on TV. It feels like we've visited!"

Immediately she brings up the book she's reading by a novelist she's just discovered, Richard Russo. "All these years, I never heard of him." She's incensed that I haven't read the book, which she gave me the week before. "I know you'll love it. He's funny and smart and he won a Pulitzer." Then I can sense the switch going off in her head. She's turning from literary raconteuse to matriarch. From that point forward, either to show me once again that there's no other meaning to life, or because it's just the patter of a ninety-year-old lady, her conversation will not be budged from the subject of her grand-children and great-grandchildren. No matter what's on my agenda to talk about, the subject of newborn babies prevails. She puts forth another story about one of her "delicious" great-grandchildren: "Nothing's formed yet. No defenses. You know? They're not people yet. Just pure, fat, happy babies."

I interrupt her and bring up Kitty, our new dog. I know how concerned she was for me when I lost Harry and she seems genuinely happy for Arnold and me that we're past the ordeal of letting him go. I always thought that in my mother's mind it was better in so many ways for me to be the cliché of a gay man who was obsessed with my dogs than it would be for me to parent an actual baby. She was against my fathering a child those years before with Sandra. But here and now she surprises me.

She says, "Why haven't you had a child?"

I shrug and look wide-eyed at Arnold.

"You're not too old," she goes on, "and Arnold definitely isn't too old. He can do all the heavy lifting."

It's the first time she's actually advocated for our having a child. Arnold and I had been over and over it and rejected the idea. I was always afraid of being too moody, too unstable, too dramatic, and I worried about exposing a child to that kind of life. I even went as far as to say, "Whoever that unborn kid was, she was spared." But now that my mother's brought it up, I start thinking maybe I'm less self-involved, more stable. Maybe I'm readier to think these thoughts. Is that because she suggested it? Is it because after all these years, even *she* thinks it might be a good idea?

I ask her why she brought up the subject.

"I don't want you to regret anything. And

I only want you to be happy."

She starts talking about her great-grandchildren again. She's expecting two more in the next few months, and her departure for Florida for the season is predicated upon these arrivals. The conversation gets very existential, as it does more and more these days. "I'm not even sure I'm going to wake up in the morning," she says, fishing for an optimistic rejoinder. "But you know, I still have so much to look forward to."

Rather than allow the conversation to be again dominated by the subject of great-grandchildren, I whip out my smartphone. It's something she does not have — else there'd be nothing but pictures of pure, fat, happy babies all night. I show her a picture of Kitty. I say, "Here's a picture of your *newest* granddaughter." A long pause, and then with a squint, she says:

"She has my eyes!"

32

I get to the Carlyle sometime around four thirty in the afternoon and make my way to the room provided for me on the eighteenth floor, a room that hasn't been redecorated since the early 1980s and feels more luxurious and chic for it: muted floral chintz curtains that match the quilted bedspread and tufted headboard, shellacked colonial revival desk and shiny brass table lamp with ruched lampshade, a padded, lead-weighted leather binder with *Room Service Guide* embossed in gold serif type. This is the room that Eartha Kitt and Elaine Stritch used for the same purpose. And Bobby Short. Waiting there for me are two little sandwiches and a chocolate Pavlova cookie from Sant Ambroeus, left there by my associate, who preceded me there to check out a few last-minute details, a few last-minute reservations she's trying to accommodate.

For the next four hours I stay in that room and alternate between cursing my fate, wondering how I could have agreed to something as crazy as this, and blessing my lucky stars. This is a once-in-a-lifetime event (which will hopefully recur a number of times over the course of my life). I'm playing the Café Carlyle for two weeks. Ten shows. Ten opportunities to sing songs, tell stories, bare my soul onstage, in front of very distinguished, hypercritical audiences full of strangers and, even scarier, friends.

I warm up my voice. Up and down scales. I warm up my facial muscles, "chewing gum" and rotating my tongue the way they taught me in Performing Arts high school. I do my "circles" rolling my neck, then my hips, my feet, etc., like we learned in Luigi's class. I assume downward-facing dog and warrior poses to stretch my groin and hamstrings. I retreat to the bed, covering my head with the hotel comforter in mortal fear. Then under the covers I practice punch lines softly to myself, eyebrows undulating, face twitching in expectation of landing the joke. Then I rationalize: Tonight, again, no matter what, the secret of my fraudulence will be kept safe from the world, and I will prevail.

I dress. My diamond ankle bracelet first.

(An Ayurvedic psychic told me I should wear diamonds "starting on a Thursday.") Then I put on my tuxedo and wrap a white silk scarf around my neck, a cross between a nineteenth-century stock tie and something you might see on Tom Jones circa 1968. My black patent Belgian loafers are slipped on, and I'm ready. I proceed to the living room where Shanleigh Philip, my associate in charge of development, is seated on the couch opposite *Gypsy,* which plays on TCM. She's engrossed in a text and doesn't look up when I enter.

"All ready?" she asks after sending the text. I don't answer. Which is my answer.

After I spend about ten tense minutes standing in the living room so as not to wrinkle or smudge anything, the call comes from Darwin, the stage manager, saying the house is seated and they're ready to start. I know that already Ben Waltzer, the musical director, and the band have assembled onstage and done their scales and warm-ups. I picture the new trumpet player, Benny Benack, decked out in his black suit and orange-striped socks, which I got a glimpse of earlier. I convince myself that I can make it across the hallway. No trace of my usual claustrophobia on the trip downstairs in the tiny elevator — for the time being it's edged out to make space for the massive stage fright that has crowded in. On the main floor I traverse the lobby and up a few stairs to the holding spot outside the "stage entrance" to the cabaret, where I await Darwin's cue. I peek in, which somehow stabilizes my nerves. The hallowed room. The pink lights from the table lamps and the dim ambers on the cool jades and tangerines of the Marcel Vertès murals. The ancient Greek minstrels, the cherubs, the donkeys, and pussycats staring into the audience. The old waiters from central casting. It could be any time. Eternal. Anything could be happening outside on the street, but the stage light washes away everything harsh: politics, news, reduced through a squint, declawed, leaving only humor. People drinking, laughing, happy. And I want to be one of them. I hear my intro music and I roll my neck. I'm clutching at the black curtain and kicking my feet in exhilaration. Then. I compose myself. If I reveal too much too soon, it'll be over before it starts.

The door opens and now I can see the entire room. The boys playing onstage. Benny is there in his striped socks, already in the set. All I have to do is traverse that small path from the door to the stage. Once

I get on there's no more fear or dread. I can be on that stage, I *must* be on that stage. The first entrance, acting like, *pretending,* you're not nervous. Then life imitates art, and I'm *not* nervous anymore, and I'm able to do it. I'm able to hear tones and remember lyrics and punch lines. No more superstitions. Nothing in the way. At this moment, this seventy-minute moment, everything stops. It's not about objects, or clothes, or obligations, or any other ideas the world will have you believe it's about. It's not about achievement, or money, or position, or power. In fact it's *the opposite of what success is supposed to feel like.*

Of all the satisfying creative experiences of my life, the next seventy minutes are the reward for what's come before. I spent the last three years working on my museum retrospective with amazing curators, fabulous architects, and filmmakers who helped put it together. It represented my creative life: fashion, film, show business, publishing — all aspects. And for all that, for all that evidence of my illustrious past, this is what I'm left with, this is my future. For all the speculation about who I am, what I do, this is the real answer. Just me and the audience and time at a standstill.

After the first number I settle into the set.

Now there's no possibility of failure. I wind my way through eight tunes and five monologues. Time has still not started ticking normally yet. It's an eternal evening with them and me. Then the finale. The last song of the night. It's not a big finger-snapping, toe-tapping, leave-them-with-a-feel-good number. I made the decision not to pander, not to be in their face and demand smiles. I risk ending the show on an almost-somber note. The song is also not an abstraction. It says what it means. Not corny, not ironic. Just the shortest distance between me and the audience. It's a tiny song that stayed with me from my hundreds of Liza records. A wending tune written by John Kander, with a very sane, very meaningful lyric by Fred Ebb. The lights in the room come down. I'm in the spotlight. I'm not fat. I'm not selling anything. I'm the minstrel singer that was predicted in the Mexican tarot. The song is the most important thing at that moment. A little truth telling.

I realize more while I'm singing. Not only the idea of the song, I realize the rightness of my being there, right there, communicating these words. My other self is able to fly up into the corner of the room and observe. This is the moment in the evening I've been waiting for. When I see myself the way a camera does, the nonperfect version, the real me. I'm telling the whole truth and I've got them in my hands. Complete silence. Ben pauses at the piano, he's waiting for me. And then I sing:

"Happiness comes in on tip-toe.
Well, whaddya know.
It's a quiet thing.
A very quiet thing."

ACKNOWLEDGMENTS

I'd like to thank David Kuhn, whose idea this was in the first place. Also Peternelle van Arsdale, for her constant and beautiful editorial eye. Thanks, too, to Shanleigh Ciena for her diligence in seeing this through to the end.

A special thanks to my dear cousin Arlene Maidman, who convinced me that my story came across okay, having reread the manuscript a number of times. And thanks to Caroline Weber, who convinced me the book would be okay, not having read a word.

Special thanks to Amy Einhorn for her intuition and precision.

More than anyone, thanks to my husband, Arnold Germer. He read every word of this book several times and listened to me talking about it at all hours of the day and night. Without him, the story might've had a much less happy ending.

ABOUT THE AUTHOR

Isaac Mizrahi (Libra) performs cabaret across the country, has written two books, hosted his own television talk show, and made countless appearances in movies and television. He has directed and designed many productions for the stage and the screen. He founded his design company in 1987, was the star and cocreator of the documentary *Unzipped,* and the subject of a large-scale, mid-career survey at the Jewish Museum in New York City. He currently develops projects for television, theatre, and literature through his own production company, Isaac Mizrahi Entertainment.

The employees of Thorndike Press hope you have enjoyed this Large Print book. All our Thorndike, Wheeler, and Kennebec Large Print titles are designed for easy reading, and all our books are made to last. Other Thorndike Press Large Print books are available at your library, through selected bookstores, or directly from us.

For information about titles, please call:
   (800) 223-1244

or visit our website at:
   gale.com/thorndike

To share your comments, please write:
   Publisher
   Thorndike Press
   10 Water St., Suite 310
   Waterville, ME 04901